I0199957

Embedded Faith

Embedded Faith

The Faith Journeys of Young Adults
within Church Communities

CARLTON JOHNSTONE

With a Foreword by Andrew Root

WIPF & STOCK · Eugene, Oregon

EMBEDDED FAITH
The Faith Journeys of Young Adults within Church Communities

Copyright © 2013 Carlton Johnstone. All rights reserved. Except for brief quotations in critical publications or reviews, no part of this book may be reproduced in any manner without prior written permission from the publisher. Write: Permissions, Wipf and Stock Publishers, 199 W. 8th Ave., Suite 3, Eugene, OR 97401.

Wipf & Stock
An Imprint of Wipf and Stock Publishers
199 W. 8th Ave., Suite 3
Eugene, OR 97401

www.wipfandstock.com

ISBN 13: 978-1-4982-6780-9

Manufactured in the U.S.A.

Scriptures taken from the Holy Bible, New International Version®, NIV®. Copyright © 1973, 1978, 1984, 2011 by Biblica, Inc.™ Used by permission of Zondervan. All rights reserved worldwide.www.zondervan.com. The "NIV" and "New International Version" are trademarks registered in the United States Patent and Trademark Office by Biblica, Inc.™

A version of chapter 2, "Embedded Faith," has been published as: Johnstone, Carlton. "Faith Crossroads and Social Networks: The Transition from Inherited Faith to Owned Faith," *Journal of Youth and Theology* 8 (2009) 43–59. Used by permission of the publisher, International Association of Youth Ministry

A version of chapter 6, "Worship and Modes of Engagement," has been published as: Johnstone, Carlton. "Modes of Engagement with Worship," *Stimulus* 18 (2010) 10–18. Used by permission of the publisher, Laidlaw College.

A versions of chapter 8, "Church Two Timing," has been published as: Johnstone, Carlton. "Understandin the Practice of Church Two-Timing," in *International Journal for the Study of the Christian Church*, 9:17–31, 2009. Used by permission of the publisher (Taylor & Francis Ltd, http://www.tandf.co.uk/journals).

To Sarah

With whom I have the pleasure of living out this precious faith,
As well as passing it on to our beautiful kids, Max and Holly.

Contents

Foreword

For an American, New Zealand is a magical place. An island nation in another world filled with majestic mountains, beautiful seas, and hobbits. Few Americans will ever get the chance to visit this enchanted land, but most would love the opportunity. To many of us it has been so fused with the Lord of Rings that we imagine it is as charmed as it is beautiful. And having been there myself, I can testify that the magic of its beauty can only be matched by the hospitality of its people.

But it is also a place where secularization has soaked in deep, and church institutions feel the loss of an age of institutional strength that can now only be remembered as if science fiction. In a small church basement in Australia, a church leader said to me, "We Australians are about decade ahead of America when it comes to the loss of connection of young people to the church. But, in New Zealand, they're about a decade ahead of us."

This may signal that we all in the western world have something to learn from New Zealand. Perhaps this magical land where secularization has soaked in deep can teach us all a bit more of how to faithfully engage in ministry with young people. It is because of this I couldn't be more excited to present my friend Carlton Johnstone's important book *Embedded Faith* to an American audience. Carlton is a Kiwi from head to toe, he is as thoughtful as he is sharp, as friendly as he insightful. I'm confident that you will find all these characteristics in his important book.

His book is of upmost importance to us in America because we have seemed to be overtaken of late with millennial anxiety. Blogs and magazine articles bleed fear that we are losing millennials, shouting like some reverse Paul Reveres that "the millennial are leaving, the millennial are leaving!" Anxiety about their departure from the church has become *en vogue*. It has inevitably led to distortions and misunderstandings about who young adults are and what they are seeking from (or outside) the church. It is as though those us with millennial anxiety believe that the presence of millennials in our churches is some kind of magical ring that will give us the institutional power that we need to reach vitality. But this anxiety, in my mind, only reveals that we are more drawn to the youthful spirit of young people than willing to look for the Holy Spirit in and through the concrete experiences of young people in the world and church. We often fail to stop and think more deeply, peering more closely at who young adults are and what they are seeking in the church.

Carlton's book is a great gift in helping us think about who millennials are and how we might minister to them, respecting at every turn their spiritual depth. Carlton's voice is free of sensationalized anxiety and clear to wrestle with the big questions of ministry to young adults. This is a project located in the sociology of religion, but nevertheless has rich theological and ministerial implications. Carlton is not shy to offer rich directions for preaching, relational contact, and congregational life. I'm confident that it will challenge all those who care about young adults and seek to understand with more depth their association with the church.

Picking up a book is often like a journey, and with Carlton as your guide into the faith life of young adults, you are in good hands. He writes with a keen perceptive that is thoughtful and visionary in style. I believe all of us in the western world need this book and I think both Carlton's skill as scholar, and his location in New Zealand, make him particularly positioned to help us wrestle further (and more faithfully) with the faith life of young adults.

Andrew Root
St. Paul, Minnesota (USA)

Acknowledgments

This book would not be in your hands without the support, encouragement and assistance of a number of people. It has developed out of my doctoral research in the sociology of religion. To my doctoral supervisors, Tracey McIntosh and Martin Sutherland, thank you for the invaluable advice and feedback you provided throughout the doctoral journey. I am grateful to The University of Auckland who provided me with financial support in the form of a doctoral scholarship that made undertaking a PhD a reality. Thanks to John Tucker, Martin Sutherland, Peter Lineham and Andrew Root, who saw the importance and value of my thesis becoming a book and wrote supporting letters to help get it published. And thank you Andy for then taking the time to write a foreword for this book. It means a lot.

To all who participated in this research, thank you for you openness, transparency, and sharing of your faith journey. You have provided a richness and depth of 'data' that has been tremendously rewarding to work with. I hope I have remained faithful in the retelling of your stories … and that church leaders listen to what you have to say.

I am grateful to my wife Sarah for your encouragement and graciousness in allowing me time to write. Thanks for patiently reading over chapters and revisions and making helpful suggestions. You are a gift beyond measure. Thanks to my delightful kids, Max and Holly. I am abundantly blessed. I hope when you guys become young adults your faith will still be embedded within a church community that nurtures, sustains, and inspires your faith in God and love for others.

Introduction

Young adults have been described as constituting a "black hole"[1] in con-gregational life. Although some churches are fortunate enough to have young adults as part of their congregation, on the whole they are under-represented in church life. Research reveals a significant drop in church attendance for young adults in comparison to adolescents. This noticeable absence of young adults in church congregations is of particular concern to churches and church leaders as they seek to address this ever-expanding "black hole." This has evoked a constant stream of literature proclaiming ways for churches to stem the out-going tide and begin to reduce the black hole that goes by the name of young adults, or by their generational titles of GenX and GenY.[2]

Fundamental to any investigation of church growth and decline in modern society is having a clear understanding of why people become involved, stay involved, or drop out of church life. The vast majority of books published on generations X and Y, and even more generally, young adults and religion concern how particular religious groups might "reach" the current generation of young adults and reverse this church decline by being culturally relevant and outlining generational differences. The church itself is often blamed for generational decline. Barna argues that religious institutions are irrelevant to generations X and Y because "their personal interest is in people, not trappings. For them, faith is a macro-value, not an entire, independent dimension of life."[3] Hahn and Verhaagen claim that, "Our generation [GenX] does not know God. Yet this is a generation that yearns and searches for spiritual reality. So far it is not finding it in the

1. Belzer et al., "Congregations," 1.

2. In the New Zealand context Generation X is defined sociologically as those born from 1965 to 1979, and GenY as those born from 1980 to 1994. The upper and lower end of the GenX scale varies somewhat in America with a range from 1961–1984.

3. Barna and Hatch, *Boiling Point*, 64.

church."[4] In GenX Religion Miller and Miller draw attention to "the terrible job" that the mainline denominational church has done of holding on to GenX youth in the 1990s. They blame this on an "obvious clash of cultures . . . one more rigid and traditional, the other marked by innovation and progression."[5] Ralph Moore argues that because Generation X are a "generation with no fundamental belief in absolutes" they are "put off" traditional church practices (which communicated absolute truth).[6] In Virtual Faith Tom Beaudoin describes churches as being "laughably out of touch" with generation X (and by extension generation Y), due to their, "Hopelessly droll music, antediluvian technology, retrograde social teaching, and hostile or indifferent attitudes toward popular culture."[7]

Are such criticisms valid and accurate? Do GenXers and GenYs find churches "irrelevant," "absent of God," "too rigid," "doing a terrible job," and "laughably out of touch" with their lives? Some churches no doubt are "out of touch" and "irrelevant" and even doing a "terrible job" where young adults are concerned. But such churches do not represent the whole, especially in a "spiritual marketplace" catering to a wide range of lifestyles, traditions, and stylistic preferences. In other words, GenX and GenY have plenty of other church options to choose from if they are not attracted to churches "laughably out of touch" with their lives. Such generational accounts often fail to make an important distinction between the churched and unchurched in relation to generational distinctiveness. This is a distinction often drawn by sociologists of religion pointing to two quite different cultures, "one communally orientated and closely tied to a church, temple, synagogue, mosque, or other religious institution; and the other less religiously based and orientated towards personal freedom."[8]

4. Hahn and Verhaagen, *Reckless Hope*, 17.

5. Miller and Miller, "Understanding," 2. Despite this clash of cultures Miller and Miller go on to say that "Many young adults are finding their way into churches, temples, and synagogues, but the medium that communicates the message of these traditions has changed radically," "Understanding," 2. Furthermore the editors of GenX Religion admit that their study leaves out GenXers who have remained in more traditional religious settings, attending churches, temples, and synagogues in which they were raised (Flory and Miller, 231).

6. Moore, *Friends*, 134. What is evident in Moore's description of GenX as having no moral absolutes (and other authors writing on Gen X) is their uncritical transfer of a characteristic of postmodernism onto GenX.

7. Beaudoin, *Virtual Faith*, 13.

8. Carroll and Roof, *Bridging*, 81.

Generation X, if the literature is to be believed, is the first truly post-Christian generation. We are, (apparently), very interested in spirituality but not institutional religion—which is usually what is meant by the phrase "I'm spiritual, not religious." Those that are interested in God, it is argued, are not finding God in churches. However, at the time of writing up my research I was part of a church that would regularly have over 300 people in attendance from generations X and Y. Something does not add up. They are talking about me and my generation, and yet a whole subset of us, a "generational unit" to use Manheim's term (discussed below), does not fit this generational profile. This generational unit is "religious and spiritual" to flip the phrase, remixed in ethnographic style.

Despite the resurgence of religion over the last three decades churches are concerned by the growing number of young adults that are leaving the established church. However, there remains a significant number who choose to stay for a variety of factors in the face of social shifts and trends not always favourable towards faith and church life. I was interested to explore why twenty-and-thirty-somethings go to church, why they change churches and what they look for in a church. I wanted to know where they were engaging and disengaging with church life. How did stage of life and life experience impact on one's experience and involvement in church and church practices such as worship and preaching? So began a three and a half year research journey for a PhD in sociology of religion through the University of Auckland. Young adults who go to church, and why, is the focus of this book.

Our biography, our sense of identity, is formed through telling our stories which are embedded in the story of the communities in which we participate. This book explores the way Christian faith journeys of members of generations X and Y are embedded within church communities. In-depth religious life story interviews were carried out with fifty members of generations X and Y who are currently involved in a church community. Conducting life story interviews provides insight and understanding into how faith is impacted and changed through life experiences and stage of life transitions.

This book offers the reader a detailed description of young adults' engagement with congregational life and religious practices such as rituals, worship, and preaching. Understanding the reasons why young adults connect and disconnect from worship and preaching will enable those working with them in a church context to give shape to a ministry that strengthens, enriches and grows their faith and deepens their sense of belonging to a faith community.

This book provides the first detailed description of multiple church switching and the religious practice I have called church two-timing. This is certainly not a phenomenon unique to New Zealand. I also hope the reader gains valuable insight into the relationship between geographic mobility and belonging to a faith community in a transient age. Multiple church switching, church two-timing, and geographic mobility all impact upon the life and dynamics of local faith communities. The young adults' religious biographies help the reader understand the impact and challenges these phenomena have on church life and how to respond to them in ways that strengthen the faith community and the place of young adults within it.

Chapter Outline

Chapter 1 provides a critique of the literature on generations and faith. Too often age differences are communicated as generational differences that can put us on the back foot when it comes to engaging emerging generations. I argue that it is important to have a deeper understanding of generational theory and how this can contribute to church life and in particular ministry to and with young adults. I will also introduce those from GenX and GenY that make up the "generational unit" whose life stories this book is based on.

Chapter 2 begins to develop an understanding of faith as both owned and embedded in a church community. An understanding of church as an 'interpretive community of memory' is developed. This chapter explores the transition of those growing up religious, from inherited faith to owned faith. This transition takes place at a faith crossroad, where one is faced with the decision to continue in the faith, or walk away from both faith and church. In coming to own faith for oneself a particular religious sensibility develops that includes an orientation towards church that gives it a central place in the life of faith. This chapter calls into question the prevalent myth of individualism that infuses our congregational life. I hope that you will come away from this chapter with a deeper understanding of how to journey alongside those who find themselves at a faith crossroad while facilitating the communal orientation of the Christian faith.

Rituals as practices of commitment are a significant part of owning faith and covenanted community which is the focus of chapter 3. In particular I investigate confirmation and baptism as rites of passage into a Christian faith community before going onto discuss the ritual of communion. Rituals are given their creative power through the stories that they are embedded in and in what they symbolically communicate. I hope that this chapter will encourage deeper reflection on the meaning that practices of commitment have for those participating in them and the importance of teaching young people the richness of religious rituals.

Having established the importance of embedding faith in a church community, chapters 4 and 5 explore the relationship between embedded faith and church switching. Chapter 4 establishes the declining importance of denominations for participants as a source of religious identity and church choice. The chapter then goes on to argue that multiple switching is a deliberate action motivated by a symbolic approach to embedding faith.

Chapter 5 investigates the importance of social networks and demographic relevance for our understanding of church switching and embedded faith. The impact of geographical mobility on embedded faith is explored. These two chapters provide a valuable understanding of the complexity and variety of reasons that motivate people to change churches and their desire for community which often proves elusive.

Chapters 6 and 7 investigate modes of engagement with two significant religious practices of church communities: worship (chapter 6) and preaching (chapter 7). When young adults looked for a new church both preaching and worship featured time and time again as factors in the decision-making process. Worship and preaching are some of the "pressure points" that influence decisions about staying or switching churches. What is apparent is that the changing demands on both worship and preaching reflect a critical sensibility and create different modes of (dis-)engagement.

Chapter 8 theorises the phenomenon of people attending two churches simultaneously, what I am calling 'church two-timing.' Church two-timing is an increasing religious practice. This chapter gives voice to the variety of reasons why people church two-time beyond labelling it as another expression of religious consumption. The stories of those involved in the practice of church two-timing demonstrate that while it is assisted by the nature of the spiritual marketplace it continues to be an expression of embedded faith. This chapter challenges the reader to see the missional potential of church two-timing and the need to for churches to be places of hospitality for those engaged in this practice.

1

Negotiating the Profile of Generations X and Y[1]

In 1951 when *Time* magazine was examining the "silent" generation it asked, "Is it possible to paint a portrait of an entire generation?" This question continues to hold sociological relevance. *Time* went on to say:

> Each generation has a million faces and a million voices. What the voices say is not necessarily what the generation believes, and what it believes is not necessarily what it will act on. Its motives and desires are often hidden. It is a medley of good and evil, promise and threat, hope and despair. Like a straggling army, it has no clear beginning or end. And yet each generation has some features that are more significant than others; each has a quality as distinctive as a man's accent, each makes a statement to the future, each leaves behind a picture of itself.[2]

"Don't trust anyone over thirty" (which originally was "twenty-five") became the symbolic slogan of the Boomer generation, highlighting a growing "generational gap." The term "generational gap" emerged during this time in the 1960s to explain the cultural differences and divisions emerging between Boomers and their parents. Cultural differences in relation to fashion, music, politics, sexuality, and drugs were particularly noticeable. Some of this disparity is related to the unprecedented size of this

---

1. Parts of this chapter were included in a paper presented at the Methodist Church of New Zealand's Mission and Unity Conference 2010 as "Emerging Generations and the Challenge of Being Witnesses in Our Time" held in Auckland, NZ, June 18–19, 2010.

2. "The Younger Generation," par. 2–3.

birth cohort, which gave it unprecedented power and a significant voice and influence. However, since then, Margaret Mead has argued that the "generational gap" has undergone domestification.[3] Not only has this original generation gap undergone domestification, but a generation later, the Boomers found themselves in the uncomfortable position once occupied by their elders.

Unlike the Baby Boomers, who became *Time*'s 40th "Man of the Year" in 1967, the collective portrait of Generation X has been strikingly less complimentary.[4] The name "Generation X" was born out of a Douglas Coupland novel by the same name. Coupland got the idea from the last chapter in a book on class by Paul Fussell, and in his article titled "Generation X'd," Coupland explains the sociological influence of the term:

> The book's title came not from Billy Idol's band, as many supposed, but from the final chapter of a funny sociological book on American class structure titled *Class*, by Paul Fussell. In his final chapter, Fussell named an "X" category of people who wanted to hop off the merry-go-round of status, money, and social climbing that so often frames modern existence. The citizens of X had much in common with my own socially disengaged characters; hence the title. The book's title also allowed Claire, Andy, and Dag to remain enigmatic individuals while at the same time making them feel a part of the larger whole.[5]

"Generation X" has become the moniker that has stuck. It could be argued that at least X has a history to its name, unlike the unfortunate succeeding generation, labelled Y. This is telling in itself, as there is no specific defining event that has shaped this generation enough to provide them with a more descriptive name than that of the alphabetical letter following Generation X.

The sociological profiles of Generations X and Y are somewhat ambiguous. Generation X and Gen Y are somewhat floating signifiers, created, Sherry Ortner argues, by "the politics of representation":

3. Mead, *Culture*. By "domestification," Mead is arguing that the generation gap has lost its original importance and meaning from its expression in the 1960s, when it was perceived as part of larger social movements.

4. Generation X, like their generational predecessors, also graced the cover of *Time* on July 16, 1990 as "Twentysomethings."

5. Coupland, "Generation X'd," par. 3.

One can see the play of various positionalities, interests, political claims, and marketing intentions at work in the competing representations. One can see as well that Generation X has quite literally been brought into being in the play of these representations. Finally, one may come to feel—as the images never stabilize—that there is a kind of Baudrillardian process at work—a free play of signifiers with no referent, really at all.[6]

In a similar manner, Lovell contends that the notion of "generation has never been so ubiquitous in public discourse as in our own present day."[7] The politics of representation has resulted in Gen X being misrepresented over the years. Coupland blames this on

boomer angst-transference . . . who feeling pummelled by the recession and embarrassed by their own compromised 60s values, began transferring their collective darkness onto the group threatening to take their spotlight. As a result Xers were labelled monsters. Their protestations became "whining"; being mellow became "slacking"; and the struggle to find themselves became "apathy."[8]

Theorizing Generations

Karl Mannheim's now-famous essay, "The Problem of Generations," has become the central reference point for many contemporary discussions in sociology and politics concerning generational issues. Mannheim argues that a distinction between the categories of "generation location," "generation as actuality," and "generation unit," is required for any in-depth analysis of generations.[9] Mannheim insists on the importance of specific sociological influences in the development of a social generation. Mannheim also emphasizes the importance of distinguishing between the various subgroups to be found within each generation. Being born during a similar period does not, Mannheim points out, guarantee a common life experience or worldview between members of a birth cohort.

Mannheim's distinction between generation as *location* and generation as *actuality* is an important one. Generation as location refers to the

6. Ortner, "Generation X," 416.

7. Lovell, *Generations*, 1.

8. Coupland, "Generation X'd," par. 5.

9. Mannheim, "Generations," 311.

3

broadest use of the term: coexisting or being located with others of the same age or born between a certain period. A generation as an actuality begins to become more specific, as it refers to a community of shared experiences and feelings. This shared experience of an actual generation occurs at a general level. Mannheim's concept of "generational unit" provides a more specific analysis of generations. Generational units share a similar view and interpretation about events, and in the process, a shared identity. Mannheim explains the difference between a generational unit and an actual generation as follows:

> The generation unit represents a much more concrete bond than the actual generation as such. Youth experiencing the same concrete historical problems may be said to be part of the same actual generation, while those groups within the same actual generation which work up the material of their common experience in different specific ways constitute separate generation units.[10]

Mannheim also speaks of the phenomenon of "stratification," or life stages when various generations can experience certain historical processes together, yet do not share the same generation location due to their social situatedness. Social stratification such as class, gender, race, and religion all influence the way one responds to and interprets significant social and cultural changes and events. This is something often overlooked in the literature on Generations X and Y, rendering them seemingly homogenous generations. Ortner is a notable exception to this, at least in relation to class and ethnicity, for Ortner argues that popular representation of Gen X in American public culture "is an attempt to deal with profound changes in the U.S. middle class in the late 20th century."[11] Beaudoin, who argues that a defining characteristic of Gen X is their common engagement with popular cultural events,[12] concedes that participation in the forms of popular culture that he discusses in *Virtual Faith* requires "at least middle-class status (because it often requires access to disposable income)."[13]

10. Mannheim, "Generations," 304.

11. Ortner, "Generation X," 420.

12. Beaudoin's argument that engagement with popular culture is a defining characteristic of Gen X is questionable. See Strauss et al.'s exploration of Gen Y's engagement with popular culture in *Millennials*.

13. Beaudoin, *Virtual*, 28. I am surprised by Beaudoin's argument here regarding class, given that the discipline of cultural studies, which includes popular culture, emerged out of studies on working class forms of (popular) culture conducted by the Birmingham Center for Contemporary Cultural Studies.

Alongside class, Ortner has noted the whiteness of Generation X: "Race is virtually absent from further discussions of the supposed characteristics of Generation X, except for some flimsy references to 'diversity.'" Rapper and hip-hop music producer Dr. Dre also highlights the whiteness of Gen X: "I haven't heard anyone in my hood taking about [Generation X]. The only X I know is Malcolm X."[14] A recent study on the worldview and spirituality of Generation Y acknowledged that the study focused on a generational unit consisting of predominantly white young people described as being "socially included," which could also read, "middle-class."[15] Those that make up the generational unit of this book are also predominantly white, middle-class New Zealanders.

Even within socially stratified groups, Mannheim argues that there is not usually one monolithic worldview within the various subgroups, but rather several. Therefore, the salience of significant social, cultural, and political events will have different meanings and interpretations as they interact with one's personal experience and social situatedness during one's formative years. From the perspective of the sociological imagination, one needs to take into consideration a person's whole biography—and not just age—as it intersects with history.

Esler points out that this existence of such subgroups and diverse generational responses to historical events is frequently cited as an objection to the whole generational approach.[16] Lovell, however, reminds us of the sociological significance of generations outside of generational descriptions, "generational consciousness," and the existence of subgroups:

> For all that generations are hard to pin down, to write about them is more than an exercise in hair-splitting intellectual and cultural history. They are closely bound up with politics and economics— that is to say, with the distribution of power and resources in a given society. Generations can have considerable coercive power once they have taken shape as distinct social constituencies or interest groups. If your age marks you out as a member of the youth cohort, it is hard to avoid being treated as a "young person."[17]

For Mannheim, such disparity is not an argument against generational analysis, but rather sociological common sense. However, such common

14. Cited in Giles and Miller, "Generalizations," 66.

15. Savage et al., *Generation Y*, 8.

16. Esler, *Youth Revolution*, xii.

17. Lovell, *Generations*, 5.

sense is often absent in the literature, which is full of what Everett Carl Ladd has called unsubstantiated "silly assertions," and "a sea of baseless assertions."[18] As Ladd's opening paragraph reviewing generational research makes scathingly clear, "Social analysis and commentary has many shortcomings, but few of its chapters are as persistently wrong-headed as those on the generations and generational change. This literature abounds with hyperbole and unsustainable leaps from available data."[19]

Bennett et al. agree with Ladd's observations, especially as it pertains to media commentaries on Baby Boomers in the late 1960s and Generation X today, saying that "too often, anecdotal evidence has been accepted as if it were proof that the patterns observed were typical among young people."[20] Andy Crouch argues that "generation misinformation" is common in descriptions of Gen X.[21] Alex Ross has described the "ongoing symposium on generational identity . . . [as] a fruitless project blending the principles of sociology and astrology."[22] Others have concluded that popular literature on generational differences may be "engaging, entertaining, and intuitively appealing," but they are in actual fact "little more than caricature—exaggerated and distorted to engage popular interest."[23] In their 2006 Hudson Report, Lester Levy et al. found that "the belief that there are large and dramatic differences among youth cohorts in different generations has not been supported by high-quality longitudinal research."[24] Generational characteristics and attitudes have found to be overstated in relation to politics, work attitudes, religion, and life values more generally.

Generational effects need to be evaluated against what are called "period effects." A period effect takes place when the consequences of an event or major social change "ripple through almost every group in society irrespective of age"[25] and impact the entire population in a similar way.[26] However, when a period effect occurs that affects people across age

18. Ladd, "Twentysomethings," 14–15.

19. Ibid.

20. Bennett et al., "Generations," 39.

21. Crouch, "Generation," 83.

22. Ross, "Generation Exit," 102.

23. Levy et al., *Generational Mirage*, 26.

24. Ibid.

25. Craig and Bennett, *Boom*, 6.

26. Roof, for example, has traced the way in which Boomers "became the carrier of cultural and religious values that would permeate 'upward' to older generations and

groups, it is generally accepted that certain events and changes will exert their strongest impact on the young. In other words, there is an interaction between age and experience. Craig et al. point out that "As a rule of thumb, analysts should not interpret signs of change among the young as a generational effect without first determining whether the same kinds of changes have also taken place (and to about the same degree) among older people as well."[27] Wuthnow questions whether there is any evidence that Generations X and Y have been decisively shaped by a particular historical event in the same way, for example, that the Baby Boomers were by the Vietnam War.[28] Furthermore, generational influences also need to be differentiated from life stages. Confusion often arises from the failure to distinguish between generational experiences on the one hand and the effects of the life cycle on the other.

It is generally accepted that adolescence and early young adulthood are the most impressionable and formative years in relation to "generational imprinting"[29] from social, cultural, and political events. Early impressions and experiences often shape later views of the world. Craig and Bennett advise that

> scholars must exercise caution when trying to identify the dynamics of generational change in this or any era. Young people sometimes think and act differently from their elders simply because they are young and not because they have spent their "formative years" being influenced by the tides of history. In other instances, the attitudes and behaviour of young and old alike will shift in a similar direction (and perhaps to a similar degree) because both have been exposed to and affected by the same historical forces and events. Finally, generational scholars must be careful not to describe all members of a given birth cohort in terms of traits and tendencies that may apply to only a relatively small percentage of them.[30]

'downward' to those born after them" (*Spiritual Marketplace*, 50).

27. Craig and Bennett, *Boom*, 7.

28. Wuthnow, *Baby Boomers*, 4–5.

29. Schuman and Scott, "Collective Memories," 378.

30. Craig and Bennett, *Boom*, 3.

Meet a Generational Unit

Because people have defined Generation X and Y differently and attributed sometimes sweeping generalized characteristics to each, there is an increased need to engage with generational units that make up an actual generation. This need is especially significant when talking about specific generations and religion. When I speak of Generations X and Y in this book, I am referring to a generational unit who share a particular type of faith—a faith that is owned and embedded within a church community. At the same time, however, embedded faith does not provided a homogenous experience of church and faith. What this generational subset, or unit, (i.e., the participants of this research) does provide is an alternative narrative to the growing body of literature that argues that Generations X and Y are not interested in religion, particularly church, despite being interested in spirituality. This generational unit shares an orientation towards church that gives it a central place in the life of faith.

Our biography, our sense of identity, is formed through telling our stories, which are embedded in the story of the communities in which we participate. This book explores the way the Christian faith journeys of members of Generations X and Y are embedded within church communities, including an investigation of why young adults change churches and what they are looking for in a church. In order to understand why Generations X and Y choose to embed their faith in a church community, I conducted in-depth religious life story interviews. I considered such interviews to be the best methodological approach.[31] Religious life stories allowed me to investigate how young adults' life experiences impact their understanding of faith, involvement in church, and church practices such as worship and preaching. These issues are all explored in this book.

I interviewed fifty members of Generations X and Y who are currently involved in a church community. Thirty males and twenty females were interviewed. The majority of participants (thirty-five) were in their twenties. The rest were in their thirties, with one participant on the top end of the Gen X birth cohort at forty-one years old. At the time of the interview, thirty participants were married and one was going through a separation. Twelve couples were interviewed, eleven together and one separately due to convenience. Thirteen participants had children. Nineteen were single. The interviewees were predominantly New Zealand European

---

31. See Appendix for more on methodology.

from middle-class backgrounds. Nineteen had formally studied theology in some capacity. Thirty-eight were employed full-time and four worked part-time. Seven were studying full- or part-time. Three (all women) were caring for young children full-time.

The majority of participants had grown up affiliated with church communities and come from families with strong church backgrounds. Many grew up attending children's ministry or Sunday school and participating in youth groups, and those that studied at university were often involved in the student ministry of the church. For some, growing up religious had been a periodic experience rather than a continuous one. They recalled early experiences of going to church, usually as a child with their parents, or a parent, or grandparents. There were periods where church attendance was not part of their life. By adolescence, however, many had chosen faith and church affiliation for themselves. Indeed, five or six participants came from non-church/religious backgrounds. In some cases, the participants' parents were declared atheists.

The denominational representation covers all the largest denominations in New Zealand as well as many non-denominational, independent churches. The average number of churches participants had been involved in was five. The collective life stories of the participants involve over 160 different churches.

2

Embedded Faith

Embedded Faith: A Challenge to Individualism

What do I mean when I speak of embedded and owned faith? It is helpful to contrast embedded faith with the more privatized understanding of faith and religion popular in the sociology of religion. Religion in modern society is considered a personal matter, privatized such that neither church nor the state has the right to interfere. Emile Durkheim drew a distinction between "a free, private, optional religion, fashioned according to one's own needs and understanding" and "a religion handed down by tradition, formulated for a whole group and which is obligatory to practise."[1]

Evidence clearly supports that the religious landscape has continued to move in a privatized direction.[2] Spirituality has also been separated out from religion as people pursue their own private and non-institutional spiritual journey. This individualized spiritual journey is epitomised by "Sheilaism"[3] identified by Bellah et al. in *Habits of the Heart*. "Sheilaism" is the self-named faith of one of Bellah et al.'s interview participants called

1. Durkheim and Pickering, *Durkheim on Religion*, 96.

2. For example, "a Gallup poll finds that 81 percent of the American population feels 'an individual should arrive at his or her own religious beliefs independent of any church or synagogue' and that 78 percent feels 'a person can be a good Christian or Jew without attending a church or synagogue'" (Roof and McKinney, "Denominational America," 25).

3. Besecke contends that "for the past 15 years, the famous 'Sheila,' in *Habits of the Heart* has served as a kind of scholarly totem for this phenomenon" of individualised, non-institutional spirituality ("Seeing," 181).

Sheila: "I believe in God. I'm not a religious fanatic. I can't remember the last time I went to church. My faith has carried me a long way. It's Sheila-ism. Just my own little voice."[4] This individualized spiritual journey has developed into what Roof describes as a "spiritual quest culture" facilitated and sustained by the "spiritual marketplace."[5] This individualized spiritual quest for meaning and inner fulfilment takes priority over commitment to a faith community. As already noted, it is not uncommon for people to say they are "spiritual but not religious," by which people generally mean they do not subscribe to institutional religion.

This religious transformation has led to the "spiritual revolution claim" that religion—namely Christianity—has been eclipsed by spirituality. Paul Heelas and Linda Woodhead set out to test this claim in *The Spiritual Revolution* by using the town of Kendal in Britain as case study. In relation to Britain overall, Heelas and Woodhead concluded that "around 4,600,000 are active in the congregational domain on a typical Sunday, and around 900,000 in the holistic milieu during a typical week. This means that the claim of a spiritual revolution has taken place is exaggerated."[6]

Even the church as a religious institution has been accused of embracing the modern focus and centrality of the individual. G. Ernest Wright laments in *The Biblical Doctrine of Man in Society* that church congregations are more like secular clubs, describing them as "a gathering of individuals who know little of Christian community in the biblical sense and expect little from it."[7] He goes onto say,

> The worship of the Church has been heavily influenced by individualistic pietism, concerned largely, not with social organism, but with the individual's need of peace, rest and joy in the midst of the storms and billows of life. The self-centeredness of the pietistic search for salvation tends to exclude vigorous concern with community . . . the sectarianism of the Churches, and their racial and national cleavages,[8] are further expression of an individualism which distorts the nature of a Christian society and provides excuse for the world's individualism.[9]

4. Bellah et al., *Habits*, 21.

5. Roof, *Spiritual Marketplace*.

6. Heelas and Woodhead, *Spiritual Revolution*, 149.

7. Wright, *Biblical Doctrine*, 21.

8. We can now also add age to Wright's list of church "cleavages."

9. Ibid.

Theologian Stanley Grenz argues that western evangelicals influenced by modern culture have tended to understand the gospel in terms of the enlightenment's focus on the individual. He views modern church life as being characterised by what he calls the "crass individualism of the gospel and nature of the church."[10] Bellah et al. likewise acknowledge that religious individualism runs very deep in American society and is clearly evident in church religion.[11] Philip Mellor and Chris Shilling attribute the source of individualism embraced by the church to the Protestant Reformation, which not only played an important role in encouraging the deconstruction of relations between church and state, but also in "promoting the individualism and rationalism which came to mark the Enlightenment project."[12] One of the implications for religion, they argue, was that "Protestantism sought to *abstract* people from the natural, supernatural and social environments, and encouraged believers to apprehend and actively structure their lives as individuals through a committed and fundamentally cognitive engagement with the word of God."[13]

In *Bowling Alone*, Robert Putman points out that "trends in religious life reinforce rather than counter-balance the ominous plunge in social connectedness in the secular community."[14] There is no doubt that some churches still signify an impersonal, unfriendly institution. Yet people, Grenz suggests, are no longer willing to accept this as they seek to move from radical individualism to community.[15] Some of those I interviewed had negative experiences while looking for a church. But these are not the

10. Grenz, "Community of God," 20.

11. Bellah et al., *Habits*, 232.

12. Mellor and Shilling, *Re-Forming*, 98.

13. Ibid.

14. Putnam, *Bowling Alone*, 79. However, in Putnam's later book written with Lewis Feldstein, *Better Together*, the authors explore the way churches are "moving against the tide and creating new forms of social connectedness" (x). See also Ram Cnaan et al., "Serving Together."

15. Grenz, "Community of God," 19. Andy Crouch argues that one of the myths alive and well espoused in conferences and popular books on ministry sensitive to generational differences is that Gen X and Y long for "community." Crouch writes, "This is the most frequently cited characteristic of younger people, and it is half-true. We GenXers, Millennials, and so forth do long for deep, accountable relationships that the word *community* implies. But we also fear them . . . The truth is that we want the semblance of community without the risk or cost. We want to be surrounded by friendly acquaintances, but we don't want to be entangled, whether in a job, a marriage, or a church" ("Generation Misinformation," 83).

churches where they chose to stay. They keep on looking until they find a church community that they feel they can begin to connect with. Community, for those I interviewed, is important, and many are prepared to accept the risks and pay the costs involved in belonging to a church community. Yet privatization of religion, crass individualism, and objective Christianity is not the whole story. The story of privatized religion drowns out alternative narratives about the communal character of religion that continue to find expression in faith communities of memory.

Michel Maffesoli argues that "the problem of individualism obscures, in a more or less pertinent way, the whole of contemporary thinking."[16] Individualism, Maffesoli contends, is a kind of obligatory rite of passage for those wishing to build knowledge of modernity. Maffesoli questions this approach:

> So-called experts, untroubled by caution or scholarly nuance, disseminate a body of conventional, and somewhat disastrous, wisdom about the withdrawal into the self, the end of collective ideals or, taken in its widest sense, the public sphere. We then find ourselves face to face with a kind of *doxa*, [17] which may perhaps not endure but which is nevertheless widely received, and at the very least, has the potential to mask or deny the developing social forms of today. While some of these new forms are quite obvious, others remain underground; moreover, the spectacular aspect of the former leads one to dismiss them as irrelevant, a criticism that seems to flourish during times of crisis. This of course paves the way for the lazy tendency inherent in any *doxa*.[18]

Maffesoli argues that a fundamental paradox exists between "the constant interplay between the growing massification and the development of micro-groups," which he calls "tribes."[19] The main thrust of Maffesoli's argument is "to show, to describe and to analyse the social configurations that seem to go beyond individualism, in other words, the undefined mass, the faceless crowd and the tribalism consisting of a patchwork of small local entities."[20]

---

16. Maffesoli, *Time of the Tribes*, 9.
17. "Doxa" here refers to common belief or popular opinion.
18. Maffesoli, *Time of the Tribes*, 9.
19. Ibid., 6.
20. Ibid., 9.

Maffesoli suggests that the category of individualism, which has served us well over two centuries of social analysis, is completely exhausted: "It is often said that truth is stranger than fiction; let us therefore try to measure up to the truth. Perhaps we ought to show, as certain novelists have, that the individual is no longer as central as the great philosophers since the age of the Enlightenment have maintained."[21] Maffesoli's notion of the "tribe" is part of what he calls the "de-individualisation of society." In relation to religion specifically, Kelly Besecke argues that the "individualism" lens of religion obscures the way in which people are talking with each other about religious meaning. Besecke offers a communicative lens, one that highlights the important social role of interaction and communication: "Specifically, religion in the modern world is well understood not only as a kind of social institution, and not only as an individualized meaning system, but also as *a societal conversation about transcendent meanings*."[22] Heelas and Woodhead also confirm the importance of the group in the "spiritual milieu" of non-institutional religion.[23]

Embedded Faith

My interest, and the focus of this book, is on institutional religion—the church—and the way the faith journeys of young adults are embedded within it. Like Maffesoli's notion of the tribe, embedded faith provides a welcome contrast to the unbalanced focus on individualization, which, Maffesoli argues, has become an entrenched ideology within academia. Embedded faith provides a contrasting perspective to understandings of the changing religious landscape as one of religious consumerism,[24] while at the same time providing an alternative framework for religious investigation. However, embedded faith and religious consumption both occur in the changing religious landscape that emphasises the "new volunteerism." Stephen Hunt explains,

> If people are indeed now free to choose the religion which suits them, this has been enhanced by what can be called the "new voluntarism" . . . Away from institutional and social pressures, people

21. Ibid., 10 (emphasis in the original).

22. Besecke defines transcendent meanings as "references to a context of life that exists on a plane beyond ("transcending") apparent reality" ("Seeing," 181).

23. Heelas and Woodhead, *Spiritual Revolution*, 66–67.

24. For example, see Roof, *Spiritual Marketplace*.

are now at liberty to follow a personal quest for meaning rather than embrace a *collective act of religious involvement* that has typified traditional Christianity. The outcome is that there is little or no social pressure on the individual to embrace a faith through the coercion of the community since, in the last assessment, the momentum originates with the religious "seeker."[25]

Embedded faith, unlike the personal spiritual quest, continues to embrace this "*collective act of religious involvement*" while at the same time expressing the "new voluntarism." In chapter 5, we will consider the impact of geographical mobility on embedded faith. Faith embedded within a community of memory can also be viewed in the context of Robert Wuthnow's argument for the welcomed rediscovery of the group as a corrective "to a field (religious research) in which the psychology of the individual has long reigned supreme."[26]

Carroll notes that, as part of this "rediscovery" of the group over the last few decades, "Congregations received increasing attention as important loci of religious meaning and belonging."[27] Such an understanding of congregations is central to this book; otherwise, people would not see the value in embedding their faith in such religious communities. Martin Marty suggested that an appropriate religious map for the 1970s focused attention on group identities and social belonging.[28] In this way, embedded faith as an alternative framework for religious investigation demonstrates the salience of religious group identity and social belonging.

This book explores the way in which faith is embedded in church as a "community of memory." Following Bellah and his colleagues in *Habits of the Heart*, I understand communities of memory to counter the individualism of society. The faith I talk about in this book is an embedded faith. It is embedded in church communities and in relationships. The faith journeys of those I interviewed do not make sense outside of a faith community. As Emily, a twenty-eight-year-old single woman, said,

EMILY: *Church is important because I don't want to be a Christian by myself, I don't want to be an island. Because I feel like I need other people; I learn and grow when I'm connected to other people. Yeah, I do life better*

25. Hunt, *Alternative Religions*, 11 (emphasis mine).

26. Wuthnow, "Two Traditions," 21.

27. Carroll, "Reflexive Ecclesiology," 550.

28. Marty, *Nation*.

actually when I'm . . . when there are people I can talk to, when there are people who hold me accountable; when there are people that I can help as well. I might have gone through something that I can help someone with. Or I might have a skill or ability or something that can contribute to either the life of the church, or a cell group, or individual. Something like that. And that is a new learning thing for me as well, because I have always been very independent and quite happy being independent. But in terms of my faith I need other people.

Such stories of religious commitment and involvement in a church community are an example of what Bellah et al. call the "constituted self," a sense of identity which only makes sense in the context of community. The constituted self stands in contrast to the "unencumbered self," which is based on "pure, undetermined choice, free of tradition, obligation, or commitment, as the essence of the self."[29] Theologically, this is Walter Brueggemann's "covenanted self," which he sees as a radical alternative to the consumer autonomy that has become so prevalent in our society and has invaded the life of the church in debilitating ways.[30]

The constituted self and the covenanted self are evident in participants' explanations of why they go to church and the role that it plays in their lives:

ALISHA: *I think just having that sense of family and a community is really important to me. And I think that if I don't go to church, then my faith suffers. I don't get that encouragement, and I'm not being challenged in my faith as well. So I go to get challenged.*

ROGER: *Sure, there was the spiritual side of learning more and I went to worship and serve God. But there were the friends, the whole community sort of thing. That was important. I would still go along to keep in touch with people and catch up with people. There's always been a part of me of wanting to help others. There has definitely been an element of that.*

SIMON: *I just loved the community of the church, and to be honest, my favorite part of church is the community and always has been. I would even to go so far as saying that my favorite part of church is before and after church. Meeting people before, and then meeting people after.*

29. Bellah, et al., *Habits*, 152.
30. Brueggemann, *Covenanted Self*, 1.

Faith, then, for these young adults is not seen as an individual quest, but as a way of life that is encouraged and supported through a church community and relationships. The religious practice of gathering on a Sunday, and being involved in the life of a local church, is regarded as essential rather than an optional extra.

Religion as a Chain of Memory

Danièle Hervieu-Léger understands religion as a "chain of memory." An individual believer becomes a member of a faith community through this "chain" that gathers past, present, and future members.[31] The community's existence and identity is founded on this collective memory. Hervieu-Léger's chain of memory shares parallels with what Wilfred Smith calls "cumulative tradition" on the one hand, and "faith" on the other, with the living person serving as the link between the two.[32] By "faith," Smith means a "personal faith . . . an inner religious experience or involvement of a particular person; the impingement on him of the transcendent, putative or real."[33] By "cumulative tradition," he means the historical deposit of past religious life of a community—temples, scriptures, theological systems, dance patterns, legal and other social institutions, conventions, moral codes, myths, and so on—that can be passed on from one person, one generation, to another. Passing on the faith from one generation to the next provides a vital link in the chain of memory. It is one of the tasks of any community of memory to pass on its stories, rituals, and practices to those coming after them. Failure to do so results in a break (and potentially missing links) in the chain of memory, resulting in what Hervieu-Léger calls "amnesic societies."[34]

Jan Assmann suggests that just as we can speak of "collective memory" of a group of people, we can also speak of a "connective memory."[35] This simultaneous "collective" and "connective" memory is the bonding nature of memory expressed, Assmann points out, with "particular clarity in the English-language words *re-membering* and *re-collecting*, which evoke the idea of putting 'members' back together (re-membering and

31. Hervieu-Léger, *Religion as a Chain*, 81.

32. Smith, *Meaning and End*, 156.

33. Ibid., 157.

34. Hervieu-Léger, *Religion as a Chain*, ix.

35. Assmann, *Religion and Cultural Memory*, 10–11.

dis-membering) and 're-collecting' things that have been dispersed."[36] In this way, church communities keep alive a memory that has no support in everyday life.

Churches, as communities of memory, keep alive an openness to experiences and "signals of transcendence" while at the same time keeping at bay the wider social situation observed by Peter Berger in *A Rumour of Angles*, wherein he argues that "transcendence has been reduced to a rumour."[37] When the gods are forgotten, as they are in amnesic societies, their existence vanishes from the minds and practices of society. This is analogous with Durkheim's argument that the existence of the gods is kept alive through people gathering to remember and celebrate them: "the gods would die if the cult were not celebrated. The purpose of the cult, then, is not only to bring profane subjects into communion with sacred beings, but also to sustain those sacred beings in life, to restore them and to ensure their perpetual regeneration."[38] Thus, "communication," as Besecke points out, "is what makes God socially real."[39]

Churches, then, are communities of memory that have a history, one that is remembered and retold. Although beyond the scope of this study, it is worth noting that one of the challenges to both the social form of church and Christian theology in a spiritual marketplace full of competing and alternative stories is to regain confidence in its own story and religious heritage. As Volf writes, "The social form of the church must find its basis in its own faith rather than in its social environment. Only thus can churches function effectively as prophetic signs in their environment."[40]

Church congregations are communities of memory that retell their stories on a regular basis, remembering the scriptural stories of faith, as well as those of people within the congregation who have embodied and exemplified the meaning of the community. Such stories can also include more painful memories of loss, failure, struggle, and doubt. The stories we tell are embedded in the story of the communities in which we participate. Memories decisively shape our identities. This occurs at an inward and outward level; as Volf points out, "Inwardly, in our own self-perception, we *are* much of what we remember about ourselves . . . In similar fashion,

36. Ibid., 110.

37. Berger, *Rumour*, 119.

38. Durkheim, *Elementary*, 256–57.

39. Besecke, "Seeing," 190.

40. Volf, *End of Memory*, 15.

outwardly, in the way others perceive us, we *are* what others remember about us . . . Memory, as the argument goes, is central to identity."[41]

Storytelling is an important aspect of embedded faith. People share their own faith journey with others within a community of memory as the community itself tells its own story that shapes its collective identity. The stories people share are often centered on life and faith and how to integrate the two. Doubts, struggles, hopes, successes, and failures also make their way into various stories. Grace spoke of the way that church keeps her faith growing rather than stagnating:

GRACE: *My reasons for going to church are . . . one is the social network of being with other Christians. And I think I grew a lot more through just being with other Christians than I do just from the sermons in church, you know, just talking about life and their faith, and you're hanging out with Christians more. And the other reason for going to church is to help me keep becoming more like Jesus. I think if I stopped going to church and tried to do it on my own I wouldn't be challenged. I wouldn't see messages that challenged me, or hear something through somebody else's viewpoint that made me think. I would miss the worship and drawing close to God through that, and being able to support other Christians in their faith as well.*

Talking about life, faith, and God takes place inside and outside of the church's Sunday gathering. Besecke argues that when looked at culturally, "religion looks like a *conversation*—a societal conversation about transcendent meanings."[42] But religion within a community of memory is more than simply a conversation; it is also a learning community.

For Weber, a ritualistic religion such as Christianity (his example was Judaism) may exert an ethical effect in an indirect way by requiring that participants be schooled in their religious tradition.[43] Being part of a community of memory involves a process Stanley Hauerwas and William Willimon describe as being initiated into a community of language, where ethics—and, I would add, faith—is a way of *seeing* before it is a matter of *doing*.[44] This is what Bellah and his research team have called "second languages" of moral life; the first language being that of the self-reliant

41. Ibid., 24.

42. Besecke, "Seeing," 190.

43. Weber, *Sociology*, 154.

44. Hauerwas and Willimon, *Resident Aliens*.

individual. Second languages are the languages of tradition and commitment in communities of memory.[45] There are, Hauerwas and Willimon point out, "ethical aristocrats," whose habits and way of life are worth observing, imitating, and copying.[46] Faith journeys are embedded in church communities as individuals learn the language of faith and what it means to be a Christian.[47]

Becoming religious involves becoming skilled in the language, the symbol system of a given religion. Embedded faith learns to see, to observe the way of faith, and comes to speak the language that comes with its own interpretive community dialect. Becoming Christian involves learning the story of Israel and Jesus "well enough to interpret and experience oneself and one's world in its terms."[48] But, as Stanley Fish's theory of "interpretive communities" makes clear, there is no single way of telling this biblical Christian story, only what Fish describes as "extensions of community perspectives."[49]

Interpretive Communities

Communities of memory are also what Fish calls "interpretive communities." In attempting to identify the *real* reading experience, in relation to which others were deviations or distortions, Fish came to see that "the identification of what was real and normative occurred within interpretive communities and what was normative for the members of one community would be seen as strange (if it could be seen at all) by members of another."[50] Fish's concept of interpretive communities helps us to see that how the biblical Christian story is told is an extension of community perspectives. Different churches, denominations, and faith traditions have slightly different memories, and will therefore tell and interpret the scriptural story differently. An evangelical church will interpret and tell the story differently from a liberal church, which will again tell the story differently from

45. Bellah et al., *Habits*, 154.

46. Hauerwas and Willimon, *Resident Aliens*, 98.

47. Discussing the implications of Israel receiving the Ten Commandments at Sinai, Brueggemann writes, "When one embraces Yahweh, one embraces not only a very different God, but also membership in a very different social practice" (*Covenanted*, 26).

48. Lindbeck, *Nature*, 34

49. Fish, *Is There a Text*, 6.

50. Ibid., 15.

a Catholic church. Church, then, is an interpretive community of memory. By combining Bellah et al.'s notion of communities of memory with Fish's notion interpretive communities, it is possible to develop an understanding of churches as "interpretive communities of memory."

Fish emphasizes the social character of interpretive communities and argues that meaning comes already calculated

> not because of norms embedded in the language but because language is always perceived, from the very first, within a structure of norms. That structure, however, is not abstract and independent but social; and therefore it is not a single structure with a privileged relationship to the process of communication as it occurs in any situation but a structure that changes when one situation, with its assumed background of practices, purposes, and goals, has given way to another.[51]

Fish argues that interpretive strategies proceed from the community to which they belong, thereby making them "community property." The individual, Fish suggests, also becomes community property, or as we could say, embedded in community, insofar as interpretive strategies at once enable and limit the operations of their consciousness.[52] In a chapter titled, "Stanley Fish, the Pope, and the Bible," Stanley Hauerwas suggests that Pope John Paul II and Stanley Fish shared a common view when it came to the politics of interpretation: "Both men assume that the text, and in this case the text of Scripture, can be interpreted only in the context of an 'interpretive community.' For John Paul II (and all the apostles before him in the tradition), the community necessary for the reading of Scripture is the Roman Catholic Church, which includes the Office of the Magisterium."[53] Hauerwas argues, along with the Catholic and Orthodox Church, that Scripture only makes sense within the practices and traditions of the church.

Interpretive activities are not free, but constrained by understood practices and assumptions of, for example, an institution, and not the rules and fixed meanings of a language system. Furthermore, the claims of objectivity and subjectivity are dissolved, Fish argues, because the authorizing agency, the center of interpretive authority, is at once both and neither:

51. Ibid., 318.
52. Ibid., 14.
53. Hauerwas, *Unleashing*, 21.

> An interpretive community is not objective because as a bundle of interests, of particular purposes and goals, its perspective is interested rather than neutral; but by the very same reasoning, the meanings and texts produced by an interpretive community are not subjective because they do not proceed from an isolated individual but from a public and conventional point of view.[54]

As we will discuss in later chapters, the way churches understand and interpret the life of faith is salient to the question about where to embed faith, or for providing insight into why a person chooses to dis-embed their faith from a particular interpretive faith community and re-embed it in another one.

Generations X and Y as a Generational Chain in Religious Memory

The task of any community of memory is to pass on its stories, rituals, and practices to those coming after them. Research, however, clearly demonstrates a breakdown in the passing on of faith as the religious affiliation of each proceeding birth cohort declines.[55] The mass exodus from active involvement in churches by Baby Boomers in their youth has been well documented.[56] Because "children born into any faith community are the primary means by which that community replenishes itself," as Roof points out, this exodus has "created a serious problem of institutional replacement."[57] Even Baby Boomers who chose to remain within faith communities, Miller and Miller suggest, were reluctant to impose religion on their children, which contributed to the generational decline in church attendance from Baby Boomers to Gen X.[58] Beaudoin suggests that for Generation X, the children of Boomers, "the step from religion-as-an-accessory to religion-as-unnecessary was a slight shuffle, not a long leap."[59] Roof points out that the religious lines dividing those born before World War II and those born afterwards are drawn more sharply than the lines separating Boomers from

54. Ibid., 14.

55. See Belzer et al., "Congregations That Get It" as well as Voas and Crockett, "Religion in Britain."

56. For example, see Roof, *Spiritual Marketplace*, or Ward, "Losing."

57. Roof, *Spiritual Marketplace*, 51.

58. Miller and Miller, "Understanding," 4.

59. Beaudoin, *Virtual*, 13.

Generation X: "Older generations remain more loyal to institutions and doctrinal beliefs whereas younger generations register higher scores on experiential measures not directly related to 'church religion.'"[60] However, research also shows that high levels of parental religious involvement, such as active church affiliation, are associated with more effective transmission of religious affiliation.[61] Even when faith is passed on, those inheriting it need to decide whether they want to remain in their parents' particular interpretive faith community or not.

The majority of those I interviewed had grown up religious. The transition from inherited faith to owned faith is in some ways a unique rite of passage for those that have grown up religious. This rite of passage occurs as people identify with the Christian faith and *internalize* it. Some of the participants who inherited faith cannot recall a time when God and the church were not a part of their life. Many embrace the faith in childhood innocence, long before they comprehend with any depth what the life of faith requires. Others simply perceive themselves as Christians because their parents are Christians, and because they go to church. Churchgoing and being a Christian are often inseparable in the early years. One is a Christian because they go to church, and one goes to church because one is a Christian. This is certainly the impression created for children by parents whose only visible form of religiosity is going to church on Sunday. Eugene, for example, made an interesting distinction when he described his family as a church-going one rather than as "a really outgoing Christian family." As Eugene explains, "Except for grace, there was not much prayer or reading the Bible at home. In many respects, I think our parents left it up to us to find our own faith." Eugene's parents illustrate the parental reluctance to impose religion on their children discussed by Miller and Miller. It is worth noting, however, that the parents of a number of participants were actively involved in passing on their faith to their children.

Even in Eugene's situation, the practice of going to church with his family provided him with a specific religious social space to make friends and belong to a youth group. It was with this youth group that he travelled to a Christian youth event in Wellington, New Zealand that provided Eugene with a stepping stone on his way to owning his faith as a fourteen-year-old:

60. Roof, *Spiritual Marketplace*, 52.
61. See Nooney, "Keeping the Faith," and Smith, *Soul Searching*.

> EUGENE: *That was the first time in worship that I experienced God. And that was one of the turning points I think—when I actually realized that I was worshipping a God that was real and I wasn't just going to church or to youth group. It was in many respects where I started to own my faith.*

Carroll and Roof make an important distinction between the churched and unchurched in relation to generational distinctiveness.[62] A person's current church involvement is strongly influenced by the extent to which they were involved in a church community growing up, for "people whose parents brought them up within a faith, or who choose it on their own when they are young, tend to remain active in later years; that is to say, youthful religious exposure is likely to stick even if predicting when it might reassert itself is impossible."[63] One of the characteristics of owned faith is that it operates at a different level of influence on the life of the believer compared to that of inherited faith.

The Transition from Inherited Faith to Owned Faith

Faith and Levels of Influence

Herbert Kelman argues that changes in attitudes and actions produced by social influence occur at different levels: compliance, identification, and internalization.[64] According to Kelman, "The three processes represent three qualitatively different ways of accepting influence."[65] Therefore, "the underlying processes in which an individual engages when he adopts induced behaviour may be different, even though the resulting overt behaviour may appear the same."[66]

Compliant behavior according to Kelman, is not based on the value of the action itself but rather on the social effect of accepting influence; namely, approval by others. Compliance therefore, Kelman explains, takes place when an individual adopts encouraged behavior, such as attending church, in order to receive the approval of another person or group while at the same time avoiding disapproval or punishment. Kelman maintains that

62. Carroll and Roof, *Bridging*.
63. Ibid., 75.
64. Kelman, "Compliance," 51–60.
65. Ibid., 53.
66. Ibid.

when an individual's behavior and attitudes are based on identification, they believe in their responses, although the why—the ideas, beliefs, and reasoning—behind them are not so important. What is important is identification with another person or group, such as a church youth group, youth leader, or a group of friends at school. People conform to social influence out of a desire to maintain satisfying relationships. At the level of internalization, Kelman argues, an individual conforms to social influence because it is consistent with their value system rather than the benefits that it may bring to their relationships. The actual content or value of the behavior is intrinsically rewarding to the individual[67]

There are parallels between internalization of belief and the shift from implicit systems of meaning to the explicit ones characteristic of Fowler's Stage 4 Individuative-Reflective faith. According to Fowler, the two essential features of this stage are "the critical distancing from one's previous assumptive value system and the emergence of an executive ego."[68] Rather than a critical distancing from a previous assumptive value system in relation to faith, what occurs is closer to a critical evaluation of faith as a way of life. However, in order for this shift to happen, a critical distancing occurs from the contrasting, alternative lifestyle value system of social groups outside of church. With the emergence of an executive ego, a relocation of authority within the self takes place. Significant others, and their judgments, advice, opinions, and expectations remain important to the Individuative-Reflective person, but are submitted to an executive ego, an internal source of authority that reserves the right to choose and take responsibility for such choices.

The Faith Crossroad

I define a "faith crossroad" as an intersection of choice between following or walking away from faith. It is at such a crossroad that adolescents and young adults are faced with making the choice about what they believe, and whether their belief is going to influence their life or not. That is, are they going to live out what they believe? This is the moral and ethical imperative of faith, of calling oneself a Christian. Adolescents and young adults face a crossroad of faith when confronted with two contrasting and conflicting lifestyle choices: to follow a path of faith, or one that rejects or abandons

67. Ibid.

68. Fowler, *Stages*, 179.

faith, or alternately, lives in a way that does not take faith seriously. Joshua found himself at such a faith crossroad during his teenage years:

JOSHUA: *Through my teenage years, like kind of most teenage boys, I got into the teenage party thing quite a bit, and a lot of my faith was important to me because it was so much of who I was through my family and all that—you know, it was definitely a part of me. But there were certain areas where I didn't live a Christian life, you know, and would be out partying quite a lot. So there was always a bit of tension there between what kind of life am I . . . I've got to make a decision at some point, but I just kept putting it off and putting it off. But I knew that inevitably I would either have to walk away from faith or walk away from just being stupid [laughs].*

Faith transitions can be a gradual process for young adults as they develop and decide upon which values are important to them and what role faith is going to play in their lives. Festinger would explain Joshua's "bit of tension"—the result of trying to hold simultaneously the different values and beliefs of his contrasting social groups—as *cognitive dissonance*. The core of Festinger's theory of dissonance holds that:

1. There may exist dissonance or "nonfitting" relations among cognitive elements.

2. The existence of dissonance gives rise to pressures to reduce the dissonance and to avoid increases in dissonance.

3. Manifestations of the operation of these pressures include behavior changes, changes of cognition, and circumspect exposure to new information and new opinions.[69]

Festinger defines the terms "dissonance" and "consonance" as referring to

> relations which exist between pairs of "elements" . . . These elements refer to what has been called cognition, that is, the things a person knows about himself, about his behaviour, and about his surroundings. These elements, then, are "knowledges," if I may coin the plural form of the word. Some of these elements represent knowledge about oneself: what one does, what one feels, what one wants or desires, what one is, and the like. Other elements of knowledge concern the world in which one lives: what is where,

69. Festinger, *Cognitive*, 31.

what leads to what, what things are satisfying or painful; or incon-
sequential or important, etc.[70]

Festinger argues that individuals strive towards consistency within themselves. This consistency exists, for the most part, between what a person
knows or believes and how they act and choose to live. The desire to resolve
inconsistencies that produce tension is apparent in Joshua's story. Despite
acknowledging that he needed to make a decision one way or the other,
he continued to postpone it. Joshua's comments suggest that a person can
remain at the faith crossroad for some time before making a decision about
which way to go.

**Did you feel a tension prior to that between what you believed and how
you lived?**

JOSHUA: *Yeah. From when I was sixteen to seventeen, I would be out on
Saturday night drinking myself into a coma and then helping out with
youth group on Sunday night, you know. Obviously the tension of
what-if-people-found-out kind of thing . . . and sometimes I think they
probably knew [laughs]. I guess the mind games you play with yourself,
where you feel that you are not being honest with yourself or with other
people. That fear of being found out you know. But at the same time, it's
like you wanted to please both people. You wanted to be cool and fit in,
and at the same time you knew that this God thing was important, but
it wasn't really cool.*

Did you have two quite distinct social circles?

JOSHUA: *Yes. I had my high school friends who are really good friends. I still
keep in touch with almost all of them today. They're all Catholics so they
are quite comfortable drinking and then going to church once a year and
absolving [laughs]. God was often the topic of conversation. We both
had different ideas of what it meant. Should it really affect the way you
live your life, I guess. They didn't seem to think so and tried to encourage
me that I didn't need to think about it either.*

The faith of Joshua's Catholic friends seems to have been at the level of
compliance. Joshua, up until he faced the faith crossroad, was operating out
of identification within both social networks: friends and church. This was

70. Ibid., 9.

motivated by his desire to fit in. The desire for acceptance is particularly strong among adolescents as they form their identity and understanding of themselves. Joshua ultimately transitioned from identification to internalization, from inherited faith to owned faith. Because compliance and identification both require social motivation and presence, there is sometimes slippage between them. The stories of those facing a crossroad suggest that the attitude of non-compliance needs to be added to the three distinctions identified by Kelman. Non-compliance runs alongside compliance. Maintaining two competing lifestyles in different worlds means that compliance in one is non-compliance in the other, and vice versa. People can also identify with two contrasting social groups in terms of behavior, resulting in a double life. Identification can be complex. As Festinger argues, people are searching for consistency. Living in competing worlds of compliance and non-compliance is a source of cognitive dissonance. It is also important to acknowledge, as Festinger does, that people "are not always successful in explaining away or in rationalizing inconsistencies to themselves. For one reason or another, attempts to achieve consistency may fail. The inconsistency then simply continues to exist. Under such circumstances—that is, in the presence of inconsistency—there is psychological discomfort."[71]

It is in choosing to venture down the road of faith that a transition from inherited faith to owned faith occurs. Belief and faith take on the understanding inherent in its semantic root. As Wilfred Cantwell Smith has demonstrated, "the phrase 'belief in God' originally meant in English a loyal pledging of oneself to God, a decision and commitment to live one's life in His service."[72] This understanding is in contrast to the meaning of "to believe" in modern English, which means to hold an opinion, whether it is right or wrong (though increasingly, Smith argues, it means to hold an opinion that is at best dubious). As a result, Smith argues, belief has come to suggest a primarily cognitive enterprise. In the transition to faith ownership, I would argue that young adults are returning to an earlier understanding of belief/faith that Smith identifies. He explains, "Through many Christian centuries the ceremonial *credo* by which one joined the Church, or the re-iterated but also ceremonial and activist 'I believe' of the Sunday service creed, was strikingly like the performative 'I do' of a marriage service, was a promise, and bore no resemblance to the descriptive

---

71. Festinger, *Cognitive*, 2.
72. Smith, *Faith and Belief*, 42.

propositionalism of a modern theorist's reporting on the current state of his opinions."[73]

Participants spoke of belief and faith interchangeably as a way of life. The spiritual dissonance experienced by young adults resulted from belief and practice being out of line. Aligning one's actions and behaviors with one's beliefs could reduce this spiritual dissonance. Faith, then, as others have argued, can be understood as a verb, rather than a noun. That is, as an active pledge of faith rather than the mere belief in propositions.[74]

At the juncture of the faith crossroad lies an ethical imperative requiring consistency between belief and practice. The transition into faith ownership is an acknowledgement that belief, as in propositional beliefs or statements, or believing something to be either true or false, is not enough. Faith ownership involves living out one's faith. What one believes therefore shapes one's practice, one's behavior, and one's attitude. What I mean by owned faith is something similar to the understanding of faith developed by H. Richard Niebuhr as "confidence and fidelity."[75] What Niebuhr means by this is "the attitude and action of confidence in, and fidelity to, certain realities as the source of value and the object of loyalty."[76] Niebuhr goes on to say that "as loyalty, such radical faith is decision for and commitment to the One beyond all the many as head and center of the realm of being; its cause, the universe of being, elicits and requires fidelity. So for faith, the kingdom of God is both the rule that is trusted and the realm to which loyalty is given."[77]

The challenge of Niebuhr's description of faith was certainly felt by many of the young adults I interviewed. Niebuhr's explanation of faith, involving loyalty and commitment to the kingdom of God, is evident in Roger's story as he describes the choices he was faced with at a faith crossroad. Roger was raised in a Christian family. His first memorable experience of faith happened when he was nine years old. He attended a children's Bible camp, where campers were invited to give their lives to Jesus and accept him as Lord and Savior. Roger responded by going up to receive prayer and making a decision to follow Jesus. He remembers that moment as a marker point in relation to his faith. Fast forward another nine years—Roger, at

73. Ibid., 44.

74. Along with Fowler, see Westerhoff, *Our Children*, as well as Parks, *Critical Years*.

75. Niebuhr, *Radical*, 8.

76. Ibid., 35.

77. Ibid.

eighteen years old, had embarked upon his overseas experience, a New Zealand rite of passage. Presented with alternative lifestyles, Roger faced a faith crossroad:

ROGER: *I remembered being there after two months, and I needed to really make a decision as to how I was going to live. And this ended up being the most significant decision that I've made. I guess just being pressured. The two main things over there were the girls and the alcohol, and with both being shoved in your face the whole time and just thinking, "Oh my goodness, I really need to sort something out and really make a decision here otherwise I'm just going to end up being a bit lukewarm," like with what I was observing what was happening to my flatmate. And so I weighed up the cost of following Jesus . . . and in light of what Christ has done for me and if all that I know is true, then I need to submit my life to Christ and not make decisions to go down this track of what was being shoved in my face everyday. So that was really meaningful for me at the time.*

Roger's decision to follow Jesus at nine was made in a different social context and stage of life—and with very different implications—compared to his reconfirmation of his commitment to faith at eighteen. At eighteen, away from home for the first time, Roger had to once again decide if he was going to keep following Jesus. His faith had remained important to him up until this crossroad. Roger's comments suggest that the stakes had become higher. There was a clear alternative path that promised a certain allure, albeit one detrimental to his faith. As Roger explains above, it was not an easy choice, but a decision that he wrestled with. What is paramount in Roger's choice to *keep* following is that when faith is understood as a journey, rather than a one-off conversion experience (that is, a "once saved, always saved" mentality), is that one needs to keep choosing the path one is on, especially in a pluralistic society with many paths to choose from.

Geographic Mobility and the Faith Crossroad

It was not uncommon for young adults I interviewed to face their first significant faith crossroad when they moved away from home for the first time, either to travel or to attend university. De Vaus argues that when geographic mobility frees a person from coercive pressures, then it is likely to lead to changes in compliant behavior. Church attendance for some young people is based on compliance, because attendance is often required by young peoples' parents rather than as a free choice.[78] In contrast, beliefs and attitudes based on identification and internalization will be more re-silient against the effects of geographic mobility on religious commitment and change. When a person has internalized beliefs and values, then they will continue to identify with them despite having moved away from their referent group and social support network. They will, however, seek out a similar social network in the place of destination, which I will come to shortly.

Sophie had already transitioned from inherited faith to owned faith before she moved away from home when she was eighteen to go to univer-sity. Sophie met some people at the hostel she was staying at, and together they went looking for a church to attend. Not long after moving away from home, Sophie faced a faith crossroad.

What about the church? Was your faith growing during that time? Was university challenging your faith?

SOPHIE: *That was probably quite a big time. Because it's a time when you can just say, "aw nah," and just walk away, and just join the rest of the university and living it up. And you have to make a very intentional decision to be a Christian when you are there. And so that was quite significant.*

How did you live out that intentionality of being a Christian?

SOPHIE: *Well, a lot of it was just the way that you live, because you get to choose how you live at that point because you've left home. So you are living in a hostel [with people] that are getting very drunk, or a lot of sleeping around or whatever. So I guess it is just your lifestyle decisions, as well as about what you want to do, and so then that becomes quite ob-vious to them that you're not doing what they're doing. Which is always a hard call when you are trying to fit in.*

Once again we see the ethical decisions that people often face at the faith crossroad. Choosing how one is going to live has a reflexive dimen-sion, as people reflect on how they are currently living and whether they want to continue living like that or make different choices for consistency

---

78. de Vaus, "Impact," 391–403.

between belief and practice. This reflexive practice involves questions of identity that lie at the faith crossroad that adolescents and young adults face in making decisions about who they are and who they want to become.

Describing oneself as a Christian takes on added significance as young adults begin to think through the implications of this identity category. This was the case for Imogen:

IMOGEN: *I had finished school and I went up to university. And my first year of university . . . I mean I loved being away from home, and I remember being on class camp and meeting this completely zany, weird as Christian girl. I was like, "I don't really know if I want to be a Christian if I am going to be like her." But she sort of asked me point blank, you know, "Are you a Christian?" And I sort of stood there and thought, this is a decision time. I can say "Yes I am," and that's the path I am going to go down or I can say "No," and I can choose to walk away. And I thought, well I don't want to walk away from this, and so I chose to say, "Yeah, I am a Christian."*

Internalization of faith occurred for Imogen as she decided that the content of her faith was worth living out. Stages of the life cycle require us to make different choices regarding faith. Young adults face particular questions about whether to follow their faith or not, especially through the transition to university or overseas travel and moving away from home.

The Faith Crossroad and Social Networks

Social networks are influential in the decision-making process that occurs at the faith crossroad. For example, Santos inherited faith from his parents. He was socialized into faith and church from birth. He has strong memories of being dragged along when he was younger, despite not wanting to go. Going to church was a family affair, and so he was required to be there. Santos attended out of compliance in order to avoid the disapproval of his parents. More positively, he says he went because his mother encouraged him to keep going. Otherwise, there was a strong possibility he would have stopped going to church altogether. Santos began to appreciate church more as he moved into his teenage years and began attending the youth-focused evening service at Flaxbush Baptist. Santos' primary social network, however, remained outside church, particular his sporting and school network.

Church and faith were not central to Santos' life, one of the characteristics of inherited faith. The main impetus for going was his mother's encouragement, which created a sense of duty, a family obligation, something not yet freely chosen. As such, church did not play a significant social role for Santos. As Santos tells it, "It was very loose, in terms of social network. I would turn up and there were people that I would say hi to every Sunday. But if I didn't say hi to them, or if I didn't see them, it wasn't a big deal. I wasn't seeing them outside of church or anything along those lines. It didn't fulfil that same role."

This changed during Santos' university years. The catalyst for change was what could be called "ethnographic reflexivity," that is, the ability of someone like Santos to stand back and see where life is heading by observing others within their social group, their life, behaviors, and the consequences of particular actions. Reflexivity encourages use of the sociological imagination. The first fruit of the sociological imagination, according to Mills, is that an individual can understand their own experience and begin to assess their future by locating themselves within their time alongside others in similar circumstances.[79]

SANTOS: *The friends that I had been maintaining through my sport I started to see as a lot more destructive, a lot more harmful than I had realized them to be in that they had some impacts on me that I wasn't very happy with. So I took some pretty strong steps to remove myself from those friendship circles and in particular the rugby one, with its strong drinking influence and a lot of things in the culture that I didn't particularly enjoy that much. So I stepped away from that a lot, but in doing so had a great big friendship void and that's what the church helped fill for me. It was awkward but it took a lack of another friendship circle to really start and make something happen within the church. And so there was a large drive I suppose, or enthusiasm from me to try and find some friends within that group. And they're some of my stronger friends today. So you know, there was a great connection that we are sharing today.*

Employing the sociological imagination, Santos assessed where his life was currently heading with the friends that he was keeping within the rugby scene. He observed the destructive impact their behavior was having their lives and the influence it was having on him. Realizing that his life was not heading where he wanted it to be, Santos took steps to change it.

79. Mills, *Sociological*, 5.

"But of course," Santos went on to say, "as soon as you start thinking about changing it, you need to start thinking about where you are changing it to. And to me it was easy at that time to change it to where I was getting input that was coming from the right place and that was from the church."

Social networks influence behavior for good or bad. Removing himself from what Santos judged to be a harmful social circle left a friendship void. This provided motivation to begin to make friends within the church community. Santos began to develop some strong friendships within church that have remained to this day. Santos' newly emerging social circle during this period resulted in church taking on a new importance in his life:

SANTOS: *Church became a lot more integrated into my life than it had been. Then of course, then you start becoming a lot [more open to church]; I suppose I started absorbing a lot more what was being fed to me rather than it was something that I had to do, there was something that I am actually choosing to do. I'm choosing to spend time with my friends. I'm choosing to go to this church and what it is I'm getting out of it. Often, it's tied in with the university time where you start taking on things for yourself and choosing things for yourself, and that's a lot of what I was doing then.*

Transitioning from inherited faith to owned faith for Santos also involved changing social circles, or at least forming a new social circle that supported his faith.

Carlos, who had also grown up in church, embraced the drinking party scene when he was fifteen. In part, he wanted to experiment in areas that the church did not encourage. Carlos was leading a double life. As he explains, "I was still going boozing on a Friday night and going to Sunday church." Exploring this drinking party scene is typical for many New Zealand adolescents. I asked Carlos whether this experimentation created any tension for him in relation to his religious beliefs and practice, to which he replied, "Not really. I wasn't aware of the tension at the time. I think there were so many other Christians doing the same thing in the church that I was going to that it never really had that much of a lasting tension where I couldn't reconcile my lifestyle to Christianity."

After a while, however, this newly adopted lifestyle failed to provide Carlos with a sense of meaning and purpose. Carlos began to take his faith and church more seriously following a dramatic experience of God that he felt when he was seventeen:

CARLOS: *One night I had gone out boozing and came home and felt really quite empty because I had gone to this party and didn't really know many people. I felt quite outside of the circle, quite ostracised from the drinking lifestyle which I had embraced. And I just had, I guess, a God experience, where I came home, looked up at the sky, and just remembered that God was still there. I dropped the non-Christian lifestyle, and within a couple of months, I was back into church full steam ahead.*

So almost like a conscious line in the sand?

CARLOS: *Yeah it was. And that affected a lot of friendships that I had outside of church because I was no longer going out boozing and I wasn't hanging out with these people that I had developed quite strong friendships with over the year. And then I got baptised when I was seventeen. I invited some of the friends that I had been hanging out with who are non-Christians along, and that was very much a line in the sand. They did come. Some of them supported it. But it really was quite a big line in the sand. And it did sort of damage a lot of the friendships that I had.*

Intentionally, or just the way it worked out?

CARLOS: *Just the way it worked out because you can't continue that lifestyle. And also because I think they've got a lot of ideas on church, and probably have got a lot of stigma attached with church, and don't want to be involved or associated with it.*

Carlos' experience of God and his "returning to the faith" is what Richardson and Stewart have described as "the conversion trajectory."[80] Kilbourne and Richardson explain that "the trajectory notion was developed to explicate those conversions where the individual 'returns home,' so to speak, to an initial religious tradition after experimenting with some combination of different beliefs, lifestyles, or associations."[81] Carlos' transition from inherited to owned faith involved both passive and active elements. His experience of God was something that happened to him and not something that he sought out. The experience was also facilitated by his socialization in the Christian faith. The active element was Carlos' response. Following this experience, he recommitted to the church and began

80. Richardson and Stewart, "Conversion Process."
81. Kilbourne and Richardson, "Paradigm Conflict," 6.

to take his faith seriously, getting involved in leadership and deciding to get baptized as a public declaration of his decision to follow God.

In this chapter, we have laid the foundation of embedded faith for what follows. Faith is embedded in church as an interpretive community of memory where people learn to speak the language of a faith community. Fish's concept of interpretive communities helps us to see how the way the biblical story told is an extension of community perspectives. It became clear from a number of participants' stories that faith ownership was not a one-off experience or decision. Rather, ownership of faith is better understood as an *ongoing decision*. This might be understood to some extent as a clarification of belief, or a re-examination of belief, as one enters a different stage of life (such as young adulthood) and has different life experiences, encounters new ideas at university or in the workplace, and interacts with people from different backgrounds with different worldviews and beliefs.

3

Rituals as Bonding and Collective Memory

Practices of commitment in the form of rituals such as confirmation, baptism, and communion give shape and expression to people's common life together in a faith community. According to Durkheim, the moral vitality and self-identity of human communities are significantly strengthened by individuals' participation in ritual acts.[1] These rituals help "define the patterns of loyalty and obligation essential to any faith community and express their life together."[2] As such, rituals help to create the community that enacts them, for "they both *express* who we are and *make* us who we are."[3] Rites of passage and rituals embed faith in a Christian community. Grenz describes baptism and communion as "visual sermons" insofar as they symbolically re-enact the story of the death and resurrection of Jesus Christ.[4] In participating in these acts of commitment, our personal narrative becomes integrated into the larger biblical story and the story of a faith community. The role these rituals play in people's faith journeys, and the meaning they ascribe to them, provides further insight into our understanding of owned faith and the way it is embedded in church community.

1. Torevell, *Losing*, 22.
2. Bellah et al., *Habits*, 154.
3. Ammerman, "Culture," 84.
4. Grenz, *Created for Community*, 263.

Confirmation: A Rite of Passage to What?

Jesuit Priest John Kavanaugh explains that "the Sacrament of Confirmation, while not historically instituted and practiced as such, can be considered to be a celebration of mature commitment after a period of years of formation in Christian practice."[5] But is this how people being confirmed understand it? What does confirmation symbolize for those being confirmed? Ruth was eight years old when she first started going to an Anglican church with her parents. Her parents were brought up in the Church of England, but had long stopped going by the time they immigrated to New Zealand. They thought it was time to revisit church again with their young daughter, and so Ruth was baptized and confirmed within her first year of attending church. Ruth explains that for her, the significance of confirmation was "because of the formality that you go through, and the ceremony that's associated with it . . . so yeah, it was quite a big deal." I asked Ruth whether confirmation shaped her faith in a significant way. "Yeah, I think so," Ruth replied. "I think it started a curiosity, but also a respect . . . for something bigger than me I suppose. As a kid you have your parents' faith and it's not until much later that you make your own decisions for it." This respect and curiosity for something bigger than herself has continued with Ruth throughout her faith journey.

For Ruth, confirmation was meaningful and captured the imagination of an eight-year-old. However, for most of those I interviewed who had been confirmed in the church,[6] the symbolic significance of confirmation did not have the same religious depth as it did for Ruth. In fact, one participant stopped attending church almost immediately after being confirmed, while another participant had already stopped and only returned specifically to be confirmed.

Ritual Inattention

Wendy was baptized into the Catholic Church before she was one year old. She identified her father as Catholic, explaining that he had attended church regularly up until she was twelve years old, when he stopped going altogether, and adding that her mother had no denominational identity. Although her mother had had some affiliation with either the Methodist

5. Kavanaugh, *Following*, 158.

6. Five of the young adults interviewed went through confirmation.

or Presbyterian Church as a child, she had not practiced any religion since then. However, her mother attended Catholic church services with her family periodically and was supportive of Wendy's baptism. Although Wendy attended a Catholic primary school that taught religious education as part of its curriculum, church did not have much personal meaning for her growing up. This early experience of church and faith did, however, leave Wendy with the sense that there is a God.

Wendy enjoyed going to church when she was young, not because she enjoyed learning about God, but because "I used to take my little books with me and just sit there and read books while Dad focused on whatever." Wendy had not yet internalized faith; it was still at the level of compliance. She went to church because of her father, and she enjoyed church as long as she could read her books. Wendy engaged in what Samuel Heilman describes as "ritual inattention," whereby she was physically present during the church service and its ritual practices, but what was taking place was of no concern to her.[7] Not only was it of no concern to Wendy, but she was also disconnected from and disinterested in what was taking place. To a certain extent, children that are engaged in ritual inattention during a church service create their own rituals that create memories of church being fun, such as reading books, playing games with the hymnals, or dressing up in nice clothes. These positive early memories of church are sometimes self-created and quite independent of the organized aspects of a church service.

Wendy cannot recall what taking communion for the first time meant for her, but she does remember church becoming more boring for her as a result. Communion for Wendy signified not being able to read her books anymore and an expectation of responsibility far more than it signified re-telling the story of Jesus. Her attendance at church declined, as Wendy's dad was a way with work for long stretches at a time. Her mother made an effort to take Wendy and her siblings, but none of them were particularly interested or motivated to go. No longer attending church raised questions for Wendy about whether to get confirmed or not. With her father no longer around much, she was conscious that it was completely her choice to become confirmed, which raised the question of whether she wanted to continue following the faith or not. Although Wendy comprehended that it was her choice to be confirmed, this distinction did not translate to an understanding of a personalized faith. This was to come later on in her faith journey. Wendy was thirteen when she decided to get confirmed, choosing

7. Heilman, *Synagogue*, 48.

to undergo religious training over the course of a couple of weekends that included teachings on the Holy Spirit and Pentecost. Our interview conversation then turned to questions of meaning. I asked Wendy what confirmation meant to her and why she decided to get confirmed. "Perhaps in the absence of an alternative," she said. "Like maybe I should just do it, because, you know, I've been brought up a Catholic, why not just carry on. More as a matter of tradition I guess." Following confirmation, however, Wendy stopped going to church.

Wendy's motivation to be confirmed largely centered on a perception of Catholic identity and duty. While Wendy's confirmation acknowledged this Catholic identity, it was not sufficient enough to motivate her to go to church. It is this identification of a religious identity that makes possible Grace Davie's notion of "believing without belonging."[8] For people like Wendy, rites of passage such as the confirmation ceremony that signified her Catholicism do not always find expression in a religious way of life. It would seem however, that religious affiliation and identity for someone like Wendy remains a more attractive alternative to being irreligious.

Sophie was confirmed when she was fourteen, a couple of years after she had stopped going to church. Sophie was brought up in a Christian family and enjoyed going to the Anglican Church with her parents and siblings. Her early memories of church are of doing memory verses, getting stickers in Sunday school, putting on plays in church, and the "hymn books." "Hymn books?" I asked. Sophie, laughing at the memory, explained, "We amused ourselves during church by having races through the hymn books. You know, we would go '293!' and between my sisters we would race to see who could get there first."

Sophie stopped going to church when she was too old for Sunday school, at around the age of eleven. The church services were, in her words, "too boring." The transition from Sunday school into the main service is often a difficult transition for children, who, having been used to playing games and having fun, are now required to sit still and listen to a sermon that they may struggle to understand.

They [your parents] kept going and you stopped?

Sophie: *Yeah. And it coincided with moving cities as well. And then I must have been about fourteen or so—it was the age where you get confirmed*

---

8. Davie, *Religion in Britain*.

at church, like the Anglican Church. You confess your faith kind of thing because you get christened as a child and so that's your public declaration of your faith and they asked me if I wanted to do that and I was like, "Yeah, sure." And so I went and did a course. And it just seemed the thing to do.

Did it mean anything to you? Why did you do it?

SOPHIE: *It kind of did and it didn't. Like, it did and I took a friend along from school to witness it. But at the same time it didn't, 'cause then I don't know, I continued on not being involved in any church and I don't think I was, yeah, probably not a practicing Christian I guess, you know. I still believed, but just wasn't doing anything about it.*

For both Wendy and Sophie, confirmation bought with it a transition into the adult world of church, even though neither of them were adults yet. The language both use in telling their story reveals a qualitative shift in their experience of church. Adjectives such as "fun," "good," and "playing" signal positive associations that encouraged church attendance in contrast to that of "boring," which deterred from it. It is not surprising then that Wendy and Sophie both stopped attending church when they were able to decide for themselves whether to go or not. Yet their early experience of church, as the remainder of their stories make clear, left residues of faith. Both continued to believe in God, although their understanding and image of God changed later in their faith journey.

Confirmation did not signify the kind of mature faith Kavanaugh talks about for either Wendy or Sophie. This is the polysemic or mulitvocal dimension of rituals,[9] in that they are susceptible to multiple meanings even when one has gone through a course to learn about the intended meaning of a ritual like confirmation. Both Wendy and Sophie engaged in confirmation with the kind of "ritual inattention" discussed by Heilman in *Synagogue Life*. Ritual inattention has similarities to Goffman's concept of "civil inattention," as Heilman notes.[10] Goffman describes civil inattention as "a kind of dimming of the lights" between two strangers as a signal of their awareness of one another. This "dimming of the lights" is then followed by each stranger withdrawing attention from the other to signal that neither

9. See Turner, *Dramas*, 55

10. Heilman, *Synagogue*, 48.

has made the other "a target of special curiosity or design."[11] However, in ritual inattention, Heilman points out, because there is "no other ego which must be defended from invasion, the emphases is on the dimming of attention rather than on signalling."

Ritual inattention can include inattention to the ritual itself, even among the participants. We see such inattention in Wendy and Sophie; because confirmation did not represent a journey into mature faith for either of them, the effect of the ritual was divorced from any ethical implications as a consequence of their ritual inattention. The effects of most rituals, according to Weber,[12] are ephemeral, having only a negligible effect on everyday behavior and ethical living once the ceremony is over. Such rituals lacked any inner motivation for the believer to live according to religious norms. The ritual inattention of Wendy and Sophie towards confirmation turned the meaning of the ritual from a practice of commitment to a life of faith into an ephemeral one, either because of a "lack of an alternative" or because it "seemed liked the thing to do." That both Wendy and Sophie chose not to continue attending church highlights the ephemeral nature of the ritual for them. It is also possible that confirmation coincided with a transition into adolescence within a church that had no, or very few, young people and therefore no peer support.

Even when confirmation happens at a later stage in life, as it did for Cameron at the age of nineteen, the ritual can become one of ticking the boxes, merely fulfilling the requirements of a particular community of memory. I asked Cameron whether confirmation was significant to the development of his faith and understanding of what it meant to be a Christian. "Not really," he replied, "because I already knew it all. In some ways, it was a bit of going through the motions. But it was an important step to say this is where I stand." As a public declaration, Cameron's confirmation was thus a claiming of an identity that was embedded in his faith community.

The choice or motive to become confirmed for Wendy, Sophie, and Cameron was influenced by their involvement in church. Confirmation was expected as a natural progression of spiritual maturation within the life of the faith community that each of them belonged to. Confirmation is a normative action in the life of certain denominations. Its meaning and the motives behind it can be very different for some participants than for the faith community itself. Nonetheless, each of the participants was religiously

11. Goffman, *Behavior*, 84.

12. Weber, *Sociology*, 152–53.

motivated to be confirmed, even when confirmation was not an expression of a mature faith, or involved ritual inattention.

Baptism

> Therefore go and make disciples of all nations, baptising them in the name of the Father and of the Son and of the Holy Spirit, and teaching them to obey everything I have commanded you. (Matt 28:19)

Believers' baptism, like confirmation, is understood as a public declaration of faith and one's commitment to following Jesus. Baptism held a significant place in the faith journeys of those I interviewed. Getting baptized was often remembered with clarity by participants and understood as being important. As C. Wright Mills points out, "along with rules and norms of action for various situations, we learn *vocabularies of motives* appropriate to them. These are the motives we shall use, since they are part of our language and components of our behaviour."[13] However, switching from one interpretative church community into another that has a different perspective and theology of baptism created a dilemma for some of those I interviewed. This was particularly the case for those who had been baptized as infants.

A Second Baptism as an Adult: Tension Between Church Traditions

Nelson was baptized into the Anglican Church as an infant and so was not required or encouraged to be baptized as an adult. When Nelson switched to a Pentecostal church in his thirties, he encountered a very different perspective on baptism.

NELSON: *I came to New Hope Church and there, the idea is very much that you need to make the decision consciously. The parents doing it for you was infant dedication. Then there was a little scratch where I began thinking about it. That went on for eighteen months or so. Then I eventually made a decision to be baptized again. No amazing moment of heaven opening. But there was a qualitative change in my life. Stuff that had been there before wasn't there in the same way, some issues. For a long time I had issues of trusting God. And that seemed to change. It also connected*

13. Mills, "Situated," 909 (emphasis mine).

with the way I understand God, and the nature of God and who God is has changed. I don't know if baptism opened doors that weren't opened in the past that I was able to move into. It has done something to my relationship with God and being able to trust God in ways that I wasn't able to before, and in ways that I can't really articulate. It has changed the quality of my relationship with God.

New Hope Church, as a different interpretive community, influenced Nelson's decision to be baptized as an adult. Not only did the church place a different importance on baptism, it also re-interpreted Nelson's infant baptism as a baby dedication, which followers of the New Hope Church consider to be a very different religious practice.

Deciding to be baptized as an adult was an interesting journey for Esther. Coming from a Presbyterian upbringing, Esther's parents had baptized her as a baby. Esther describes her journey to getting baptized as an adult:

ESTHER: *I was brought up Presbyterian, so adult baptism was an option but not required. When I was seventeen (before leaving home) I went through a "Growth Class" with my minister at home, and at the end of it everyone else got baptized except for me. I had decided to "respect" the christening I had been given as a baby and not to get baptized again. This was partly because I knew my mum was a bit offended by the idea that people felt they needed to do again what she and Dad had done for us, and I didn't want to hurt her feelings. She definitely was comforted that I wanted to do this at the time I think. But maybe I was also living off their faith a bit.*

So then I left home and went to a few Baptist churches where adult baptism was such a big thing, and after a few years I realized it was something that had become important to me too. I wanted to make a public confession of my faith, and it almost felt like I wouldn't move on or grow unless I did this—I think this was something God challenged me at the time to do. It certainly helped me stand on my own decisions of faith and separate from my parents, so it was a good thing. And my parents were happy for me to do this after all. Nothing amazing happened at the time really, except that I did feel like there had been a seal placed around my spirit (more of an imaginative intuitive thing than any real physical sensation) and a peace that I had done the right thing. Who knows how much my environment influenced these thoughts and experiences, but I still feel it was a good thing to do.

Denominations such as the Baptists form interpretive communities surrounding matters of faith and practice. Baptism based upon one's confession of faith in Jesus Christ is strongly encouraged and taught in Baptist churches. Esther suggests that her church environment influenced her thoughts on baptism. Baptism for Esther was also about making a public confession of her faith. Like others, she felt personally challenged by God and that this was the right thing to do as an act of obedience. She felt she needed to be baptized as an adult in order to grow in her faith. For Esther, baptism also became a marker of owning her faith independently of her parents.

Unlike Esther, Cameron decided against getting "re-baptized" as an adult. For him, confirmation served the Christian symbolic function of a public declaration of faith:

CAMERON: *I was baptized as an infant in a Presbyterian church; a decision which my parents, as believing practicing Christians, undertook as their commitment to bring me up in a Christian way. I have never been baptized as an adult. At eighteen, I affirmed their actions and my own faith as an adult by undergoing a course organized by my Presbyterian church, which concluded with a special service where we took vows and assumed full church membership. We were given the option of being baptized—which I didn't feel was necessary. After I left the Presbyterian Church, I joined a church which had a large number of ex-Baptists, and I did feel like adult baptism was the preferred option from other people's point of view. However it wasn't required for membership, and while I wrestled with choosing not to have it, I have maintained that for me it wasn't necessary.*

As Cameron explains, adult baptism can become an initiation rite, particularly into another church denomination or tradition. Knowing that adult baptism was "the preferred option" at his new Living Water Church and yet deciding that for him "it wasn't necessary," demonstrates the way church switching involves selective adherence, as well as the diversity of interpretive positions and understanding of faith that are possible within a congregation. The fact that Cameron wrestled with choosing not to be baptized as an adult suggests that not only do new members experience a pressure to conform to the teachings of their new interpretive faith community, but that there is also a process of justifying one's own thinking (or that of a previous interpretive faith community) when one chooses not to.

Cameron went on to explain that his experience of baptism in the Holy Spirit, evidenced through his speaking in tongues was, for him, more significant than having to be water baptized as an adult. Cameron expressed being baptized in the Spirit as "God putting his stamp on us." As Hervieu-Léger suggests, this priority placed on the subjective religious experience by both individuals and church communities (especially those influenced by the currents of the charismatic renewal) "short circuits the doctrinal and ritual expressions of faith by the regulated establishment."[14] That such "short circuiting" occurs is not in doubt. However, as the remainder of this chapter will show, baptism and communion as doctrinally informed ritual expressions of faith have an important cognitive dimension that is not by-passed or "short circuited" in favour of an emotional expression of faith. In many instances, this cognitive dimension actually enriches the emotional aspects of religious expression and engagement.

Baptism as a Line in the Sand: "This Is Where I Stand"

Some participants were conscious that how they were living did not always match up with what they believed. Baptism became a symbolic statement of the desire and choice to live a consistent live between belief and actions. Grenz has outlined the ethical demands of baptism: "This act declares that we are to live in accordance with the new identity God has freely bestowed on us. It challenges us to allow the Spirit to transform us into the community of those who belong to God—which we are. And it admonishes us to live in accordance with the grand vision of who we *will be*."[15]

This emphasis on behavior and on thinking through what it means to live as a Christian was evident in a number of participants' narrative account of their baptism. Grace was baptized as a fourteen-year-old after developing a particular understanding of personal faith: faith as a personal choice that needed to be lived out. Baptism for Grace was a way to publically declare her faith. What made Grace's baptism particularly significant and special for her was experiencing the presence of the Holy Spirit for the first time. She describes the experience as being difficult to explain but feeling "a real sense of heat and love and contentment."

14. Hervieu-Léger, *Chain*, 58. She suggests that this search for an emotional expression of subjective religious experience is a response to the loss of the language of belief in modern society.

15. Grenz, *Created for Community*, 237.

Grace gave her testimony the week before being baptized. A few days later, her older brother challenged her on whether she really believed what she had said by pointing out how frequently she would come home and argue with her parents. Grace discusses the challenge of living out what she believed:

GRACE: *I really did believe it, but it was just harder to put into actions the sort of person I wanted to be. You know, because my faith should be changing my actions towards others in what I say and how I love others. And I knew that some of the stuff I was doing as a Christian, I should be doing better. Things like, you know, relationship with my parents and that sort of thing. I knew that. But actually making the changes was quite hard.*

Grace found the ethical demands of faith a challenge, but one that she has committed to overcoming as she grows in her understanding of faith as a way of life.

Eugene got baptized when he was seventeen. Eugene says that "for me it meant a public confirmation that I was a Christian." Eugene's decision to be baptized followed from a greater realization of who he was in Jesus Christ. One of the turning points in terms of his faith came when he was dating a non-Christian girl, which was a big issue for friends and leaders in his youth group. Eugene did not think it was such a big deal. As Eugene explains,

EUGENE: *But I actually remember consciously putting God in a corner as saying, "It's OK, I will figure this out." And it is quite funny because it didn't last very long at all because I was a knucklehead. But that kind of taught me that I remember being very, very convicted about that and saying, well, kind of God saying, "Well you are either for me or against me and I don't want you sitting on the fence anymore," kind of like that message became very clear in my own mind. And that was when I decided that I wanted to follow Christ and be a real believer as such and not just kind of wishy-washy. And that's when I got baptized as well, during that year.*

The notion of being a "real believer" is an interesting one. There is a stage where faith becomes personal, where belief shifts from a "knowing" to "a way of life." Baptism for Eugene was a significant turning point, when he describes his faith as becoming "a personal thing for the first time I think. Like actually having a personal relationship with Christ and kind of wanting to pursue that." He compares this realization with what his faith had been prior to this turning point: "It's almost living like a Christian but not really believing it. I didn't make that step, didn't make that commitment. And I think that was a big thing that made a difference."

Toby explained that baptism for him was also very important step, although at the time he didn't fully comprehend exactly what it involved, especially in light of his present understanding. Nonetheless, he understood that baptism was an act of commitment that he was making to follow God for the rest of his life. Toby goes on to say,

TOBY: *And I think that while that understanding of what it means to be committed to God has changed as my view of faith has changed over the years, there was the sense that it was a significant sort of step or sign in my life—that this was a decision that I had made and this was the way I was going to continue making choices in response. And so for me I think it's been a matter of integrity to recognize that was something that I chose to do and has therefore shaped the decisions that I have continued to make down the track.*

Like others, baptism for Toby was closely associated with a conscious ownership of faith. However, Toby faced a major faith-life challenge when his parents separated not long after his baptism:

TOBY: *A month after my baptism my parents separated, and I think for me that was a pretty significant time in my life that I look back now on as sort of the crossroads of my faith, the foundation of my faith today. And the pain that I was experiencing just conflicted so much with what I had been brought up to believe—in terms of a God who loves me and accepts me, and seeing that lived out in my family with my parents, and experiencing an environment of love and acceptance—and that sort of shattered all those preconceptions, all those beliefs that I had been brought up to believe.*

So I found myself in a position where I could either just throw all those away or I could trust in God to help me through it. And at the time of my baptism I was given the verse in Proverbs 3:5–6 which is, "Trust in the Lord with all your heart. Lean not in your own understanding; in all your ways acknowledge him and he will direct your path." And for me that has become a really meaningful verse, particularly during that time where I didn't have any idea what was going on but I chose to trust God in it and I continue to do that and see him bring redemption and healing. From that time my faith in him and his faithfulness has grown.

Facing a faith crossroad in this traumatic event so soon after publically declaring his faith through the act of baptism was unexpected. Toby's experience does highlight the ongoing choice required to keep believing in the face of doubts, suffering, and a religiously pluralistic society. Toby, at a faith crossroad, made a decision to continue trusting God, even when life did not make sense.

Baptism as a "Motivated Act"

Nelson Foote argues that people's action and choices are made on the basis of the individual's understanding or perception of who they are.[16] If they are Christian, then baptism is seen as a "natural" step in their faith journey (depending on the particular faith tradition). Following Foote, baptism, then, can be understood as a "motivated act" based on identification. For some participants, baptism was considered the "thing to do," an "obligation," as well as an important step in their faith journey. For Theo, baptism was not a marker point in his faith. Yet he still considered it personally important as a public confession of faith. Theo considered baptism as an obligation that Christians needed to undergo. In this regard, baptism is still seen by many as an act of obedience and commitment to the Christian tradition. Theo recounts his baptism:

THEO: *I got baptized when I was seventeen, when I first joined the Baptists. Yeah, they were keen to baptize me.*

Was it significant for you?

THEO: *No. Oh well, I knew I needed to do it, because I was a Christian and these people were telling me that Christians do this. So it was important to tick it off. And I enjoyed the chance to get up in front of the church and say that I believed, because I did. I was a Christian and so I was happy to undergo the obligations of being a Christian.*

For Joel, baptism was significant because:

JOEL: *You buy into the importance which is promoted at the time. Which is that it is an important step that you almost need to take, was how it was promoted, if you are to continue in your journey. But I mean it's a pretty*

16. Foote, "Identification."

big decision to make in hindsight, at that age to go, "Right, I'm going to commit the rest of my life to a particular cause" as such. So at that time you don't particularly understand the commitment you are making.

The remainder of Joel's interview suggested that the meaning of baptism and the commitment it signifies has deepened for him over time. For Weber, motive is "a complex of meaning, which appears to the actor [themselves] or to the observer to be an adequate ground for [their] conduct."[17] The "intrinsically social character" of motive that Mills highlights from Weber's definition is also articulated in Theo and Joel's baptism discourse. Each of their faith communities told them that baptism is something Christians do and that it was an important step of faith.

Explaining the significance of his baptism, Timothy says:

TIMOTHY: *It was from the point of view that I had to, obviously I made the decision, but it was kind of the youth group thing to do, you know. But I think the most significant thing was that my Dad came to it. Because he comes from a family that has no concept of God and suddenly I'm a Christian and I'm already at odds with my Father so that just heightened it in some ways because he wouldn't understand what I was doing. So for him to come to the baptism was a big thing. I don't think he understood it. I mean, he does now. He looks back and was appreciative that I hung around with those sorts of people rather than drug-takers and stuff like that. So he appreciates it from that point of view.*

Timothy's account of his baptism suggests that its significance is not always in what the ritual signifies but in those that attend in support the person being baptised. Timothy's baptism is analogous to Sophie's confirmation in that its significance for her came from the friend she invited came along to support her. In Timothy's case, it was his father, with whom he does not have a close relationship. Although Timothy implies that some of his motivation for baptism was a result of peer pressure, "the youth group thing to do," it was still a public expression of his faith, which was becoming increasingly important to him. Furthermore, inherent in Timothy's language of baptism being "the youth group thing to do" is an expression of (and desire for) group affiliation and identity; a motivated act based on an understanding of this religious group's Christian identity. Even though Timothy's father might not have fully understood what baptism meant, he

17. Cited in Mills, "Situated," 906.

did understand that it was important to Timothy and therefore came to support him.

Calvary Bible Chapel, where Christina attended church growing up, consisted of about twenty to twenty-five people. It was a close, family-type church, where Christina found love and acceptance. Christina's sense of belonging increased after she was baptized at sixteen, despite her later realization that it was "for all the wrong reasons . . . The guy I was dating thought it was a good idea. Everyone else was doing it . . . Seemed to be the thing to do. It was like a milestone that you kind of reached in our church when you were roughly sixteen, so it seemed to be the thing to do. So it wasn't something that I sought actively." I asked her if she knew what baptism meant or symbolized. She answered,

CHRISTINA: *I had some idea. I had never seen a baptism before I got baptized. That was a little freaky. I had a lot of unpleasant experiences growing up. Mum had a lot of violent relationships that I witnessed. I was molested by my stepbrother growing up. So [through] all those things the church was my place of peace, you know, my refuge. So although I didn't really know what I was doing becoming baptized, it fitted into place with everything else that was happening.*

Did you have a sense of belonging at that church?

CHRISTINA: *More so after I was baptized. Everything just fitted into place so much more and I felt more of the family than I had before.*

Christina is perhaps being overly hard on herself in describing her baptism as being motivated "for all the wrong reasons." Calvary Bible Chapel was Christina's "safe haven" from her regular world of chaos and abuse. It is not surprising then that Christina decided to be baptized, understanding it not only as "the thing to do" but also as something that would strengthen her bond with this faith community. "Institutionally different situations," according to Mills, "have different *vocabularies of motive* appropriate to their respective behaviours."[18] The vocabulary of motive for baptism within a church is religious. It is this religious motive that is absent from Christina's discourse and precisely why she concludes that she was baptized "for all the wrong reasons." And yet, I would argue, a religious motive *is* there subtly, almost unconsciously in her comment, "It was like a

18. Ibid.

milestone that you kind of reached in our church when you were roughly sixteen, so it seemed to be the thing to do." Her decision or motive is based on her observation of others within Calvary Bible Chapel, and she looks to them for the appropriate guidance for religious practice.

Baptism for Hayley has become a marker point of remembrance of her decision to follow God. Something qualitatively took place for Hayley during her baptism that changed her perspective on how she views God and her faith. In some ways, it brought a strength and confidence in her belief in God that had been missing prior to her baptism. "Anyway," Hayley says, continuing to tell me her story, "then I decided to get baptized. I don't know why. I don't know what possessed me to get baptized. But anyway, I did. Before I got baptized, I was still wavering. I was still going, 'Aw this is too hard, I feel too miserable, God's rejected me; I might as well just give up.' But since I've got baptized I don't think I seriously considered giving up."

By the time Jack reached thirteen, he had decided that his faith "isn't just something I do, it is actually something I want to be about." Getting baptized signified this decision and understanding of faith for Jack. As he tells it, "It was just a step; it was a growth step. It wasn't necessarily a significant step in terms of I had reached this incredible moment in time and now . . . I just saw it as a progression of my faith and I had come to an understanding where I felt, yeah, this is what the rest of my life is going to be all about." However, what Jack felt his life was going to be all about began to take an unexpected turn. "It was pretty much from my baptism," Jack said, "I felt like my faith almost started to crumble and as my support structures around me began to sort of disappear, like those who kind of did talk to me slowly disappeared out of my life."

This disappearance was the result of the people who had made up Jack's social support structure growing older and attending church less frequently. Consequently, Jack's own attendance dropped as he began to play weekend sports. Jack eventually stopped going to church for a number of years. It is interesting to note that, for Jack, there was a definite dissonance between his expectations of baptism's significance and its eventual reality.

Communion

Remembering the Jesus Story: Communion as Bonding Memory

While confirmation and baptism are only practiced once (sometimes twice when those that have been baptized as infants decide to also undergo adult baptism) communion is practiced on a more regular basis. The Lord's Supper is a reminder of the story of the life, death, and resurrection of Jesus. As Jesus instructed his followers, "Do this in remembrance of me" (Luke 22:19). Communion is a "bonding memory," a symbolic action that functions as a memory aid. Drinking wine and eating bread are potent symbols of the revival of a memory that has the potential to be forgotten. Bonding memory, as discussed earlier, has a unifying quality.

According to Assmann, bonding memory has a "normative, contractual character," that commits the individual to fulfil the obligations that they have committed themselves to. Bonding memory is not without its challenges, as Assmann points out:

> The context may have changed so much from one day to the next that nothing reminds him of the commitment he has made and of the interests that led him to make it. The memory disappears because it ceases to be supported by the new situation. It must therefore be carried through in a hostile environment, where it no longer seems appropriate but instead has receded into the distance and become alien or irksome.[19]

The "re-membering" and "re-collecting" nature of bonding nature of memory, Assmann suggests, interprets memory as the restoration of lost unity. For Assmann, this restoration, or prevention, of lost unity is what is at stake with bonding memory:

> It refers to cultural efforts that aim to establish connections and consolidate togetherness . . . When collectives "remember," they thereby secure a unifying, "connective" semantics that "holds them inwardly together" and reintegrates their individual "members" so that they possess a common point of view. Wherever people join together in larger groups they generate a connective semantics, thereby producing forms of memory that are designed to stabilize a common identity and a point of view that spans several generations.[20]

19. Ibid.
20. Ibid., 11.

This bonding memory of the communion ritual contributes to the sense of communitas, for "it is only through the power ascribed by all to ritual, particularly to the Eucharistic ritual that the likeness of lot and intention is converted into commonness of feeling, into 'communitas.'"[21] The story of Jesus is central to the Christian faith around which church communities gather to remember. Stories and sacred myths give embodiment to rituals in religion. These stories, central to a community of memory, have a representational content. It is this representational content of a religious myth or story that Polanyi and Prosch argue "must seem possible to us (i.e., be actually possible) if we are to be able to accept it."[22] Polanyi and Prosch suggests that the incompatibilities involved in various rituals such as communion, which considers the same physical objects to be both flesh and bread, blood and wine, are fused together by our imagination, which gives meaning to the whole ritual and moves our religious feelings so powerfully.

Grace had just partaken in communion the night before answering my question about its importance to her.

GRACE: *Communion is very important to me because the cross—the death and resurrection of Christ—is central to our whole faith. Without it, Christianity would be just another dead religion. So when I take communion, it is a chance to reflect on the importance of the cross, and I am reminded once again of the amazing love Jesus has for us to die on the cross. It is also a time to ask forgiveness of my own sins. Of course I can do this at any time, but I like the quiet reflective space that communion creates to do this. It is also something Jesus commanded us to do: "Do this in remembrance of me."*

The language people use to explain and describe their experience of communion is articulated through a particular vocabulary: sin, forgiveness, Jesus' death and resurrection. These words are all endowed within a religious context, the language of faith, which participants learned through their church communities. Hauerwas and Willimon argue, for example, "that sin is not natural but rather we must be taught by the church to be a sinner."[23] Sin, and a particular understanding of sin, is the beginning of the Christian identity in that we acknowledge ourselves as sinners saved by

21. Turner and Turner, *Image*, 13.

22. Polanyi and Prosch, *Meaning*, 158.

23. Hauerwas and Willimon, *Aliens Live*, 77.

the grace of God.[24] Communion symbolizes this understanding of sin and grace and forgiveness. Using the reflective space created by communion in a church service, Grace thinks not only about the symbolism of the cross but also the ethical implications that Jesus' death and resurrection pose for her. This reflection is expressed in the act of confession. Confession is a reflexive practice, as it demands that the one confessing think about how they have been living in relation to what they believe. In this way, the ritual of communion and its symbolism intersects with the everyday experience of living religion.

This intersection of ritual and the everyday is something that Esther finds helpful. "Communion," Esther said, "helps me to focus on sin and confession, which I probably didn't do much of elsewhere in my faith life. I wonder actually if it would have been better to do this more often, as I sometimes feel out of touch with my own sinfulness." Esther finds both freedom and a challenge in practicing communion on a regular basis, for she remembers the death and resurrection of Jesus and uses it as a time of confession. Esther now considers that "communion is more important than I was brought up to believe." Esther enjoys a growing appreciation of the sacredness of communion, which had sometimes been lost on her in the elements used to represent the blood and body of Christ in her youth group days. "Also, I have been through phases of using pretty much anything for communion, such as coke, and chips—mostly in youth group times. But I now believe much more in the symbolism of communion, and the sacredness of it, and that these things are important to the experience and reflection of Christ's work on the cross."

The church environment and the space created for communion can change the meaning and of the ritual's reception depending on what the context signifies about the ritual, such as its seriousness, sacredness, or even seeming triviality. Participants' imagination is significantly stimulated by the environment the church creates for taking communion. Cameron's comments demonstrate the way that a church can set the "mood" using the environment of communion, as well as the way that "mood" influences symbolic reception:

---

24. Hauerwas and Willimon, view the confession of sin as "a theological achievement," because "sin is not some generalized assumption that we all do something wrong somewhere . . . Rather, sin names the discovery, when confronted by the gospel, that my life has not been lived as a gift from God" (*Aliens Live*, 77).

> CAMERON: *As communion is a more formal part of faith practice, I enjoy it more as a solemn moment, and while it takes concentration, it is often quite cleansing to the soul—although this also depends on the reverence with which is it conducted by the person who is leading it. Some churches are more formal than others, and the less formal ones it seems like it isn't as serious an issue, which for me has less effect.*

The way communion is practiced impacts its experiential depth. There is a correlation between an informal, casual approach and a formal, serious approach and the type of experience Cameron has had in participating in communion.

Weber, as mentioned earlier in the chapter, understood the effects of most rituals to be ephemeral and lacking any inner motivation for the believer to live according to religious norms. The exception to this phenomenon, Weber notes, are rituals that require ethical purity before participation, such as the Lord's Supper. Weber attributes this ritual fear and respect associated with the Lord's Supper according to the doctrinal teachings of Paul, that "whoever eats the bread or drinks the cup of the Lord in an unworthy manner will be guilty of sinning against the body and the blood of the Lord" (1 Cor 11: 27).[25] This condition of ethical purity, Weber believed, could exert a strong influence on everyday behavior. While those I interviewed do not come to the Eucharist with a "terrifying fear," as in Weber's account of the ritual, they nonetheless participate in it with reverence and use it as a time of inner confession. It is this inner confession and desire to live a life that honors God following the example of Jesus that Weber attributes to the mystical character of this "ritualistic piety."

Bodily Knowing

In addition to the ritualized environment, some people find preparing themselves for communion to be an equally important part of the ritual process. Emily places a lot of importance on communion, explaining that "I always take it seriously and make sure my heart is in the right place to take it, sometimes skipping it if I feel I would just be doing it for show." She

25. In this passage in Corinthians, Paul is responding to requests from the Corinthian church for guidance concerning table fellowship (what Martin Luther calls *Haustafel*, literally "house table," as cited in Foster, *Celebration*, 102). Paul's response regarding the Lord's Supper was that if their meal failed to reflect the overcoming of social stratification, then they would bring condemnation upon themselves. See Yoder, *Body Politics*, 18.

went onto describe that what goes on for her during communion is "a time of reflection, prayer, and thanks, and always that overwhelming feeling of 'I don't deserve this.' I still don't really understand the kind of love that drives someone to do this for me." Experiencing communion emotionally, as Emily does, is a form of "bodily knowing" that Winifred Whelan defines as "a kind of knowing that is *felt* by the body before, after, or alongside the understanding of the mind."[26] It is also what Rudolf Otto describes in *The Idea of the Holy* as "creature-consciousness" or "creature feeling," which he defines as "the emotion of a creature, submerged and overwhelmed by its own nothingness in contrast to that which is supreme above all creatures."[27] Such an overwhelming feeling can be difficult to articulate, perhaps explaining Otto's position that it "must be directly experienced in oneself to be understood."

Likewise, as Eugene came to understand more about faith and take more ownership of his own faith, his appreciation of communion's significance began to grow. For Eugene, as for others, it is a time to focus on the cross and what Jesus did there, as well as on Jesus himself. However, Eugene does not use the time just for pouring over his own sin and issues. His headspace at the time affects how meaningful participating in communion is. He admits there are times when he gets "a little blasé about it," but for the most part, the experience of communion is very real and has a deep impact. According to Eugene, "there are other times when I really kind of feel it. Feel it and experience it in terms of actually visualising Christ on the cross. And that really helps me." The experiential dimension of rituals can be difficult to articulate, because "feeling it" and being "overwhelmed" by a ritual such as communion is a form of "bodily knowing."

Nelson experiences communion by means of bodily knowing more than through cognitive engagement:

What goes on for you when you take communion?

NELSON: *I don't know. Not a great deal intellectually. I don't think about it a great deal. I experience it emotionally. It kind of feels bigger than I can think, if that makes sense. It is one of the few things in life where I experience something more through the filter of my emotions than through the filter of my intellect. I run most things through the filter of my intellect.*

26. Whelan, "Bodily," 274 (emphasis in original).

27. Otto, *Idea*, 10.

> *It works that way round in terms of communion, I connect with it the other way. I used to go to those voluntary communion services at school. I used to love going to them.*

In developing this idea of bodily knowing, Torevell suggests that ritual "is never a precisional or analytical form of cognitive communication, but works by appealing primarily to the sensual and fleshy bodies, emotions and feelings of the participants."[28] Or, as Assmann puts it, "Rituals dramatize the interplay of the symbolic with the corporeal."[29] Ritual can even transform everyday consumables such as coke or chips, as they did in Esther's youth group experience, when used to represent the blood and body of Christ. It is this tangible, bodily knowing aspect of communion that endows the ritual with such powerful symbolism, for as Joshua explains, "you've got bread in your hand and it focuses your thoughts quite clearly about Jesus, you know, on the cross, which is what it is designed to do."

Wine and Bread as Dislocated Symbols

Christians learn that the symbols of communion—wine and bread—signify Jesus' spilled blood and his body broken. The creative power of these symbols, and of the communion ritual itself, is founded on an understanding of the story of Jesus' death and resurrection. All of the participants I interviewed know the story well. Many have been brought up hearing it. But what happens to the symbolic signifying power when the story does not make sense? Or when people struggle to comprehend the meaning of Jesus' death?

Hayley understands that communion is supposed to be important, but the experiential reality is quite different. Pressed by the demands of children and her awareness of people arriving for the second church service, communion is robbed of its reflective dimension. In Polanyi and Prosch's terms, Hayley's imagination is distracted and not free to resolve the incompatibilities between the symbolic elements and Jesus' blood and body. In addition to these distractions, Haley faces theological questions, such as "What kind of happened on the cross exactly, in theological terms?" The meaning and significance of communion can often become lost in everyday life and the kind of concerns that regularly trouble Haley. Communion

28. Torevell, *Losing*, 32.
29. Assmann, *Religion*, 10.

loses its symbolic power for Hayley in her struggle to make sense of the various theological explanations of Jesus' death that Haley encountered in her study of theology.

Some of those interviewed were going through a period of deconstructing their faith to examine their beliefs. Theo has been deconstructing his faith for the last couple of years, and still has questions concerning Jesus:

THEO: *So I still believe in Jesus; I don't know whether he was the son of God because that relationship between Jesus and God is quite unclear to me. However, it is clear that it was significant and Jesus was certainly in a very special category. And so it doesn't matter to me so much whether he was God or whether he was, you know, some proxy of God. The reality of what he was trying to achieve is still there. The moral of the story is still in place: that God was somehow trying to reach out to us and, you know, show us a better way to live. And I accept all of that. Although I think a lot of Jesus' death on the cross was more symbolic in what it achieved. Because if God is God, I think God doesn't need to transact something. I think he can do it by sheer act of his will, albeit painful for him. I no longer hold to an idea that God needs to have to crucify part of himself to actually achieve something. I think that's more just there to show us something. Therefore, showing us becomes a symbolic thing of the length that he is prepared to go to.*

In light of this deconstruction, Theo still considers Jesus' teachings to be very significant and something that he needs to act upon.

Likewise, Belinda now finds the concept of Jesus dying on the cross "quite crazy. And I still really struggle to come to terms with it. But I am grateful for it because that means that I can be connected to God." Rebecca's understanding of Jesus has changed to the point where, she says, "I don't know who Jesus is now. I don't know what it means for him to be God." She used to just accept the doctrine of Jesus as it was taught in church and "just go, 'Well, that's what a Christian believes.'" As Rebecca has deconstructed her faith further, she now wonders if she is in fact allowed to call herself a Christian: "I don't understand who Jesus was and I don't understand what he did and I feel like becoming enlightened or growing spiritually doesn't necessarily have to mean . . . doesn't have to . . . the focus doesn't have to be on Jesus atoning for sins or something."

Some of the questions that Antonia and Santos have been asking as they deconstruct their faith concern the divinity of Jesus and how much it matters. Although Santos says he no longer needs all the answers, including to questions concerning Jesus' divinity, in order to have confidence in his faith in God, he still wonders, "How much does it influence you? Does it affect your concept of God and your ability to call yourself a Christian?" Antonia agrees and emphasises that she continues to find Jesus' teaching amazing and valuable. However, "The kind of whole death and resurrection and just, the whole way that fits into your Christian faith—it's a hard fit, it's quite hard to come to a point on."

Wondering what exactly happened on the cross, finding it crazy, and being unsure how it all fits into everyday life are theological concerns that suggest the meaning of the communion symbols as the blood and body of Jesus can become dislocated and lose their signifying power. In this state of dislocated meaning, communion has the potential to "disorientate and undermine as well as to build up a community, if their significance rests upon assumptions no longer accepted by the actors."[30] The creative power of ritual, Torevell points out, "is partly based on acceptance of those actions and what they rest upon and signify."[31]

Having established that participants' owned faith is embedded in church life and the role that rituals such as confirmation, baptism, and communion play in understanding this faith, we now turn our attention to why young adults switch churches and what they are looking for when they do change.

---

30. Torevell, *Losing*, 47
31. Ibid.

4

Church Switching

Thinking About Where to Embed Faith

One of the dominant forms of both church growth and decline is in church transfer, as people switch their allegiance from one church to another in a phenomenon that has been referred to as "the circulating of the saints."[1] Religious switching has a short but rich research history within the sociology of religion. Since Rodney Stark and Charles Glock's[2] landmark 1968 study exploring patterns of religious commitment, denominational switching has been the focus of numerous studies. Researchers have explored various influences on religious switching such as social status, parental divorce, marriage, social networks, and economic factors.

Having established the importance of embedding faith in a church community for participants in previous chapters, how then do we make sense of young adults' church switching? In this chapter, I argue that church switching needs to be understood as an intentional act, motivated by a conception of church as centrally important to a life of faith as a Christian.

The Multiple Switcher and Religious Commitment

Research documents an extensive religious mobility within Christian churches.[3] Interestingly, researchers are unanimous in finding that switchers

1. Bibby, "Circulation."
2. Stark and Glock, *American Piety*.
3. See for example, Hadaway, "Denominational Switching"; Stump, "Regional Migration"; Roof and McKinney, "Denominational America."

are afterward more committed church members and more religious than non-switchers. The reason most often cited is that switching requires a conscious decision and a certain amount of "religious initiative," so that switchers tend to be people with more "religious motivation."[4] Stayers, by comparison, are viewed as having "inherited faith" as well as the church of their parents. It is argued that they attend more out of tradition than personal religious fervor. However, the transition from inherited faith to owned faith means that those who have stayed in the church they have grown up in through young adulthood evidence deep commitment and involvement in their church. Nonetheless, the point is that church switching does not signify a lack of commitment. Switchers evidence a strong belief in the importance of church and in seeking out a church that corresponds with their beliefs. Switching then, represents a deliberate action.

The religious initiative that motivates participants in finding a new church was clearly evident in the interviews. This initiative included asking around, tapping into social networks, and seeking recommendations, which we will discuss in more detail in the next chapter. If participants did not have their own transportation, they would often find a church within walking distance. Others searched for a church in the phone book or online, or heard about a church on the radio. For some, the process of finding a church was one of trial and error until they found one that they felt they could belong to.

Research on church switching suffers from a widespread failure to distinguish between single verses multiple switching. Roof, a well-respected sociologist of religion, finds this failure and lack of available data on multiple church switching surprising, given the extent of religious mobility and "the general recognition by scholars that religious switching is a phenomenon of some importance."[5]

Religious life stories have made it possible to track the *multiplicity* of church switching that occurs in the course of a person's faith journey. Roof criticizes quantitative measures of switching for being "insensitive to 'number of times a person has switched,' and thus tend to overly simplify people's religious biographies," resulting in "misguided generalisations."[6] In contrast, the qualitative approach I employ in my research has been conscientiously sensitive and attentive to multiple switching within participants' religious biographies.

4. Hoge et al., "Denominational Switching," 253.
5. Roof, "Religious Switching," 530–31.
6. Ibid., 530.

Multiple Church Switching

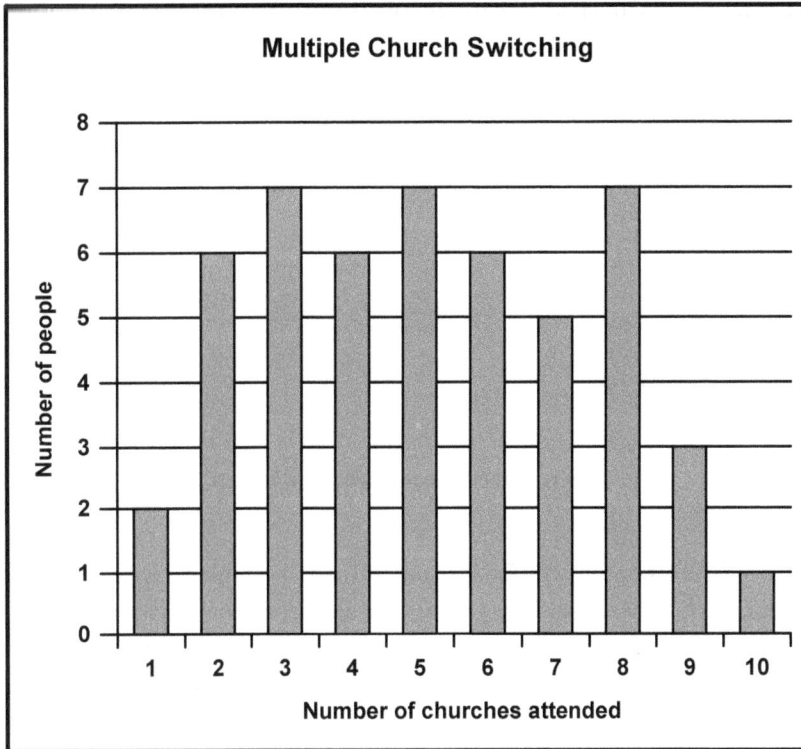

Figure 1. Number of Churches Attended by Participants

The above graph (fig. 1) shows the number of times young adults I interviewed have switched churches. Over 160 different churches are represented in the collective switching histories of the young adults interviewed. Out of fifty young adults interviewed, only two people have never officially switched churches. Even then, one was involved in church two-timing, and the other underwent a period of exploring other churches with his wife, who had been discontented with their current church. For young adults who switched churches multiple times the reasons for switching were not usually consistent for any one person. Rather, individuals cited a variety of reasons for switching at different moments in their faith journey. This affirms the complex nature of religious mobility that the research acknowledges. Geographic mobility includes variables such as work, family, university, and travel. Stages of life, and changes in a person's faith journey, also influence people's decision to switch churches in different ways.

Tracking a Multiple Church Switcher: A Case Study

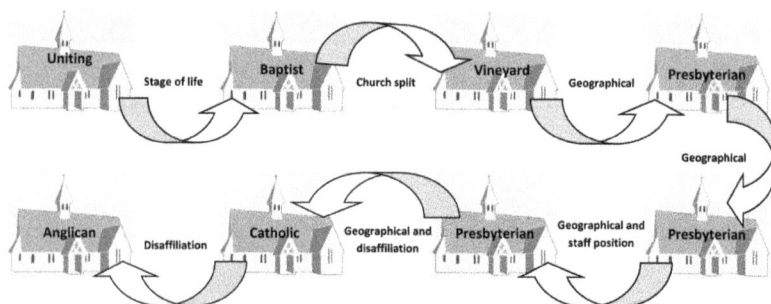

Figure 2. Theo's Church Switching History

The diagram above (fig. 2) tracks Theo's switching history. He has switched churches eight times across six different denominations. A brief overview of Theo's religious biography puts these church switches in context. Theo's parents sent him to a Presbyterian-Methodist church when he was younger. They themselves did not attend, but his father had been affiliated with the Methodist church earlier in life. Theo had a spiritual experience at an Easter camp when he was fifteen years old, which opened his eyes to a dimension of Christianity that he had not been aware of. This experience made Theo aware that there was more to church than he had previously encountered, and so, as Theo put it, "I went looking for it." Theo found what he was looking for at Willow Baptist Church, where the congregation, he explains, was "dabbling in charismatic things." Theo had also heard from schoolmates that Willow Baptist had more young people than his current church, providing further motivation to switch churches.

Theo is an active seeker similar to those Hadaway describes, who "once having had a religious experience, sought a church that coincided with their beliefs and reinforced the character of their experience."[7] In seeking out a church that coincided with his new beliefs, or at least new experience of faith, Theo switched interpretive communities to find one that provided a charismatic understanding of faith. Theo's switch was also motivated by the increasing isolation he felt as one of the few young people attending the

7. Hadaway, "Denominational," 452.

Presbyterian-Methodist church. The switch not only provided Theo with a church culture and an interpretive faith community that would coincide with his new beliefs and reinforce the reality of his experience, but also with an important plausibility structure in the form of a peer social network.[8]

Theo describes the impact of encountering these new spiritual experiences:

> THEO: *It was pretty earth shattering actually to begin with. Because probably my faith—while I was very much a zealot, I was also very fragile. And at the time it felt like I had finally got some evidence that God was real other than my subjective sense of what was truth. And that was very important because whenever I experienced doubt I was able to immediately dispel them by, "Oh, what about those super natural things that happened?" And so that was a huge relief I guess at the time.*

Reflecting back on his experience, Theo acknowledges the importance of having his faith embedded in a church community with a peer group that sustained and supported his faith. As a consequence of being on his own, with no Christian friends in his previous church and no peer-based plausibility structure, Theo says he was "definitely feeling shaky about whether I was going to stay in church." He recognized his current congregation as a "dangerous place" for his own faith, despite his experience of God at camp, and he felt the temptation to walk away from church and faith. When he began to make Christian friends at his new church, Theo ended up completely changing social circles, much to his regret as he reflects back on this period of his faith journey. He described his experience of switching churches as "a bit of a social and brain implant." Although at the time Theo experienced a strong sense of belonging in his new church, he now thinks that "they let me belong too much. There wasn't enough encouragement to belong to the other parts of my life." Theo's critique on belonging suggests that the life of faith can become *too* embedded within church life, to the detriment of other areas such as friendships outside the world of church. In the next chapter we will explore in further detail the relational and social dimension of church switching.

Theo's next church switch was the result of a church split that he attributes to "personality and stylistic differences," particularly personality differences. One half of the church became a Vineyard and the other half

---

8. A plausibility structure provides the social support and confirmation that makes faith plausible. See Berger, *Heretical*, 16.

remained a Baptist church. Theo was nineteen at the time, and chose to go with the Vineyard group. He attended this church for eight years, up until he got married in his late twenties and switched to a Presbyterian church following a geographic move for work. Together, Theo and his wife, Jody, surveyed the new area, visiting Salvation Army, Baptist, Apostolic, and Presbyterian churches. This wide range of church denominations illustrates that the denomination may not have been a contributing factor in choosing which church to join. They ultimately decided on Saint Ignatius Presbyterian church, not so much because Jody had previous affiliations with this denomination, but because "that was the church that probably wanted us the most." Theo elaborated:

> THEO: *We had way more opportunity to give. I mean the minister said that I could preach as often as I pretty much wanted to, and was happy to give me lots of opportunities. Their music was in a dire state and Jody and myself are both musicians. And so there was a real sense of here is a place where we can give. We kind of recognized that we weren't going to get much out of church, but we could give a lot.*

Was that important to you, having that space to give?

> THEO: *Yeah, it was. I mean I've got the skills, and you know, I wanted to put them into action. Like, if I am ever going to be involved in church I actually want to be involved. I'm not really that happy passively sitting. It just makes me critical of how they're not doing it right; whereas at least if I'm involved in it I'm a lot more sympathetic to it being done badly.*

Active involvement and contribution to the life of a local church community is a characteristic of embedded and owned faith. We will return to the importance of contributing to the life of a church community shortly. Soon afterwards, Theo and Jody spent a year working overseas and began attending the same church as some of their work colleagues. Another important factor in their choice of church was geographical proximity: "It was the closest church; we made the decision a wee while ago to always go to the local church even though there might have been better churches farther away."

Returning home to New Zealand, Theo was offered a staff position at a Presbyterian church in the area of young adult ministry. While Theo enjoyed his work, dealing with the church politics and senior leadership was a disheartening and frustrating experience:

You mentioned that it didn't end well for you and you gave up something you were really enjoying. How did that impact upon your understanding and perspective of church?

THEO: *Well, because of my difficulties in dealing with the mother church, you know, I found that very demotivating and I started to get really cynical with the church, you know, and just its unwillingness to change. And how difficult it was even within different services within the same church to combine on things and to share things, and the authoritarian structures within church were really hard for me to live with . . . There were a lot of* fait accompli *in the church I was working for where basically you could make all the points you wanted but at the end of the day the decision was going to get handed down from on high which you had to accept.*

Sometimes you got to give your input just so you would feel good about it, but it wasn't taken seriously. He [the senior minister] did what he wanted to do and that was it. And I guess some work places are like that, but increasingly not the good ones—you know, I just wasn't listened to. And that was really disappointing because I felt like things could have been done a lot better. And people weren't open to that at the top. And I realize now why so few young people go to Presbyterian churches, because I don't want to go there myself either.

Theo and Jody became what we might describe as "reluctant leavers," as a result of relational conflicts with some of the church leadership. Theo enjoyed what he was doing and the group of people he was serving, many of whom were involved in an alternative church service that Theo was responsible for. When people leave a church reluctantly, there is often a residual element of anger and hurt. In Theo's case, he left Saint Dominic's Presbyterian Church feeling "really angry with the church; with the Protestant Church." Theo emphasized the tendency of Protestant churches to split when there is a major disagreement. Theo said he was saddened by the fact that "People cannot allow room and space for other people with divergent ideas." In this current state of angst towards Protestant churches on the one hand and of continuing to value the importance of church on the other, Theo says, "I was attracted to the idea of going to a Catholic church."

Theo was interested in learning more about the Catholic way of doing things and "to see what was in it for me. What could I learn from them that might help me in my state." Theo found was able to ease his anger by un-embedding his faith from Protestant churches and re-embedding it in the Catholic tradition for a time. As Theo expressed it, "I didn't have any negative feelings towards the Catholics. So it was a nice way of staying in faith while putting some of my own baggage over to one side and have a little bit of a holiday with the Catholics." However, all good holidays come to an end and Theo's "vacation" in the Catholic church was no exception:

THEO: *It didn't work out. Although it did help me deal with the anger, which was good, and got me over that little hump. But really the Catholics were very boring, and if you talk about the Presbyterians being unable to change their dinosaur structure, the Catholics have got a lot they could learn from the Presbyterians with that regard. And the community in the Catholic church was actually really, really poor in the one that I attended. It was the worst of all the churches that I have ever been in. People didn't even know each other. They were in the door, did the business, out the door. You go to mass to fulfil your spiritual duty. There was no sense of networking or, you know, trying to figure out who the other people were and to see if you could help them in their crisis and they could help you in yours.*

Once I got to know the routines . . . I wanted to learn the routines and I found them useful for awhile, I enjoyed the more meditative style, I just need the emotional turmoil in myself to calm down and the Catholic service was a good one for allowing that to happen. It gave me space and time to pray in a place where no one was telling me what to do all the time: like, "Now stand up and sing this song," "Now come up and do this," you know. There was lots of space. And you could just sit in the back and no one thought twice of it, you know, and just soak up the atmosphere and do your own little prayers or thoughts about what to do. So I enjoyed the space.

But in the end, after I went through that phase, I got bored with that. It didn't work out for my family anyway because it was very family unfriendly. And we ended up . . . I guess I was ready to rejoin the Protestants. And we looked around and we went to a Lutheran church and a few others. But we ended up at an Anglican church, which was a nice compromise because it was still very Catholic, giving me a little bit of space and giving me some well-chosen words to say. Because they are well-chosen, as opposed to more by the hoof Baptist charismatic churches which, you know, make up their words a lot more freely and a lot less thought-out and often offend my theological sensibilities a bit more.

But I still find the Anglican church quite deficient. I mean, certainly the preaching is very simplistic and whatnot, but at least it's short.

Internal Leavers

Theo is currently what Alan Jamieson[9] describes as an "internal leaver," by which is meant that his faith is not currently being supported, encouraged, or developed by his church. Theo articulates this when he says, "I've been going to church for nearly twenty years now. And, you know, I am not wanting to lose my faith, because I still have a faith, it's just a faith that is not particularly helped by church." Theo meets all of Jamieson's five criteria describing the experience of being an internal leaver: disenchantment, disillusionment, disengagement, disidentification, and disorientation.[10] Disenchantment is "the sense of not enjoying church anymore because it no longer fascinates or interests them."[11] The boredom Theo experiences in church and the effort it sometimes takes him to even go to church are characteristics of disenchantment. The anger and hurt that Theo experienced as a reluctant leaver from Saint Dominic's Presbyterian led to a sense of disillusionment with church. For those experiencing disillusionment, Jamieson points out that "What was once *life-giving*, now feels *lifeless* and they can wonder if, after all, they are wasting their time."[12] Theo captures the sense of disillusionment characteristic of internal leavers when he says, "Because of my difficulties in dealing with the mother church, you know, I found that very demotivating and I started to get really cynical with the church, you know, and just its unwillingness to change." Theo felt let down by the leadership and saddened by the lack of willingness within the church to change. Disillusionment leads to disengagement from the church, in that people no longer feel connected to what is going on in the life of the church community or structures.

Disidentification is another criterion describing the experience of the internal leaver. Theo's disembedding from the Protestant church is a strong expression of disidentification. Although he has since returned to a Protestant church, this switch has not been accompanied by a sense of identification with the church, their practices, or the people there. Typical of

9. Jamieson, *Called Again*, 12.
10. Ibid., 14
11. Ibid.
12. Ibid.

disidentification, Theo expresses his observations as an outsider. Another characteristic of the internal leaver, according to Jamieson, is that of disorientation—"the sense that they don't know where they belong anymore."[13] Disorientation, Jamieson explains, is sometimes linked to feelings of loss and uncertainty that can result in anxiety. Theo certainly feels a sense of disorientation in not feeling like he "fits" into church anymore. The sense of losing one's bearings and sense of uncertainty regarding faith and church comes through clearly in Theo's discourse surrounding his current faith: "I need to get comfortable with a faith position for myself. I have to get there. The sooner I get there, the better, you know, to be a lot less confused and to be a lot more certain about things would be wonderful progress."

Jamieson suggests that disorientation is typically linked to a "sense of freedom, curiosity about the future and excitement about possibilities ahead."[14] This more positive side to disorientation is also evident in Theo's interview as he discusses where he hopes he will end up:

THEO: I'm hoping that I might come out at some point where I feel very comfortable with a lot of things and where they won't cause the same sense of irritation. I will be able to hold them a lot more loosely but find the things that are really core to be incredibly enriching and rewarding and that church won't be so much of an irritating place for me. But once again a place where I can give and let all the other stuff go that causes me pain at the moment.

Jamieson argues that if circumstances, such as family, friends, or work, were different, then internal leavers would probably leave the church altogether.[15] Why does an internal leaver like Theo still go to church? There are often a variety of reasons why internal leavers continue to attend church. When I asked Theo for the reasons behind his decision, he answered with a mix of seriousness and humor, "It keeps my wife happy." Qualifying his reasons further, Theo said that

THEO: Even if I took that out of it I might still go anyway, because I'm really scared about what might happen if I don't go altogether . . . I'm worried though that if I don't go to church at all that I may lose the habit of being spiritually focused. At least it keeps it on the table in terms of

13. Ibid.
14. Ibid.
15. Ibid., 12.

unanswered questions, something that needs to be dealt with. If I stop going to church altogether, it might just turn into something that doesn't have to get dealt with at all and I will just sweep it under the carpet, which would be a shame.

In addition, Theo wants his children to have the same grounding in the Christian faith as Jody and he had. Attending church sometimes feels unhelpful to Theo's faith and often, he says, "offends my theological sensibilities." Nonetheless, choosing to embed his faith in a local church—albeit a precarious embedding—acts as a memory aid by reminding Theo that his faith is important enough that he needs to work through and process some of his unanswered questions about church and faith that could easily be ignored without the accountability that comes from the gathered congregation.

The Decline of Denominational Importance

All of my interviews support research that argues for the decline of the importance of denominations as a source of religious identity, or as a factor influencing church choice. Because of the perceived cultural and theological similarities (more so than the differences among denominations), people often base their decision on the "substance" and "style" of individual churches rather than an understanding of a denominational position or doctrine. As long as they do not feel a church's theology is "off-track" then it remains a contender.

Based on my interview findings, I would suggest that one of the reasons why denominational identity is increasingly unimportant is due in part to a lack of knowledge about denominational differences. To paraphrase and adapt Hervieu-Léger, there has been a break in the "denominational chain of memory" resulting in "denominational amnesia."[16] When Roger was asked as a fifteen year old at a Christian camp what church he went to, he said, "Greenwood Interdenominational Church [laughs]. And the leader who went to a neighbouring church said, 'No, no, just tell them what church you really go to.' So I said, 'Greenwood Baptist Church.' I guess I didn't really know anything at all about other denominations." Having studied at a Baptist theological college and been involved in Baptist youth

16. See also Prothero, *Religious Literacy*, for a discussion of the impact of religious illiteracy on denominational identity.

camps over the years, Roger says that he is now "really committed to Baptist churches." In this regard, Roger is an exception to the majority of the participants. But he also illustrates Ammerman's argument that there is a correlation between the communication of denominational narratives and denominational identity.[17]

Nathan likewise shares a sense of denominational loyalty. Nathan, who is now in his thirties, has been affiliated with the Baptist denomination all his life and used to think that he was a Baptist by default. "And I was," he says, "being brought up in a family that had been involved in Baptist churches for two or three generations. So there is a lot of identity as being part of a Baptist church."

For Sean, who switched from a Baptist to an Anglican church, the only perceived denominational difference was, he says, "subtle variations in the way people do communion," suggesting that the denominational narratives are not discussed and that they have set aside their traditional liturgical practices. If there are no clear distinguishable denominational characteristics for church switchers such as Sean, then it is quite possible that it no longer clearly "means something different for an Episcopalian [Anglican] to become a Baptist, than for a Baptist to become an Episcopalian," as Hadaway argues.[18] For Sean, the denomination "doesn't make any sort of difference." What does make a difference is the "realness" of the people that make up a church community. For Sean, such realness is present when people are honest and engage with life's struggles and hardships rather than just ignoring them or spiritualizing them in a way that suggests such realities are trivial.

The multiple church switching of my participants supports research that suggests that denominational switching usually involves "fairly short theological and cultural trips."[19] According to Rokeach, individuals form cognitive maps of the apparent distances of other denominations from their

17. Ammerman, *Pillars*, 245.

18. Hadaway, "Denominational," 453. Ammerman highlights the fact that "Not only do congregations with more eclectic worship practices lose a strong sense of identification with their denomination, but they may also lose more adherents to future intergenerational switching" (*Pillars of Faith*, 244–45).

19. Bibby, "Going," 292.

own, which they use in choosing a church.[20] Babchuk and Whitt[21] likewise found that denominations perceived as being similar were chosen far more often than those that are perceived as being more distant religious bodies.

When I asked Harry, who has predominantly been involved in Baptist churches, how important the denomination was to him, he replied, "Not particularly. I did go to an Anglican church in the UK. Not particularly important. I guess I want a good Christian church. I'm not interested in the Catholic church. It is more about the substance of the church and what they affiliate to." Obviously for Harry, the Catholic church is not a good "Christian church," or more likely, the cognitive distance between the Catholic church and Harry's predominant involvement in Baptist churches is just too wide to cross. Likewise, denomination is not important for Wendy or Ruth, and yet both discounted certain denominations as possibilities:

WENDY: *The actual denomination is not important at all. It would depend on the actual individual church. Their theology is quite important. Even through I say denomination is not important, I would hesitate a little bit before going to a strictly Pentecostal church until I found out that they had good theology* [laughs].

RUTH: *It is not important. It is more about the theology behind the church rather than the title of the church. I mean we couldn't go back to a Brethren church now; there would just be no way.*

My findings suggest that even when a person's faith journey has been predominantly embedded within one denomination, there is still a reluctance to ascribe to a denominational identity.[22] Peter's comment on the importance of the denomination expresses this reluctance: "I don't identify as a Baptist, but I've been involved in Baptist churches." Nelson has switched churches eight times, but has only been affiliated with one

---

20. Rokeach, *Open*. Rokeach found that people were able to rank denominations based on perceived similarities to their own. The order of percieved relatedness is: (1) Catholic, (2) Episcopalian (Anglican), (3) Lutheran, (4) Presbyterian, (5) Methodist, and (6) Baptist, with the addition of sectarian bodies, such as Pentecostals, in the seventh position. This is sometimes referred to as the R-Order, after Rokeach (Babchuk and Whitt, 246).

21. Babchuk and Whitt, "R-Order."

22. Hoge and O'Connor emphasize that "denominational identity" is not the same as "local congregational identity," or involvement in one's local congregation ("Denominational Identity," 84). My findings confirm that local congregational identity, even if it is seasonal, is more significant that denominational identity.

other denomination, a Pentecostal church. The other seven churches were all Anglican churches. Nelson's religious mobility mirrors his geographical mobility, which was the reason for seven of his church switches. Nelson's last switch to date was from the Pentecostal church back to an Anglican church, a choice that was motivated by his wife's struggle to identity with the style and size of his Pentecostal church. Given Nelson's heritage with the Anglican Church, we could assume that the denomination held some significance for him.

Is the denomination important to you?

NELSON: There is a familiarity to the Anglican form and Anglican traditions. But ultimately I was quite happy not to think of myself as an Anglican, especially when I was at New Hope Christian Church. What is more important is the substance and the content rather than the actual term. It is quite nice to be back in an Anglican church again and connecting with it . . . but it [the denomination] is not hugely important to me.

Nelson does not identify himself as an Anglican, even though the majority of the churches he has attended have been Anglican and he has come to appreciate Anglican traditions; that is, the Anglican "way" of doing church that he has experienced and come to know. All the same, Nelson does identify with the various individual churches he has been involved with over his lifetime. Thus, church switching that occurs as part of people's religious biographies within this study is better understood through a symbolic approach to embedded faith rather than that of denominational identity or preference.

The Search for Community: The Symbolic Approach to Embedded Faith

Hadaway argues that "Simply trying to be 'the church for all people' in a community is no longer enough in the new religious marketplace. The day of the great generalist is gone. The market savvy specialist is more in keeping with the times. Openness to change is required, as is an open orientation to the world."[23] Research has shown that the increased range of religious alternatives may actually enhance overall religious participation rates by

23. Hadaway, "Church Growth," 351–52.

raising the likelihood that matches between individual commitments and preferences and institutional programs will be possible for a greater range of a diverse population.[24]

In *Congregations: Stories and Structures*, James Hopewell suggests that there are four approaches from which to examine a potential dwelling and a church congregation: contextual, mechanical, organic, and symbolic. A church as a dwelling simulates its environment (contextual), performs tasks (mechanical), supports the life of its inhabitants (organic), and conveys meanings (symbolic). Hopewell explains,

> In househunting terms, the symbolic search is one undertaken to find a residence that reflects the identity of the family, a place that expresses the self-understanding of its occupants and their trans- action with the world . . . They ask: What, in any circumstance, does this place say about us? What does it express about our values and the way we engage the world?[25]

This symbolic perspective of a church community is the primary ap- proach advocated by Hopewell. The symbolic approach to studying con- gregations focuses upon their identity, the way the congregation operates as a discourse through the exchange of symbols that express the views and motivations of a faith community. Symbolic studies investigate a church culture or personality. Churches can have similar contextual, mechanical, and organic features and yet display remarkably different personalities— much like siblings who grow up in the same household and end up being very different people. Shifts in religious preferences provide insight not only into changing patterns of religion, but also into how people view their own identity, group loyalties, and commitments. This symbolic approach to finding a church to embed faith within comes through consistently in my interviews with participants. Questions of style and the type of com- munity characterize the symbolic approach to finding a church and church switching.

People look for different things in a church, just as they look for dif- ferent things in considering a home to buy. Or perhaps more accurately, people place different value and importance on particular features of a local church. Community was considered an important aspect of church for all those I interviewed. However, the type of community each person was looking for was sometimes quite different. The type of community one

24. Ammerman, "Organized Religion."

25. Hopewell, *Congregations*, 29.

looks for provides insight into the practice of church switching, as well as an understanding of the importance of community in choosing a church.

Peter's experience of finding a church articulates the *feel* of different types of church communities. He had already heard positive rumors about Spurgeon Baptist from his friend Imogene before he moved. Upon arriving, Peter found he liked Spurgeon Baptist and wanted to settle there as a place where he felt like he fit in. Some of his friends, however, were not so sure about their personal fit and so, as Peter explained, they all went "shopping for a church together." I asked Peter for his impressions of the various churches he looked at. One church he described as being very streamlined, slick, and polished, but "it just didn't sit right with me. Maybe I just wasn't used to a really slick, polished church. It didn't feel very real." Peter described another church as being "quite grungy, with great music." In contrast to the other church, this one seemed more real, but sometimes "too real," because as Peter explained, "you sort of got the impression that it was OK . . . it felt like it was OK to sleep around and do drugs because they were just so accepting. I don't know if that was the case, but that was the impression that I got. So that kind of didn't fit either for me." The problem, according to Peter, was that,

PETER: *I didn't stay where I felt like I fitted. Instead I moved around. And because I didn't get linked into anything, I ended up getting into trouble really. Because I started going out with this non-Christian girl, and then I didn't really get linked into church, and it wasn't particularly a helpful time as far as my spiritual growth went.*

Some of Peter's friends settled in different churches and he eventually went back to Spurgeon Baptist with another friend. The importance of the symbolic dimension to church can be seen in the language Peter uses, such as "fitting," and the phrase, "seeing what feels right," which were both common responses throughout the interviews to questions about what participants were looking for in a church.

Community of Otherness

While some people seem to stumble upon what they are looking for in a church by chance, others, such as Antonia, have a clear idea what they are looking for and conversely, what they are not looking for in a church. Whether or not church switchers have a clear idea of the type of community they seek, those I interviewed knew when they had found it. There was something about the church community they connected with, be it meeting likeminded people at a similar stage of life, theological resonance, something about the "feel" of a place, an aesthetic dimension, or a particular style. When Antonia returned home from a period overseas, she was looking for "something out of the ordinary" in relation to church. She explained, "I didn't really feel like going to a church that had a strong pattern; you know, half-hour worship and then, you know, all the rest of the things that sort of line up in a row and then have kind of another half an hour of songs at the end where you're allowed to go home." Antonia went to a church she had been to a couple of times before heading overseas, which she knew as a community that "was fairly artistic and a different cultural model than other churches in Auckland." Antonia said that the church enabled her to "experience different things and different worship styles and different ideas with quite a lot of intelligent thought around Christian issues."

The Logos Baptist Church culture that attracted Antonia and her husband, Santos, is led from the front by the church leadership. The couple described the pastor as being "very flexible, he was very similar to us, he was quite happy to have a range of interpretations and yet still hold onto a Christian faith." This openness was important to Santos and Antonia, and was reflected in the faith community as a whole.

ANTONIA: *I think one of the cool things about Logos Baptist for me is that is doesn't try to pin people down to any definition [laughs]. It doesn't try and define people at all. Like you're not forced to go, "Oh yes, out of options A, B and C this is the one that I believe."*

SANTOS: *Which is so engaging, isn't it, when you don't feel you have to mold yourself to be able to participate? You can just engage where you are. And that's so connecting.*

ANTONIA: *I think it recognizes the faith journey a lot. In that people are at all different stages and coming to knowledge about different bits of it and experience different things, you know, without trying to gather everybody from all these different places and end up with everybody on the same road, going one direction, down one path, it's actually just recognizing that everybody's on different paths and that's OK.*

The understanding of faith communicated by Logos Baptist resonates with Antonia and Santos. The church allows and encourages a space that

Antonia and Santos feel connects with their current place in their faith journey: one of questioning faith and life, but also one of intellectual engagement. Both have been involved in churches that were not as comfortable with people questioning certain areas of faith or with having unresolved issues. Antonia, commenting on past church experiences, said that, "There was actually nobody to talk to if you had a question because everybody had the answer already, so you weren't allowed to ask the question." Both Antonia and Santos are comfortable living with contradictions and tensions and unanswered questions. They are now in a faith community where questioning without having the answers is encouraged.

In many ways, Antonia and Santos have found a church community akin to what Friedman calls the "community of otherness," where space is opened up for members who view things differently, or who have come from a different interpretive community denominationally, and for members who potentially belong to multiple interpretive communities. Friedman explains that the community of otherness "is the community that confirms otherness within climates of trust."[26] Arnett likewise suggests that "An invitation to human community needs to permit and encourage the emergence of human uniqueness."[27] Friedman contrasts this community of otherness against communities of affinity or like-mindedness:

> The community of *affinity*, of *like-mindedness*, is based on what people feel they have in common—race, sex, religion, nationality, politics, a common formula, a common creed. The community of otherness, in contrast, does not mean that everyone does the same thing and certainly not that they do it from the same point of view. What makes community real is people finding themselves in a common situation—a situation which they approach in different ways yet which calls each of them out.[28]

In this way, the type of people that make up a church shapes its culture and determines whether it is a church community of affinity or one of otherness.

26. Friedman, *Confirmation*, 153.

27. Arnett, *Communication*, 22.

28. Friedman, *Confirmation*, 135 (emphasis in original).

Church Community: A Place to Call Home

The language of home participants use to describe church illustrates that the religious sensibility is one of investment and commitment rather than one of consumption. While similar language might be used in relation to finding a church to describe what an individual is looking for—preferences, needs, style, etc.—when framed by the religious sensibility, this language changes from one of consumption to one of community. In searching for a new church, participants sometimes spoke of their experience of a church as feeling like home. Such talk of church as home suggests that some people do in fact view church as a dwelling. One pastor in a church that Sophie attended made a direct comparison between church and home by encouraging the congregation to treat the church like home. I asked her what that sense of ownership looks like. She answered, "The church is kind of like your home." Sophie elaborated,

SOPHIE: *When I was still at my church in Wellington we were encouraged to consider the church like our home. So when you welcome someone in, like if you notice if something is slightly amiss, you'd sort it out, you know? So if there was a bit of rubbish somewhere, you'd just pick it up because it is like your home. And, you know, you have a bit of ownership there. And then you are concerned for the things that are going on there and the people that come in. I don't know if that's what I normally feel, or is that a today feel?*

Intertwined with Sophie's understanding of church as home is a sense of ownership and investment. Ownership is something valued by young adults. When people feel that they have ownership of something, then there is also the responsibility to look after it—an investment in place and people. As Sophie explained, "you notice if something is slightly amiss, you'd sort it out." Sophie's ambiguity about whether she normally feels church is a home to her or not suggests that home, at least as a feeling, is not altogether permanent, fixed, or stable. Rather it is something vulnerable, exposed to the elements of an accelerated culture of high-speed change and extensive geographic mobility.

For Emily, the experience of church as a home was a first impression of a church she attended in the UK. The experience of home took Emily by surprise. Some friends had invited her along, an invitation that she accepted reluctantly because she wanted to make her own way in London, including finding a church on her own. As Emily explained, "But I went along to their church and the first day I walked in and I went 'Aw, this is home,' and I never left." I asked Emily what made it feel like home. She answered,

EMILY: *The people, it is hard to describe . . . but it is probably the most healthy example of a church that I have ever been connected with. And I'm still not quite sure what was so different. I think that because a lot of the people there were from other countries, or not even—a lot of them were English, but they weren't from London, so everybody was kind of new to London or strangers in London and there just seemed to be a genuine commitment to genuinely building community . . . people realized that they needed it. They're away from family and friends and everybody just worked at it.*

The church acted as a surrogate family for Emily during her time in England. Emily is describing an experience of Turner's concept of communitas created by a state of liminality, an in-between place of existence.[29] Emily and other members of Saint Francis' Anglican were geographically away from their home country, only in the UK for a season before moving on again. Communitas requires a consciousness and intentionality of the sort describe by Emily, where "people realized that they need it . . . and everybody worked at it." "Communitas," Turner states, "is a relationship between concrete, historical, idiosyncratic individuals. These individuals are not segmented into roles and statuses but confront one another rather in the manner of Martin Buber's 'I and Thou.'"[30]

The transformative and deep communal experience of communitas described by Turner also comes through in Cameron's story. Having been invited by a friend, Cameron went along to a church for the first time in several years. "And from the first time I went there," Cameron explained, "something within me . . . I had this huge or overwhelming sense of arriving home. I said at the time and for quite a while afterwards, it is like the eagle has landed." It was certainly not a homogenous church congregation: "It was a church made up of all kinds of people from all walks of life; if you want to use a class system, particularly the lower class. And a lot of them hadn't had church backgrounds, hadn't been brought up in faith. They had simply come to a conversion point for whatever reason. There were

29. Turner, *Ritual*, 95–97.
30. Ibid., 119.

prostitutes, surfers, druggies." Cameron's experience of "arriving home" was a mix of this diversity in addition to a strong experience what Cameron described as "the presence of God." But home, however it is described, and the experience of communitas can be temporal and sometimes seasonal.[31] Home is uprooted and sought elsewhere. Community has a fluid, elusive dimension that is unstable and changing and eventually resulted in the eagle flying yet again for Cameron. But despite community's elusive nature, people still seek it out.

One of the characteristics of a home is familiarity. Community for Christina was a place that felt like her previous church. Finding such a place proved difficult in Auckland's church scene. Christina had moved to Auckland from a smaller church and town, and she struggled with the size of the churches she looked at in Auckland. This added to her sense of geographical dislocation. It was only out of desperation for friends, a year after being in Auckland, that Christina began looking to find a church again. She had no social network to tap into and so relied on the phone book. She called one church close by to find out the time of the service, but they had forgotten to turn the answering machine on.

CHRISTINA: *So I didn't know what I was turning up to and I arrive at ten and everybody was coming out and milled around for a bit and I thought, I'll just leave. And one of the women walked up to me and said, 'You look a bit lost.' And I said, 'Yeah.' She introduced me to Joshua and Katie. And I went straight out to the mall for coffee. And then went to home group that week. And my first church was the following week. So I had been for coffee and to home group before I had been to church . . . They really wanted to know more about me and wanted me to join in . . . and just the sense of belonging was there immediately.*

A sense of belonging was something Christina longed for in the big city that had intensified her sense of loneliness and social fragmentation. Although Christina does not recognize it, coffee and the small group she went out with were part of church—ritual practices carried out on a weekly basis. The church service is only one part of a faith community's activities and interaction.

The search for *home* is a search for a place—a church—to embed one's faith. It is about finding and having roots in an otherwise mobile and

---

31. Turner regards communitas as "a moment of transition rather than an established mode of being or an ideal soon to be permanently attained" (*Ritual*, 143).

transient society. The alternative is religious "rootlessness," or, to continue with the metaphor of home, "homelessness." Yearning for and romaticization of home is evident in popular sayings about it:[32] "Home sweet home," "There's no place like home," "A man's home is his castle," and in New Zealand musician Dave Dobbyn's song, "Welcome Home." However, the feeling of home felt in some churches is not guaranteed, and as some participants found, can be hard to find. To paraphrase Bono, "A church does not always make a home." And even when it does, home as a permanent, fixed location is now confined to the realm of poetry for most, and not reality as Toffler[33] has argued. Under such conditions, to find a church that feels like home, however that might feel in contemporary conditions, is something quite extraordinary.

Contributing to the Church Community: Opportunity to be Involved

Finding a place to embed faith has its challenges, but once found, switching churches is often accompanied by a willingness to get involved in the life of the church community. People, for the most part, want to contribute to the church that they belong to. Being involved increases one's sense of belonging. One of the things many of those I interviewed looked for in a church when switching was the opportunity to be involved. Being able to get involved in a church shortly after beginning attending was especially important to Joshua. He checked out a number of churches when he moved to Auckland for university:

JOSHUA: *I went to a number of churches and I think they were all kinda good. They were, are doing, great things . . . but I just wanted to do stuff, you know. I don't want to have to spend three years getting to know people in church before you have any sort of trust built up before they will let you do anything.*

The structure and size of a church will often influence the process and opportunities for involvement in contributing to church life, and for some, this involvement is found particularly in the church service.

---

32. Here I am building on Toffler's observations in *Future*.

33. Toffler, *Future*, 83.

Cameron ended up switching churches with some of his friends after failed attempts to get involved:

CAMERON: *We made an attempt to get involved in leadership initiatives that weren't accepted for whatever reason. And after that we thought, well, if we can't be involved—because we were clearly leadership material; one of them was a psychologist and people that had things to offer—we all left and went somewhere else.*

It is possible that the church leaders did not "clearly" view Cameron and his friends as "leadership material." It is also possible, however, that the leadership did not consider the initiatives they suggested as contributing to the church's vision, or perhaps they wanted more control over membership involvement. Whatever the reason, a lack of opportunity for involvement has a tendency to marginalize people and create a sense of disconnectedness. Involvement creates a stronger feeling of connection to a group. Often people remain uninvolved not because of a lack of willingness or because they are simply "church consumers," but rather as the result of a lack of opportunity. Space needs to be created for people to find and explore areas that welcome church involvement.

The ability to contribute to the life of a faith community can sustain a person's affiliation and commitment to a church. This was certainly the case for Zack and Bianca, a couple in their late twenties:

ZACK: *I think there has to be some . . . you have to have some spiritual input from somewhere that doesn't necessarily have to be from the church you're attending. You might get snippets every now and again, and if that's complemented by your own quiet times and with other friends or with the home group, then I think that's enough. And for the rest, the main reason we are there is because you feel like that's where you can contribute.*

BIANCA: *I don't know. I still think it's important. If you are getting connected, if you are getting challenged, then it's kind of where you want to go, isn't it? But then if you think there's room for you to contribute to that church then that's also a good thing. You kind of need both for me.*

While the preference is to be in a church that grows and challenges faith, as Bianca pointed out, this is no longer a priority for people like Zack, Theo, and Jody. What is important is having the opportunities to be involved. Growing spiritually remains important, but these participants seek spiritual growth and challenge through other means, such as friends or personal study.

Dis-embedding Faith

Moving Beyond Role Expectations

Involvement can be confined and limited by role expectations and assumptions about who someone is, or what they have been involved in over the years. Toby found changing churches to be a liberating experience, because it freed him to get involved in areas that he had previously not had the opportunity to. Toby said that, "it has been freeing, just because through a sense of people's expectations and not recognizing the changes and growth that has gone on in me, I felt restricted in ways which I could actually begin to live those out."

Toby changed churches for ministry reasons. But reflecting back on the change, he comments on how it has enabled him to grow and mature into a different person than he would be if he had remained at Flaxbush Baptist.

Toby: *But as I look back again on it I can see as I've taken a step of faith and trusted in God that it took me out of my comfort zone and placed me in situations where I hadn't necessarily had the opportunities to be involved. The growth that's gone on within me has been incredible, and I think in a way, through my experiences of these and theological study, I've placed myself in a box at Flaxbush in terms of how people perceive me in terms of my pastoral care role. I was quite comfortable with not being in an up-front role and being more relational—I'd always shied away from the upfront sort of leadership and hadn't the confidence and that sort of thing. And to be given opportunities to begin doing that where people have no expectations of who I was or what I'd been involved in allowed me to try new areas of leadership, and that has allowed me to develop in ways that I don't think I would have if I had continued to be at Flaxbush.*

Toby suffered from what Helen Ebaugh[34] calls "identity hangover" from his previous pastoral care role. Identity hangover occurs when a past

34. Ebaugh, *Becoming*, 5.

identification with a social category or role lingers in some form (e.g., role residue) in the lives of people leaving a previous role or social category. Tension develops between an individual's past, present, and future as they struggle to incorporate past identities into present conceptions of self. Toby faced the challenge of incorporating a previous role identity of pastoral care and working behind the scenes into the new self-concept that opened to him through switching churches. In fact, at the new church, Toby was expected to be upfront and to even preach periodically. As a result, Toby gained new confidence in areas limited by his previous role.

Role expectations can limit church involvement. Rebecca found the expectations placed on her by her former church to be suffocating, which was one of her main reasons for wanting to switch churches. She had recently returned from doing mission work overseas:

REBECCA: *One of the reasons I wanted to leave after that was because everybody thought I was a certain sort of person, and I didn't.*

Did you feel constrained by that in comparison to the sort of person you were becoming?

REBECCA: *Yeah. I think so. Or I felt that I would have to start disagreeing with things that people would talk to me about. And I didn't want to be seen like that because they might give me the label "sinner," or try and convince me otherwise. And I was quite comfortable with the fact that I knew that it was OK to think differently, but I didn't feel that I would be allowed to do that. I didn't feel that it would be approved of.*

Rebecca's sense of herself was changing, as was her understanding of faith, which had broadened during her time overseas. She therefore wanted to move beyond the expectations and assumptions that people in her church had of her. Ebaugh explains that "The ex-role creates a unique sociological phenomenon in that the expectations, norms, and identity associated with it do not so much consist in what one is currently doing, but rather stem from expectations, social obligations, and norms related to one's previous role."[35] Through dis-embedding their faith from their previous church and re-embedding it in their current church, both Toby and Rebecca were creating new identities independent from this "ex-role."

35. Ebaugh, *Becoming*, 149.

Changing Church Cultures: From Doing to Being

In contrast to those who seek out a church that offers opportunities for involvement, others seek out a church where they feel they can just *be* rather than having to *do*. My interviews revealed that this choice was not motivated by a passive mentality. For those I interviewed in this situation, the choice to seek out a new church came largely from having been too involved, overcommitted and, for some, being burnt out by the church they were exiting. Sophie said that she was attracted to Iona Church because

SOPHIE: *I think the fact that you are not obliged to be involved in lots of stuff. You can just come along and they treat you like adults and sort of respect your time, so you know, this would be really good to come to but it's up to you kind of thing. Where my previous church, it was like you must come, like you know, to this or that or whatever. And so just choices and options there, nothing is compulsory. You just cruise on up.*

For Joel, who had been heavily involved in the youth ministry of his church, attending another church was liberating. Joel described it as being "Just freeing, because I could just sit there and no one would ever ask me to do anything . . . I could just *be*. I think I would walk in there and not commit to anything for two years. That's sort of how I feel. It has sort of taken the joy out of church for me, for my personal walk." Churches can project and encourage either a culture of doing or a culture of being. People that are attracted to churches that have a culture of being rather than doing do not equate to a passive-active binary. For some, such as Sophie and Joel, this freedom to *be* provides the much needed space to be refreshed from having been heavily involved in church life that, for Joel at least, took the joy out of both church and his faith in general. When people are allowed to be, there is a freedom to get involved when they are ready, without constant pressure from the front (often in the form of sermons) and from church leaders that are dependent on human resources.

Jack needed to leave his church to find some space from role expectations and rediscover who he was independent of these. He was feeling burnt out from his involvement as a youth leader. Jack switched from his Baptist church to an Anglican that a number of his friends had started to attend. However, for Jack, attending this Anglican church was not the same as belonging:

JACK: *I don't necessarily belong to a church now . . . it's a weird, weird feeling. I go to Saint Barnabas' Anglican. Every time I go there, I get this intense feeling of "just love me," you know; that I don't need to do anything in that church.*

Just letting God love you?

JACK: *Yeah, just me love God and let him love me. It's just solely about that: totally being. Back to what it was, embarrassingly, at the beginning.*

Jack still considers the Baptist church home, but said that, "I had no desire to go back there quickly because I don't actually know how to integrate myself into that church as a participant in the pews." Jack had been involved at Flaxbush Baptist for so long that he had become a certain person within this church community based on role expectations of himself and others. The attraction to the Anglican church was being able to distance himself from this role expectation of leadership. Jack liked the feel and dynamics of Saint Barnabas' but, more importantly, Jack said that "I liked the fact that I had nothing to do when I turned up there." Jack talked about the freedom that came from having no expectations placed upon him at Saint Barnabas' because nobody really knew him yet.

The Exit Process of Reluctant Leavers

The process of leaving a church can often be a difficult one. A person's identity is sometimes bound up in church involvement. Belinda's experience of leaving a church that she was heavily involved with for over seven years was caught up in feelings of guilt and having to reformulate her identity separate from what she did. Ebaugh's four-stage role-exiting process is helpful for understanding this process for people who, like Belinda, are deeply committed and involved in their church. The four stages are (1) First Doubts, (2) Seeking Alternatives, (3) Turning Points, and (4) Creating the Ex-Role.[36]

The doubting stage, according to Ebaugh, is one of reinterpretation and redefining a situation that was previously taken for granted.[37] First doubts involve a reinterpretation of reality. Previous expectations and

36. Ebaugh, *Becoming*, 34.
37. Ibid., 41.

events that were defined as acceptable are seen in a new light and take on new meaning. For Belinda, first doubts surfaced about her understanding of identity, because "it took me a while to realize that my identity wasn't wrapped up in this role that I was involved with." Ebaugh explains that "The doubting process is usually gradual in that the individual first experiences dissatisfaction in a generalized way and only eventually is able to specify and articulate what he or she finds lacking in the situation."[38] Belinda, who was burnt out from being a youth leader, was not encouraged by leadership to take some time out. There was a culture of just pushing through and relying on God for strength. The strength never came. What did come was anger: "I got involved in youth leadership and church again but I was angry, I was really angry. And I spent about a year of just being angry in church. And so I wouldn't engage in the sermon or the worship or anything. I just couldn't." I asked her why she did not just leave and go and find another church. "Because this innate thing, that I was like, I couldn't leave . . . like there's this culture where you get shunned for changing churches."

A sense of wellbeing began to redefine Belinda's understanding of identity and role expectations: "And I felt justified because I was like, actually I need to look after myself, and that was the first time that I had begun looking after my needs over and above what everyone else needed from me, or what I thought they needed from me." Being involved in church took on a new meaning as she separated involvement from her sense of self and self-worth. She gradually became free of the guilt that had resulted from not being involved as she began removing herself from certain responsibilities and her leadership position. Belinda developed a new understanding of what it meant to be a Christian that did not require church involvement.

The second stage Ebaugh discusses involves seeking alternatives. Usually after admitting dissatisfaction, this seeking becomes a conscious step in the exiting process. Ebaugh describes this stage as a comparative process in which costs and rewards of one's current situation are compared and evaluated against alternatives.[39] Belinda still considered church to be important to her Christian faith. She was just not happy with her current church's emphasis, demands, and pressures surrounding involvement. Belinda describes the process of finding an alternative church, saying,

38. Ibid.
39. Ibid., 87.

BELINDA: It's a little bit embarrassing, but when I finally did decide to leave New Hope Pentecostal I had just visited Saint Mark's Anglican for a few weeks in a row. Because I really didn't want to leave unless I decided where else I wanted to go. And I had gone to Saint Mark's a few times over the year since it had started and I had really enjoyed it. But I still felt like I couldn't leave New Hope yet, and I had a lot of friends there at Saint Mark's. Another thing was there wasn't anything for our age group for a long time.

The third stage in the exiting process discussed by Ebaugh is the turning point. Having weighed up alternatives, there comes a point where the individual makes a firm and definite decision to leave, often connected to some turning point in their life. Ebaugh explains that a turning point,

> Is an event that mobilizes and focuses awareness that old lines of action are complete, have failed, have been disrupted, or are no longer personally satisfying and provides individuals with the opportunity to do something different with their lives. Old obligations and lines of action are diminished or seen as undesirable and new involvements are seen as possible.[40]

In terms of the leaving process, the turning point for Belinda came before finding an alternative. The turning point, "the straw that broke the camel's back," for Belinda followed a series of conversations with the pastor of New Hope on the need for pastoral care for leaders which flowed out of her own experience. The pastor failed to listen and did not take her concerns or her wellbeing seriously. The church had developed a culture, in Belinda's view and experience, that only valued people when they were involved.

The final stage of the exit process Ebaugh discusses is the need to create a new identity. This new identity for Belinda was one free from expectations to be involved in church. Her identity as a Christian was now based on her relationship to God rather than trying to meet the expectations of others through serving and being a leader. Belinda said that being interviewed for this research has helped her realize that Saint Mark's is "my church but it's not the focus of my life. It's not like church used to be, and just knowing that that's OK." Belinda has a new understanding of the role that church plays in her faith journey. Church is important, but no longer

40. Ibid., 123.

as central as it once was, and she no longer needs to be involved in church to feel like she is a Christian.

The exit process as it is described in a number of participants' stories reveals that leaving a church that one considers home is a painful process, especially when negative feelings are among the reasons for leaving. What these interviews highlight is participants' deep sense of commitment and struggle through the leaving process, which often takes place gradually rather than as a sudden departure. Furthermore, a number of people explored avenues of dialogue with leadership to find a way forward that might enable them to stay. In Belinda's case, church leadership let her down by failing to listen or act to address her concerns. Such experiences of leadership intensify participants' sense of hurt and disillusionment towards church. That these people choose to remain in church is a testimony to the importance they place on church as a critical part of their Christian journey, and to their theological understanding of the place that God has given to the church as the body of Christ. These young adults continue to search for church done well and are prepared to commit themselves to being a part of that journey with a group of people.

5

The Relational Dimension
of Embedded Faith

Faith may be a spiritual matter, but in order to hold it needs mundane
anchoring; its roots must reach deep into the experience of daily life.

—BAUMAN

Peter Berger argues that "modern societies are characterized by unstable, incohesive, unreliable plausibility structures."[1] One of the consequences of this for faith has been "a weakening of every conceivable belief
and value dependent upon social support."[2] In other words, certainty is
elusive, or at least hard to come by. In a similar fashion, Zygmunt Bauman
argues that

> Our times are hard for faith—*any* faith, sacred or secular; for belief
> in Providence, the Divine Chain of Being, as much as for belief in
> a mundane utopia, in a perfect society to come. Our times are in-
> hospitable for trust, and more generally for the long-haul purposes
> and efforts, because of the evident transience and vulnerability of
> everything (or almost everything) that counts in earthly life.[3]

Given this difficult social climate for faith, it is not surprising that people seek out a faith community that will sustain and encourage their faith.

1. Berger, *Hertical*, 17.
2. Ibid.
3. Bauman, "Europe and North America," 4.

This chapter explores the importance of social networks and relationships to people's faith journey, their experiences of church, and the decisions they make concerning church.

Demographic Relevance

Parents Seeking Out Peer Support for Their Children

Parents concerned with how best to pass on their faith often want a supportive and conducive church environment for their children. Switching churches as a family constituted some of the participants' earliest memories of church switching, as their parents sought out peer support for their children and teenagers. Grace's first memory of church switching as an eight-year-old from Grace Bible Chapel to Kauri Baptist came about because her parents wanted her to be in a "good, supportive youth group." Their former church lacked young people. Grace did not know anything about the family's new church, but went "because that's where we were going." The shift was a positive experience for Grace, who made some lifelong friends through her new church. Similarly, Esther switched churches with her family because her parents wanted a more supportive environment for Esther and her two siblings. Esther explained that there was no Sunday school at their church, so her parents switched churches in hopes that their children could have some peers. Harry's family church, on the other hand, did have a strong Sunday school, but was lacking progression into youth ministry. Harry's parents switched the family to another church that could provide the support for his older sister through the church's youth ministry.

Those who had children emphasized the importance of either being in a church or finding a church that has a children's ministry. Even when they no longer consider church beneficial to their own faith, internal leavers such as Theo continue to attend church for the sake of their children.

How does having a family change what you look for in a church?

THEO: *It changes everything. Because, see, even though I've had my struggles with the church, I still want my children to have access to the faith. And I can't see how they are going to have access to faith unless they go to church; unless they have somehow trod the same path that I have gone through. So I'm kind of caught there. I want them to experience church without some of the excess that I experienced. But I still recognize that the church is a valuable ally in helping me bring up my children with Jesus in mind. It's not something I can do on my own because the power of my culture is so strong I think I will lose my children to hedonism.*

Parents will at times sacrifice their own church preferences for the sake of their children. A strong Sunday school or youth ministry becomes a determining factor in switching for parents who seek out demographic relevance for their children when they feel it is absent in their current church.

Seeking Out Demographic Relevance for Oneself

While parents switch churches for the sake of their children and their socialization in the faith, young people sometimes take matters into their own hands when their parents' church lacks young people or a youth ministry, all of which demonstrates the importance of peer groups in the life of faith.

You went to Lakeside Baptist and then Grey's Anglican. Can you talk me through those transitions and the reasons for those changes?

EUGENE: *I think when I was getting to thirteen, because I was in the youth group for a wee while and stuff like that at Lakeside Baptist, and a lot of my high school friends were going to Grey's Anglican, and basically I wanted to hang out with them more and be part of a bigger group and that kind of stuff. So it wasn't traumatic at all, it was a natural transition to going to a different youth group. I remember starting to go to Grey's Anglican and slowly phasing out of the Lakeside thing. And generally I think the youth group at Lakeside kind of finished anyway.*

ANTONIA: *I was in the youth group, and then when I was about fifteen, I changed churches to go where my friends were. At that point I felt quite happy to be in a place where there was a bit more of a youth culture and that kind of thing.*

Your previous church didn't have that?

ANTONIA: *It was probably just a bit more traditional in the youth group setting and not that dynamic. The church was a bit more conservative.*

Adapting Berger's idea of plausibility structures, Duncan MacLaren suggests that youth groups provide a plausibility shelter.[4] Alternatively, Nick Shepherd suggests that it is more accurate to view youth groups as a "plausibility source" because young people are not sheltered from their lives crossing alternative lifestyles and beliefs.[5] It is evident from my interviews with young adults that their lives do cross alternative lifestyles and social circles, which can often lead them to a faith crossroad. Suffice to say that age-based church ministries do provide a plausibility structure. Whether this takes the form of a shelter or a source depends on the extent to which a young person engages in social circles different to their beliefs and lifestyle or retreats from them. A common reason participants gave for switching to a particular church as adolescents and young adults was simply because of the presence of peers of their own generation. What youth groups also provide, then, is what I have come to describe as "demographic relevance."

Sophie stopped going to her parents' church because she came to consider the church personally irrelevant due to its demographic makeup:

SOPHIE: *Church just didn't seem relevant. Mum and Dad's new church didn't have many young families in it. There was possibly one other person my age at church. And so it was full of older people. And they were a bit more ritualistic, more into rituals than the other one. Yeah, I guess the church I grew up in was quite a family kind of community church. Where the one we moved to in Auckland was kind of like a dying church, like you know, just aging. It was just going to putter out when everyone died off sort of thing.*

Sophie's comments that church "just didn't seem relevant" because of its lack of young people, and that the church they moved to in Auckland seemed to her to be a "dying church" suggests that having peers in a faith community endows faith with a sense of relevance and belonging, particularly for young people. The demographic relevance of church, or the lack of it, frequently contributed to people's decisions to switch churches.

Sophie's impression of Christianity was radically altered when she attended a Christian youth camp and met other young Christians outside of her parents' church. Sophie explained that the camp "exposed me to the fact that not everyone was as dead and dry as my parents' church. Like, there were Christians out there that could have fun and sing some fun songs and

4. MacLaren, cited in Shepherd, "Christian Youth," 7.

5. Shepherd, "Christian Youth," 8.

there were young people that were alive," Sophie's faith began to grow independently from her parents' faith through her social interactions with her weekly Campus Life group meetings. She did not attend a church in the formal sense, but considered the Campus Life group as her church, although it would not be recognized as a church in the formal sense. This new social group provided Sophie with important social support, a plausibility source that, according to Sophie, stopped her from walking away from her faith. Leaders also kept an eye out for her and encouraged her in the faith.

Sophie resumed her active involvement in church when one of her school friends became a Christian:

So you're out of church for most of your high school. Have you got a mix of friends that believe and don't? What's happening with your social groups and influences?

SOPHIE: *Yeah, went through waves of having mainly non-Christian friends and then occasionally, or every so often, friends that would become Christians through me taking them to Campus Life, and that always spurred my faith on, even though it wasn't intentional that they became Christians. But it would keep me going because I would feel obliged to help them work out their faith. When I was sixteen, a friend became a Christian and she started going to an Elim church and I thought that I would go along with her, you know, to make sure this works out, and then I started going regularly and I was like, ah wow, this is kind of a cool church. There were other young people and it was not dry and boring, you know.*

Sophie returned to church almost out of a sense of responsibility that she felt for her friend's faith. Long before Sophie felt committed to the church, she had a deep sense of commitment to her friends. It is common for people to switch churches to go where their friends are going. This pattern is most apparent during the teenage years, when people are making friends at school and camps. For some, this meant switching to a different church from their parents.

Finding People in the Same Stage of Life

For a number of participants that I interviewed, finding a church with a strong student ministry during their university years was a determining factor in continuing to go to church, or at least a very attractive feature that drew them in. People often found an encouraging support network critical to sustaining their faith during their university years. During this stage of her life, Sophie's main social network was in the friends that she made at a university's Campus Life Christian group:

SOPHIE: *I guess the big growth thing was with the uni Christian group because we would meet weekly as a large group and weekly as a smaller group as well. And I guess, like, I hadn't mixed with those sorts of people before, like the types of people that study at university . . . like, just big thinkers and that. Most of my friends up until then, they've sort of been a different style of people. So it was constantly challenging because everyone was going through a similar thing and everyone was questioning lots of things, like the way things were done, or how we do life, and looking at the possibility of doing a community. I guess it's sort of setting yourself up for life for how you might want to do it. So it was a very important time I think.*

Questioning faith and aspects of life together within a social support circle creates an environment of safety. Doubts and questions become a valid part of the faith journey and are often part of developing faith maturity. In contrast, when an individual raises doubts and questions about faith within a church community that discourages such thinking, spiritual dissonance often results. A person can begin to feel marginalized as they face a lonely journey brought on by a crisis of faith. Finding social networks that support a person's faith journey and development by sharing a similar worldview, theology, and experience is something that young adults give significant attention to. This search for a like-minded social network is one of the major factors in church switching.

When Emily first moved to Auckland from a smaller town in her mid-twenties, she began looking for a church. She visited about five or six churches, mostly one-offs. She visited one church that one of her flatmates attended a couple of times, but quickly decided that it was "not really my group." Another church that she visited reminded her of her church back home. Again she commented that "It's not my thing." Reflecting on what she was looking for in a church, Emily said,

EMILY: *Maybe I'm looking for, I think possibly when I went to Iona Church and you could sort of see automatically that it's your demographic, you know twenties and thirties and you realize that all the other churches are missing that whole group of people. There's a gap in all the churches of that age group. Not in all of them, just some of them.*

Emily was looking for people she could connect with, like-minded people with whom she could identify. By this, she meant single people of a similar age and stage of life. She found this community at Iona and stopped looking at other churches. Emily was looking for a symbolic match: a church community that reflected her stage in life as a single professional young adult.

The Elusive Community: Stage of Life Disconnect

One of the consequences with age-segregated services is that people can, and often do, grow out of the church's targeted audience or particular de-mographic as they move into another stage of life. Participants often de-scribed this occurrence as "no longer fitting." For example, Grace returned from overseas in her mid twenties after having done missionary work on behalf of her church, which had sent and supported her. Re-entry for Grace was an extremely difficult and painful time. Many of her friends had moved on, both geographically and in terms of their life stage, with many of them married and having children. This isolation upon returning home pro-vided a striking contrast with the strong sense of belonging, community, and purpose that Grace had experienced within the expatriate missionary community:

GRACE: *I always felt when I was working in Asia as a missionary that this is where God wants me, and feeling that I was really living with a purpose for my life at that time. And I came back to New Zealand, and I think what was so hard was I just didn't have that sense of purpose. And I felt like I was drifting, and I didn't have that sense of belonging anymore in the social networks, or even in the church, because the church had changed a lot since I had been away, just in that year and a half, and there was a new minister and a lot of my friends that were there when I left had all moved on and they were no longer there.*

Grace felt the absence of people her age keenly, which would eventu-ally become her main reason for leaving. Grace left for a church similar to Kauri Baptist in terms of style, but which featured more young adults. She ended up at the Brooklyn Baptist through friends she knew there. She also began to experience a similar sense of disconnection at Brooklyn Baptist towards the end of her time there, and again left in search of people who were not just her own age, but who were also in a similar stage of life:

So what led to the decision of leaving the Brooklyn Baptist and ending up at Holy Trinity Church?

GRACE: *It was purely the social thing. I liked how the evening services were at Brooklyn and being part of that. But the people I was hanging out with at Brooklyn . . . I wasn't at that stage of life. I connected with them in the past. But we were at very different stages of life now, because all the friends—fifteen friends that I was closest with when I started at Brooklyn Baptist four years ago—had all got married within that time, all but one; and then five of them in the last six months became pregnant. And so I just found it really hard being around the talk that was always on pregnancies and babies. And with that, the girls, they weren't interested in doing the same social things that I wanted to. So that was the main reason.*

Did that involve losing a sense of belonging?

GRACE: *Yes, very much so. Because for a lot of people at Brooklyn, there's a very strong social connection, they're all at similar stages of life and they're all, you know, having babies at the same time. And so that's providing a really strong connection with each other. And I can't relate to that.*

Grace ended up at another church among more people who shared her stage of life. A number of her friends had begun going there and invited her along. Grace's main attraction to Trinity Church was social, for as she explained, "It was refreshing to have a new social circle of people that were in the same stage as life as me."

The stage of life disconnect illustrates the fluid dimension that can characterize church communities, which are never fixed or static. This is the fragile nature of community identified by Bauman, part of a "liquid modernity," in which traditional lifelong loyalties and commitments are a thing of the past.[6] As Marx observed about modern life, "everything that is solid melts into air."[7] Or, as Bauman has written,

6. Bauman, *Liquid.*

7. Marx, *Communist,* 83.

Community of common understanding, even if reached, will therefore stay fragile and vulnerable, forever in need of vigilance, fortification and defence. People who dream of community in the hope of finding a long-term security which they miss so painfully in their daily pursuits, and of liberating themselves from the irksome burden of ever new and always risky choices, will be sorely disappointed. Peace of mind, if they find it, will prove to be of the "until further notice" kind.[8]

This "liquefaction" of which Bauman speaks has profoundly impacted the stability of community, including faith communities, as evidenced by the significant religious mobility we have discussed, which in turn generates a desire for community that Bauman argues is a way of seeking safety in an unsecure world. Eric Hobsbawm makes a similar argument when he writes,

Never was the word "community" used more indiscriminately and emptily than in the decades when communities in the sociological sense become hard to find in real life. Men and women look for groups to which they can belong, certainly and forever, in a world in which all else is moving and shifting, in which nothing else is certain. And they find it in an identity group.[9]

The young adults I interviewed do search for a faith community to belong to. But their multiple switching suggests that when they find it, it does not last, at least not in the way the first experienced it. And yet, because they want their faith to be embedded in a church community, they continue to search for a renewed sense of community even as they recognize that it might not last.

Rumors of Church and Tapping into the Social Network

Ammerman found that people are willing to travel out of their immediate neighbourhood to attend a church that offers programs and styles of worship that are especially suited to their own particular needs or preferences[10]. One must first of all know of these churches' existence, which requires a well-networked membership, because "Niche congregations need members who have extensive connections in the community by way of which

8. Bauman, *Community*, 14.

9. Hobsbawm, "Cult," 40.

10. Ammerman, *Congregation*, 324.

they can recruit persons who occupy the same population or categories of identity."[11] My own findings support Ammerman's. It was common for participants to tap into their social networks in finding a church. Seeking out personal recommendations is a valuable and trusted way of finding a church. Recommendations are often sought out when a person moves geographically to a new place where they do not know many people, let alone the church scene, or even where to begin looking.

Before Peter even moved to Auckland, a friend had unofficially networked him into her church. Peter explains, "Imogene said, 'If you move up for university then you should come to Central Baptist.'" Imogene herself had been introduced to the church by a friend she had made at university. Church leaders are a valuable source of information when finding another church, for they can tap into their own church network. When Joshua was moving cities for university, his pastor recommended that he meet with a pastor of a church located near Joshua's destination. Joshua arranged to have coffee with this pastor, connected with him, and ultimately felt inspired by the pastor's vision for the church.

It is through social networks that rumors surrounding a church circulate: its culture, demographics, style of worship, preaching etc. Sometimes "rumors of a church" start to be embedded into one's consciousness even before one is looking for another church. So when one eventually encounters the "straw that broke the camel's back" as part of the exit process identified by Ebaugh, one may already have another church in place. The rumors of church that I am specifically talking of here are of a positive nature, those rumors about a church and what it is doing that circulate through various social networks. People hear good things about a church from friends, who will often encourage them to come and experience it for themselves. It was through such rumours that Sophie's friends heard about Iona Church and continued the ongoing rumor about the church. These friends had not managed to visit the church themselves, but from what they had heard, they concluded that it would be a good "fit" for Sophie. Sophie commenting on this, said, "They wanted to go to it but they've got kids and they knew they would be better off at a different service or a service with their kids because they were at different stages in their lives." Iona may have fit Sophie, but the same was not true for her friends because the church demographics were not well suited to their stage of life with children.

11. Ibid., 324.

Rumors of a church can start a chain reaction of "checking it out," as the church in question becomes a trendy and cool place to be associated with. Esther heard rumours about Zion Church a couple of months before actually going:

How did you go from Central Baptist to Zion Church?

ESTHER: *I had Zion recommended to me by a few people. Like, Larry's friend Adam went there, and he was always telling us to go. And various people had sort of said Zion was a good place to go and I knew that there were a few Central Baptist people sighted there occasionally. I thought I would give Zion a go and see. I found it really hard to start with. I was a little bit of, "Oh I'm not driving to Central, I am driving somewhere else." It's because I don't really like change. But after a little while I met people and it was pretty easy because I knew a number of people and one of my best friends came not long after that.*

Church switching can be influenced by "migrational flows" from one church to another, or groups of friends that move together in typical tribal fashion. Migrational flows happen for reasons that often go unexplored by churches suffering a migrational loss. Esther was a reluctant leaver of Central Baptist. Her reasons for leaving were substantial, but the decision to leave was not made lightly. According to those I interviewed, such migrational flows between churches are often the result of a shared sense of discontent, marginalization, or feeling the need for something more from church. When a key person in a friendship group or influential leader leaves one church for another, especially if the new church is geographically close, then there is a strong possibility they will pull others from their group over with them. If church leaders take the time to investigate the reasons for church members leaving, such as Esther's pastor did, then valuable insight can be gained into church culture and areas of discontent or disconnect that need to be addressed.

Geographic Mobility and Social Networks

Structural characteristics of modern society such as university, jobs, or affordable living tend to encourage mobility, sometimes to the point of necessity. New Zealand, along with Australia, Canada, and the United States, has one of the highest rates of geographic mobility in the world.[12] In New Zealand, young adults are the most mobile age group.[13] The young adults I interviewed moved for a variety of reasons, including their parents, university, work, and the traditional New Zealand overseas experience. When they move, they look for a new church. One of the dominant reasons behind church switching is a result of these kinds of geographical shifts, both nationally and overseas. Sometimes a shift to a different part of the same city also results in a search for another church. Geographical closeness to one's faith community is important to many participants, but not essential. This becomes even more apparent when people have children, for many parents prefer to seek a support network within a close proximity of home, school, and children's ministry, rather than driving significant distances. Geographical movement thus represents a mixed blessing for religious organizations as a significant source of both church growth and decline. This kind of transfer growth can be considered the "lifeblood" of churches. However, by implication, this lifeblood transfusion usually means the decline (even hemorrhaging) of other churches. It is not uncommon, then, for church growth to be predominantly a result of people switching rather than effectively evangelizing the unchurched.

Geographic mobility has the potential to disrupt the stable web of communal attachments that have traditionally encouraged particular behaviors and practices such as churchgoing. However, as de Vaus points out, a crucial factor in geographic mobility is the type of social groups and networks that replace previous ones.[14] De Vaus argues that geographic mobility has its greatest impact on religious change when familiar points of identification are not available in the new area. Finding a church community that one connects with is something that those I interviewed actively sought out in their new location. In a pluralistic society, it is highly likely that similar social support networks will be available through destination faith communities as they had been within the original community. Within a church context, people moving will often search for a church community to belong to that is similar to the one they are leaving. In other words, people seek out the familiar, which minimizes the sense of disorientation and insecurity

12. Bell, "Comparing," 169.

13. Statistics, "QuickStats," 2. More than eight in every ten (83.9 percent) twenty-five to twenty-nine-year-olds moved at least once in the five years prior to New Zealand's 2006 Census.

14. de Vaus, "Impact," 392.

that can come with moving to a new place. There are, of course exceptions to this pattern. For example, those who experience a shift in their theological beliefs will also often look for a church that matches this shift.

However, even when familiar points of identification in a new place are available, there is no guarantee that relocated Christians will find them. Moving to attend university in Auckland from the small town where she had attended an intimate family church created a major culture shock for Christina. She did not know anyone in Auckland, and without a car, was limited to searching for a church within walking distance. I asked her how long she looked searched for a new church:

CHRISTINA: *I must say I gave up pretty quickly. Just got to the point where it just didn't seem right. And if I couldn't find a church then perhaps—illogical thinking—I wasn't supposed to find one. I would be all right for a bit, and then it just drags on. So yeah, that first year, flatting and getting used to Auckland and uni.*

In contrast to Christina's experience, the impact of geographic mobility is minimized when people can continue to identify with reference groups that are similar to those that they belonged to prior to moving. Social networks and recommendations, or knowing someone in the new destination, are invaluable avenues for finding a church. Finding a church following a geographical move to a new town or city is not always straightforward. Sometimes people are limited in their ability to search for a church, as Christina was, due to not having reliable transportation or not having social networks to draw on in their new location.

Finding Friends: Church as a Facilitator of Social Networks

Geographic mobility, Welch and Baltzell suggest, may in fact lead to heightened religious identification and participation.[15] It is argued that individuals moving geographically are motivated, in part, to attend church in their new community out of a desire to establish a social network and make friends within that community. This hypothesis, according to Welch and Baltzell, is founded on socio-psychological grounds. Individuals are motivated to

15. Welch and Baltzell, "Geographic," 76.

attend church in the hope of forming new friendships with members of their congregation.

The following interview excerpts highlight the degree to which participants viewed church as a facilitator of friendships. Church provides a specific social space for meeting and making friends within a faith community:

Talk me through that journey to New Hope.

CARLOS: *New Hope Church was the best thing. It was a really good social network. I really loved the music. I found the preaching to be really inspiring. And I was really quite into it. Yeah, so just through having people there . . . I guess my life was based a lot around what the church had to offer in the sense that it offered friendship—social circles—so it was quite grounding.*

What made you start to look for another church?

CHRISTINA: *After God having answered my prayers [laughs] I just wanted to get back on track and sort my life out. I was just desperate to have friends again. And I hadn't had somebody that I could really call a friend for quite a few years. So just being connected to people again was quite a motivation. But that whole wanting to rebuild my relationship to God was up there.*

In your recent geographical move, how important was it for you to find a church and get involved in a church?

KATIE LOU: *To me it was important. But I also realized that we may not be there for long. It was a big church so getting involved in a small group was also important.*

So why was that important?

KATIE LOU: *I don't know. We were lonely. I think again just connecting with other Christians and to be with people you can talk about big issues in life that they would understand if you are talking in a Christian way of doing things. Whereas other people outside of church won't necessarily understand. So again looking for support within the Christian community.*

Participants also considered church an important place to look for and find a partner:

CALEB: *Another reason why I want to mix in a wide network so I will get to meet Christian girls, which I won't do if I don't. So that's important as well. I think what motivates me is actually I do want to take some risk later on in life that will develop or will further the calling of God or change people's attitudes. And that will be a lot easier if I've got, or if I'm connected to someone, or joined with someone who is in that community or on that same journey.*

People intentionally seek out a Christian community to belong to in order to sustain, grow, and challenge faith, but also for very practically motivated desires such as friendship, and in Caleb's case, finding a marriage partner who shares his faith.

Even when church ceases to develop people's faith, the practice of churchgoing is considered important to the relational aspect. This was the case for Jonathan and Rebecca. They were "over church." Moving overseas provided a timely reason to stop attending their church. At the time of our interview, the couple was not motivated by the belief that attending church overseas would help them grow spiritually. In fact, they doubted that this would be the case. Rather, Jonathan and Rebecca saw church as a convenient place to meet some Christians, hopefully like-minded ones, and begin to make some new friends in a community where they wont know anyone:

REBECCA: *And for me too in terms of growing, like I'm thinking when we go overseas I definitely want to be in contact with some Christians to do life with because we don't have our friends. But it won't have to be at a church, but of course we will look there . . .*

JONATHAN: *Yeah, well, it's convenient.*

REBECCA: *And for the idea that our children might have other friends, because usually you find families at churches. I would be actually, personally, much more interested in, say, seeing missionaries who are there and inviting them to our house once a month or something for dinner and just nutting out, just chatting, and seeing what they are doing and why are they doing it and who are they and what have they learned and what can I learn, you know, and grow that way. Or any of the charity*

> *organizations, because for me, if they are doing good then they are bring-*
> *ing the kingdom and I want that to rub off on me and help them if we*
> *can. So that, to me, is more important than joining a church.*

JONATHAN: *Yeah, joining as church would be a low priority. But going to one*
for convenience's sake, to find like-minded people, that's a high priority
and that's a pragmatic thing; it's not because it's a church.

For Jonathan and Rebecca, finding and making new friends that are Christians is more important than finding a faith community, notwithstanding that church is a good starting point to meet and make such friends. In this way, the nature of church changes from one of belonging to one that provides a social space for meeting people. Church, in other words, becomes a religious networking provider for people wanting to make friends. The kind of friends that are sought out are ones that young adults can share their faith with, discuss issues pertinent to life and faith, as well as do life with—even if just for a season. Consequently, when people begin to find some of the institutional practices of church, such as the worship service, irrelevant or discontenting, church as a whole can still remain relevant through the informal social networking that occurs.

The Social Void: Mitigating Dislocation

As de Vaus suggests, people's sense of dislocation is significantly reduced if they can find social support networks similar to those of they have left behind. When they do not find such networks, a social void opens up that can make faith harder to sustain. Daniel shared his insights on the crucial difference between having a friendship circle and not having one, and the support social networks provide for faith as well as life more generally, when he spoke about living overseas in a different culture:

DANIEL: *A real struggle time of my faith came next when, as a family, we*
moved overseas. I guess I lost that close friendship with Joel, my best
friend, even though we wrote. And I think he taught me how important
Christian friends are in one's faith journey. And I really struggled . . .
Church there was very much a traditional thing. So there were pastors
there, who wouldn't believe in the resurrection and all sorts of different
things, but were still pastors of churches, which was really weird. And

I suppose different language, and the church services were in that language. I struggled with immense loneliness.

Daniel had internalized his faith, so it was strong enough to last out a year without significant peer support. Daniel found encouragement in his time of loneliness from a spiritual encounter he had with God. "I went for a walk one night on my own. It was a beautiful night with a clear, starry sky, feeling so very much alone. And somehow on that walk, I can't really explain it, God just made himself known to me again. He made it known that he was there and that he loved me and that became another strength point that I went on from." When Daniel returned to New Zealand, he became involved in a church that had a large youth group. Daniel spoke of the significance of this time:

DANIEL: *I don't actually really remember growing spiritually in that time. But I think I learned a lot in terms of friendship and just relating to people. I remember being very, very, shy in my younger years. And I think at that youth group, God used it to break my shyness. I remember praying once, "God, will you help me to break my shyness and take the focus off myself and to be confident more?" And he really answered that prayer through that youth group. From that point on, I really started to make some good friends.*

Daniel's original connection to this youth group was through a friend, again highlighting the importance of social networks in discovering possible churches to attend. Given Daniel's difficult year overseas, finding a group of peers to share his faith with became essential for Daniel upon returning to New Zealand. Daniel was still in his formative adolescent years and could easily have ended up involved with and influenced by a social circle that did not share the same faith.

The search for Christian friends was also a motivating factor for Eugene following his own move. Geographical shifts often coincide with stage of life transitions as people move away from home for the first time, often to go to university or on their overseas experience. Geographic mobility associated with university can bring with it mixed feelings of displacement and excitement along with new friends and adult independence. University exposes people to new ideas that can broaden worldviews and provide important stimulation for rethinking faith. When Eugene first ventured to his new city for university, he only knew two people, his temporary hosts. He soon got in touch with the pastor of a local Baptist church that was known for its student ministry. The church's pastor invited Eugene to stay with him until he found a permanent living arrangement. Eugene eventually found a flat and started attending the pastor's Baptist church. However, Eugene was disappointed to find that the welcoming impression the pastor's hospitality had left him with was not apparent in the church as a whole. Eugene explained that he did not enjoy the church and struggled to connect with people there:

EUGENE: *It was a slightly alternative approach to church. You know, I remember going along one time and the pastor gave a talk and said, "Right, questions, discussion." And it's funny how that challenges your way of thinking about church. Because at the time, I was thinking this is weird, and didn't really kind of enjoy it in the end. Looking back on that now, it's like, well that's not such a bad thing after all. At the time, I thought it was a bit weird coming from where I came from.*

This different experience of church challenged Eugene's previous understanding of what church was about, or at least how the worship service should be structured. The question and discussion time did generate engagement, but it felt more intellectual than what he was used to. Attempting to make sense of that time, Eugene explained that "Looking back, I don't know why I didn't settle into that church. It was small, but not too small. I was unsettled anyway and I was adjusting. I had no friends and knew no one. Some of the people were friendly, but not overly. I remember going on and off and having a hard time basically." It is extremely difficult for someone to connect to a church if they are struggling to connect to the people who make up that church. This highlights the social dynamic of church and may explain why even churches in the same denomination can have a very different culture and tell their story in their own unique way.

During a holiday back home in Auckland, Eugene told his cousin of his struggles with church. His cousin encouraged Eugene to contact a youth pastor he knew there. Eugene did get in touch, and as he explained,

EUGENE: *It's not really like me to do that but it's kind of like desperate, desperate times [laughs], you know. And I remember doing that. And he kind of connected me with a few people and I got invited to things. And that's kind of like how it started. It was the community that I started to get connected with and ended up meeting some really, really cool people who were some of the youth leaders there and they were a slightly older couple. And I ended up going to board with them over summer. And that gave me a stronger foundation. And it didn't take very long at all to find a sense of community at that church.*

In both churches, people extended Eugene the gift of hospitality. The main reason for switching, however, was that he hadn't yet found a sense of connection. There is a strong likelihood that Eugene would now connect and appreciate the style of service that he had previously struggled with. Eugene's' story is representative of people's search to find belonging and community within a church, even if that sense of belonging is found in a smaller group within the life of the church.

Seasonal Belonging in an "Age of Transience": A Case Study

In *Future Shock*, which is increasingly being lived out in the present, Alvin Toffler argues that transience is now a permanent feature of everyday life in our accelerated culture of high-speed change. Transience has a mood all of its own—a feeling of impermanence.[16] Toffler argues that this transience, this feeling of impermanence, is experienced not only in our relationships with people, but also in the four other "classes of relationships" Toffler identifies as affected by transience: an individual's relationship with things, places, institutions, and ideas.[17] It is not surprising then that embedded faith has adapted itself to this "Age of Transience" by finding expression in seasonal belonging facilitated by geographical mobility. Seasonal belonging was a noticeable trend in the religious biographies of my interview participants. The transient nature of Sophie's religious biography is a case in point. Below is a diagram of Sophie's church switching history:

16. Douglas Coupland's novel surrounding four fictional Gen X characters is aptly titled *Generation X: Tales for an Accelerated Culture*. The characters embody transience and impermanence.

17. Toffler, *Future*, 43.

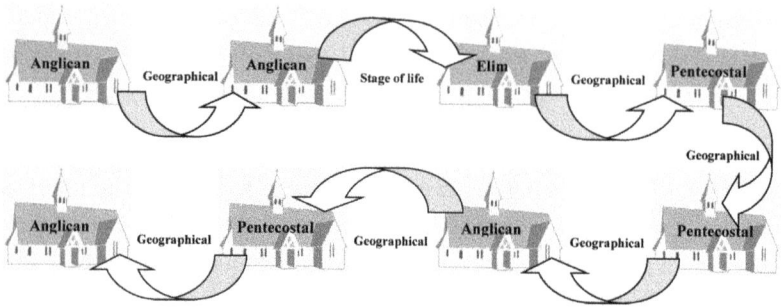

Figure 3. Sophie's Church Switching History

Seasonal belonging is a consequence of both geographical mobility and stage of life. Seasonal adherents often get involved in their chosen church for as long as they attend. This period might last three or four years during university, or it might otherwise last only a year or less. Sophie has switched churches seven times (figure 3) throughout her faith journey. All, except one of her switches (Anglican to Elim), have been for geographical reasons. She originally relocated with her family before moving cities to go to university. The other four geographic moves have all been work-related, including her overseas experience. Wherever Sophie ends up, she searches for a new church to belong to. Her social networks have been a significant source for finding a church in new locations, as she discusses elsewhere in this chapter. Sophie has yet to change churches while remaining in the same city.

Transience, Toffler suggests, can be defined in terms of the rate at which our relationships turn over; which in turn characterizes us. Life, for some, is characterized by a much slower rate of turnover than others: "low transience" verses "high transience." Sophie's religious biography and life in general is one of high transience, as evidenced by her extensive geographical mobility. This contrasts with the "low transience" of Dylan's religious biography, which has given him a very low rate of turnover. In contrast to the majority of participants, Dylan, who is in his mid-twenties, has been involved in the same church all his life. High transience affects the way we experience reality and our sense of commitment. It can even come to permeate the "feel" of a church community, as Emily perceived about Iona:

EMILY: *Whereas now, I want a church where I go along, hopefully get married, have kids, stay in the church for a long period of time. And I look at Iona, and I look at that group of people, and it still looks transitional to me. And it looks like they are all there for this time, but it might not stay that way. I don't know whether that is going to happen or not. But it is just the feeling I get. So stability, I guess—in a congregation, in a church—and something that is going to make people stick around.*

"Whereas now," contrasts what Emily now seeks in a church community with her previous affiliation to a church she knew she would be attending for a limited time, one that she describes as being "in transition." Emily's observations, while they might not necessarily represent the culture of Iona as a whole, nonetheless suggest that a church community can itself embody transience. As discussed in the previous chapter, it was Emily's liminal state that created her sense of communitas within the church among other "transients" and made church feel like home during her time in the UK. Now Emily is looking for a church "home" in a place of permanence—or at least a longer period of time than her pervious transition—and has still not found what she is looking for.

Sophie, by way of contrast, realizes that the foreseeable future of her religious biography will continue to involve seasonal belonging. Constant relocating disrupts relational webs of significance in one place and requires the establishment of new ones in another. Seasonal belonging mitigates the social dislocation that can be caused by the geographic mobility discussed above. Speaking of her most recent relocation, Sophie said,

SOPHIE: *I was looking for . . . intentionally wanting a church where I would actually meet some people my age because I knew that I would need to make some friends. And I guess, like, in doing that you'd hopefully be in a church that's sort of your style and with people your age, if people my age were still in a church, you'd hope it would be a place that they were growing in, because by some ages you just wouldn't be bothering going to church if you didn't want to be there, and to grow I guess they just all go hand in hand in a way.*

Sophie found such a church in Iona, the same church that Emily felt was made up of people in transition. Perhaps Sophie, as a seasonal belonger, contributes to such a church dynamic. However, until she moves on, Sophie has committed to Iona and involved herself in contributing to the life of the church community. In this way, seasonal belonging becomes a survival strategy for embedded faith in a transient world.

Age-based segregated churches therefore should not be surprised by in-flows and out-flows of age cohorts. Churches that recognize the patterns of seasonal in-flows and out-flows can develop responses that make the most of such flows and address factors that might be contributing to age cohort exiting. Churches that have a student ministry are examples of one effective response that can help offset the dislocation young people often feel in moving away from home for the first time or to a new city.

6

Worship and Modes of Engagement

Both liturgical theologians and churchgoers alike note the importance of
worshipping in church. While it is valuable to understand the theological reasons
for the importance of worship, it is likewise important to understand
the perspective of the worshippers themselves and to interpret
how they describe their experience.

—RICHARD WOLFF[1]

Albert Schutz, in his article "Making Music Together," suggests that an individual approaches a piece of music from a historically—or in one's own case, autobiographically—determined situation. Joshua's response to a question on worship demonstrates the way his own biography has influenced his interpretation of the meaning of worship songs:

JOSHUA: *There are some of those songs that when you're in your teenage years and you're in church and you think you're too cool for this kind of music . . . and some of them they are awful and there's no denying that . . . and some of them you thought were awful but somehow they've stuck with you. You know, Keith Green songs, or like "Amazing Grace," or whatever, and something has changed in your life that you kind of get it now. You kind of understand what they were talking about, whereas before you just thought they were awful songs.*

1. Wolff, "Phenomenological Study," 219.

The same song can come to mean something different when it resonates with new life experience or articulates feelings, desires, and reality that were not there before.

However musical meanings are not arbitrarily applied by the listener. Neither are musical meanings purely subjective. Musical meanings, Wright argues, are the product of a musical culture: "The way music is interpreted and given meaning depends upon the musical culture of the listener."[2] Musical culture, according to Schutz, is made up of a web of social relationships, past and present; where knowledge is both socially derived and socially approved.[3] This social web includes anyone who has contributed to the building up of the listener's knowledge, including teachers, parents, worship leaders, as well as what the listener may have appropriated by listening to (as well as playing) music. Worship as a musical culture and genre[4] is defined by faith communities and denominational traditions that accept the rules of the genre (or sub-genre) and whose members participate in the ritual practice of worship. A music culture, then, operates as an interpretive community in the production and creation of meaning in the practice of worship.

Worship is often regarded as being central to the life of a Christian and therefore plays a significant role in a person's faith journey. People have different experiences of church worship depending on their stage of life, lived experience, and spiritual capital. The focus of this chapter is to understand participants' experience of worship and different modes of engagement. In order to do so, it is necessary to understand that modes of engagement operate out of a religious sensibility discussed in previous chapters and which we will now examine here in relation to worship.

The Religious Sensibility

Lawrence Grossberg argues that individuals and audiences interact with texts in relation to particular sensibilities. A sensibility as defined by Grossberg "is a particular form of engagement or mode of operation . . . it defines the possible relationships between text and audiences located within its

2. Wright, "Musical," 422.

3. Schutz, "*Making Music*," 168.

4. Fabbri, "Theory," 58. Fabbri defines a musical genre as "a set of musical events (real or possible) whose course is governed by a definite set of socially accepted rules" ("Theory," 52).

spaces."[5] The sensibility of a particular cultural context, such as a church worship service, defines how specific texts and practices can be taken up and experienced. Grossberg identifies two types of sensibility in relation to popular music: the sensibility of the consumer and the sensibility of the fan. The sensibility of the consumer in relation to cultural texts operates in the domain of pleasure and entertainment. In contrast, the sensibility of the fan operates in the domain of affect, or mood:

> Affect is not the same as either emotions or desire. Affect is closely tied to what we often describe as the feeling of life. You can understand another person's life: You can share the same meanings and pleasures, but you cannot know how it feels. But feeling, as it functions here, is not a subjective experience. It is a socially constructed domain of cultural effects. Some things feel different from others, some matter more, or in different ways, than others. The same experience will change drastically as our mood or feelings changes. The same object, with the same meaning, giving the same pleasure, is very different as our affective relationship to it changes. Or perhaps it is more accurate to say that different affective relations inflect meanings and pleasures in very different ways. Affect is what gives "color," "tone" or "texture" to our experiences.[6]

Affect matters to fans because it is what gives their investment in popular cultural texts, such as music, weight and significance beyond the consumerist sensibility, whose main emphasis is the production of pleasure. The religious sensibility of worshippers is closer to that of the fan than the consumer. In this I agree with Ward, who argues that Grossberg's "notion of investment can be regarded as being similar to the commitment of worshipper to participation in worship."[7]

Church: The Social Context for Worship

The weekly church service remains the central social activity for congregational life. Worship through singing makes up a significant portion of the church services attended by the participants in this study. Worship in church is "public music,"[8] or what Helmut Rosing has called "social-

5. Grossberg, "Fan," 54.

6. Ibid., 56–57.

7. Ward, "Affective Alliance," 27. See also Ward, *Selling*, particularly chapter 11, "Participation."

8. Frith, *Performing*, 76.

interaction music,"[9] and as such, requires a material community. Church provides a particularly musical auditory environment that shapes the listening experience in a way that is qualitatively different to listening to a worship CD in the car or at home, or to a self-created worship playlist on an iPod.[10] In other words, worship in a gathered faith community provides a different experience than worshipping independently.

To grasp the meaning of a worship song is to understand a musical culture that provides what Karbusicky refers to as an "intentionality of perception,"[11] and Frith calls "a scheme of interpretation."[12] A scheme of interpretation provides the knowledge about how to hear music and specific music genres. A music culture provides not just knowledge of musical forms, but "also rules of behavior in musical settings."[13] Jody, for example, spoke of the importance of stillness in worship "so that God can speak to you."

Do you think that is a weakness [not having quite time to reflect] in churches because of the way that people aren't really given that time?

JODY: *Oh absolutely, that is a huge weakness. Like, I always used to try and provide that time in worship leading. I would always try to lure people in gently. But they still only get twenty minutes to get there. So, you know, there is only so far you can go in twenty minutes. And also if you are singing songs the whole time, that doesn't always give people the opportunity, sometimes you should just shut up and let there be silence; which I did occasionally.*

Preparing oneself to "enter into a time of worship" allows for an orientation towards the focus of worship, namely God. This practice of stillness also implies that worship is not something that should be rushed into, but rather is a musical genre that requires concentrated and focused engagement.

Different churches have different rules of behavior appropriate to worship that must be learned. This is illustrated by Cameron's contrasting

9. Rosing, "Listening," 119.

10. The influence of buildings and space on worship and congregational culture is explored by Sally Gallagher, "Building."

11. Karbusicky, "Interaction," 650.

12. Frith, *Performing*, 249.

13. Ibid., 249.

experiences of "free" worship and "structured" worship. Cameron explained that free worship:

CAMERON: *Is being able to go where you feel God is leading. If you got excited you could shout. And people shouted, absolutely. So there was a freedom of expression like that towards saying how great God is or yelling "Yeah!" or pretty much expressing yourself just the way you would do in I guess a sports kind of crowd or something like that, at a rock music concert or whatever.*

Worshippers are free to respond accordingly. Spontaneous emotions need not be kept under check in this particular worship environment. Cameron found this expression of worship liberating. Cameron has since switched to a larger Pentecostal church, where he struggles with a more structured style of worship. He explains,

CAMERON: *So from that, there is more structure to the worship. It is more, you know, two verses, a chorus back to the first, whatever, that kind of thing, that kind of approach. And the worship there is, you know, we will clap now and everybody claps, and everybody raise their hands now, and everybody stand, and everybody sit. So there is a lot more conformity to it, which I don't subscribe to at all. I prefer the free worship. But free worship is like, it is freedom of expression, it is also our ability to express ourselves . . . If worship is about meeting God and encountering God, we need to do it according to who we are as a person, not as someone tells us to.*

Cameron's criticism and dislike of structured worship was based on the feeling of having to conform, which for him reduced the enjoyment of the worship experience compared to a more personalized expression of worship. But even free worship is managed to an extent in terms of time, pre-selected songs, or particular learned expressions of worship such as shouting "Praise God!" and "Thank you Jesus!"[14] One only needs to observe young children raising their hands while singing to mimic their parents to appreciate the socialization that occurs within a church environment. In this way, learning the worship culture of a faith community is based upon socially derived and socially approved knowledge.

14. Frith argues "that 'meaning' can only be defined institutionally: the term describes not simply discursive conventions—agreements to agree—but regulated forms of social behaviour" (*Performance*, 249.)

The social structure of a local church also imposes itself upon musical meaning: the arrangement of the seating, the style of the building, the direction of the worship leader and worship band are all constitutive elements in both the environment and the guiding of the participants in regulating the practice of worship.[15] As Lucy Green argues, "Both experience of the music and the music's meanings themselves change complexly in relation to the style-competence of the subject, and to the social situations in which they occur . . . music can never be played or heard outside a situation, and every situation will affect the music's meaning."[16]

Cameron's contrast between free and structured worship highlights the way in which meaning is also determined not simply by *what* is sung but also by the *way* it is sung. In this way, Karbusicky's intentionality of perception "gives rise to different qualitative experiences having a different meaning."[17] Frith argues that different people use different music to experience different sorts of community.[18]

Worship as Collective Effervescence

It is the gathered faith community, the material community, which enables the experience of what Durkheim calls "collective effervescence." Durkheim's observation in *The Elementary Forms of Religious Life* that the very act of gathering is an "exceptionally powerful stimulant," still holds true today.[19] The most important characteristic of collective effervescence, according to Durkheim, is the fact that is it communal. Collective effervescence does not refer to a vague quality associated with any social gathering, as Tim Olaveson makes clear, but rather "to a specific and real social entity involving intention and volition"[20] as well as symbolic focus. Nelson's enthusiasm for worship captures the intention, volition, and symbolic focus required for collective effervescence:

15. See Stockfelt, "Adequate Modes," 90.

16. Green, *Music*, 143.

17. Karbusicky, "Interaction," 650.

18. Frith, *Music*, 121.

19. Durkheim, *Elementary*, 162.

20. Olaveson, "Collective," 100–101.

NELSON: *I think the most important thing for me about church is worship. That is what I would value and look for. If there was just great preaching, I would miss worship. I would feel an incredible lack for worship.*

What makes worship good for you?

NELSON: *There is something about a group of people worshipping that I really enjoy. That sense of community and a community process around worship. I like getting into the zone and being completely focused on the moment and completely focused on God and being thankful and appreciating that relationship . . . That ability that we have to connect with the creator of the universe, the maker of heaven and earth, this incredibly powerful God, who can also be our Father and our friend and our encourager. It is an amazing place to get into and space to be in . . . I think the space can sometimes be more easily facilitated by some people than other people.*

This "something" about a group of people worshipping that Nelson articulates as a "sense of community" can also be described as an experience of collective effervescence. I am suggesting, then, that "the zone" that Nelson is speaking of "getting into" through worship is an experience of collective effervescence, where he is "completely focused on the moment and completely focused on God." Collective effervescence is a temporary condition and therefore needs to be recharged, so to speak.

Olaveson suggests that there are two different types of "effervescent assembly" in Durkheim's thought:

> *Creative effervescence*, characterized by intense emotion, and in which the outcome is uncertain and may produce new ideas; and *re-creative effervescence*, in which there is also intense emotion and excitement, and a bond of community and unity among participants, such as that they feel morally strengthened.[21]

The weekly gathering for worship is an example of such "re-creative effervescence" by which moral and spiritual life are re-created and reaffirmed. In his popular book, *Celebration of Discipline*, Richard Foster writes that "If worship does not change us, it has not been worship . . . If worship does not propel us into greater obedience, it has not been worship. Just as worship begins in holy expectancy it ends in holy obedience."[22] Worship

21. Ibid., 101.
22. Foster, *Celebration*, 148.

as a powerful source for re-creative effervescence in a gathered faith community finds theological support in the writings of Niebuhr and Hauerwas, among others.[23] For both Niebuhr and Hauerwas, the act of worship encourages worshippers to re-center their lives around core values. Hauerwas, however, also extends his argument to a critique and questioning of what is *reaffirmed* in Christian worship, as it shapes the life of faith communities.[24]

John Blacking suggests that "Music is essentially about aesthetic experiences and the creative expression of individual human beings in community, about the sharing of feelings and ideas."[25] The following comments from interview participants demonstrate that Nelson is not alone his appreciation for the communal dimension, or the collective effervescence, experienced during worship:

ANDREW: *I think it is an opportunity for people to do something together, to feel like they are in community. There is definitely something that happens when a group of people, whether some are just going through the motions or not, but when the others are united in thanksgiving through song, it goes beyond the words sometimes and something deeper happens.*

TOBY: *Like, I struggle to sing, because I can't sing and so that sort of connection with worshipping God in that way doesn't connect with me at deeper levels, but at the same time, when you're a part of a people that are praising and worshipping God, there's a sense that something's happening in that time, that we are all part of God's family as we gather to worship and praise him and even though I don't . . . I find that singing isn't an expression of my style of worship, that there is still a sense of connection with his people as we do that together.*

FIONA: *I get a great sense of something indescribable, of being with a whole lot of Christians all worshiping God together and giving praise. I just love that . . . I think the great thing about singing is that it is something that everyone can do all at once. You don't have to be in tune.*

Durkheim's concept of collective effervescence and Turner's concept of communitas both give a name to participants' experience of worship going

23. See Niebuhr, *Radical*, and Hauerwas, *Better Hope*.

24. Hauerwas' concern, then, is the faithful character of worship "insofar as such worship shapes the truthful witness of the church to the world" (*Better Hope*, 159).

25. Blacking, cited in Frith, *Performance*, 251.

"beyond the words" and into something deeper, "something indescribable", and "something happening" as a result of people coming together.[26] Durkheim describes the effects of gathering as resulting in "a sort of electricity," whose initial impulse is "amplified as it reverberates like an avalanche gathering force as it goes."[27] Collective effervescence describes the bond of community and unity experienced through worship that contributes to a feeling of being morally and spiritually strengthened and is therefore character-forming. Likewise, the experience of communitas is also usually a deeply intense feeling experienced amongst a community of equal individuals. Collective effervescence is not guaranteed simply by people gathering with intention, volition, and symbolic focus. The way worship is led, and the sacred space created for worship, all contribute to people's worship experience and facilitate or hinder collective effervescence. It is to this performance aspect of worship that we now turn.

Worship as Performance

Worship in church contexts is not unlike a staged performance. There is a dramaturgical aspect to church worship, which, drawing on Goffman, requires loyalty and discipline, particularly by the worship team, "if the show they put on is to be sustained."[28] "In addition," Goffman goes onto say, "it will be useful if the members of the team exercise foresight and design in determining in advance how best to stage a show."[29] Staging a show in terms of worship is about creating a sacred space, or an environment that facilitates the congregation's worship of God and collective effervescence. Preparation is part of the ritual and practice of worship. People who are part of a worship team will practice regularly as a regular part of the church service. Goffman's dramaturgical exploration of the performance of social actors is useful for understanding church worship. Those I interviewed who are, or have been, worship leaders involved in a church worship team were certainly conscious of the performance aspect of managing or "staging a show."

26. See Olaveson, "Collective," for a comparison between Durkheim and Turner's concepts.

27. Durkheim, *Elementary*, 162–63.

28. Goffman, *Presentation*, 218.

29. Ibid.

Staging the Show: Creating the Worship Environment

A number of the young adults that I interviewed are, or have been, worship leaders or have served as part of a worship team in church. Jody was fourteen when she started playing the piano in church, albeit badly by her own admission. Her worship team was supportive, and after a few years, Jody became a very good musician. Jody was leading worship by the time she was eighteen. She then became a paid staff member coordinating the music for Saint Dominic's Presbyterian. Being involved in the music ministry brought her a great deal of satisfaction:

JODY: *I felt like worship leading was my gift. And it was the way that God wished me to serve the church. And I was worship leading so I was serving the church in this way. And I was to encourage people and help them to connect with God. And I always felt very connected with God while I was worship leading. And in those early years, I would always prepare so well. And I would pray heaps in the week leading up to it. I would pray carefully about the songs and be absolutely focused on doing the best job I could and being so connected with God that God was able to speak through me when I was worship leading. And I just saw it happen. It just came together so many times. And people came up to me and said, "Wow that really spoke to me and it was so encouraging." And you know, I thought, great. And that was awesome.*

Preparation was an important aspect of leading worship for Jody, especially finding out what the sermon was about and the passage of Scripture that would be read. Following this, Jody explains that she would

JODY: *Ask God to speak to me about it. And then I would usually get some ideas to do with the passage. Or I would just ask God for ideas and I would try and listen. And then I get ideas, I might just get one song. And then I would try and focus or bracket a certain idea, a certain song—try and build up songs that fit and that also the ideas would flow from one song to the other. So I always chose songs according to the lyrics and not according to the music.*

It was not until Jody gained employment in her church as the worship coordinator that she experienced an undesired shift in her attitude and experience of worship. Part of the problem was a growing sense of disconnection with God. Jody says that she felt more and more like a hypocrite every time she had to get up to lead worship. She hated the idea of being a "professional Christian" and having to be up front to convince everybody. Jody elaborated, "They wanted worship to be authentic and they also wanted me to be genuinely very spiritual. And I was getting less and less spiritual. I felt like I couldn't reveal that because then they would be very unhappy with having me on staff."

Jody had always enjoyed leading worship as a volunteer. But she felt being paid changed her expectations and experience of leading worship. The job involved administration, something that Jody was not good at. She felt unsupported by the rest of the staff in what she did, which added to her questioning whether what she was doing was worthwhile. As Jody explained to the senior pastor, she felt her spiritual life was terrible and felt like a hypocrite when she got up to lead worship:

JODY: *And I said that I wasn't really worshipping during the week and then I get up on Sunday and worship and it makes me feel like a hypocrite. And he just kind of passed it off. He said as long as you are actually genuinely engaging with God on Sunday, then that's fine. And so I thought, OK. And I was, I was really genuinely trying to engage with God. I was really against the idea of faking it. And I scared myself because I knew how to fake it so well. I knew everything. I knew what to say, the look on my face, I knew how to play, you know, I knew what songs to repeat. I knew how to do it.*

Jody slipped in and out of "faking it" depending on her spiritual state. For the most part she was sincere in her leading. But when she was not feeling connected to God, she knew how to give the appearance of connection.

Jody's experience of leading worship while feeling disconnected from God is not uncommon. Others I interviewed spoke of the same tension, the same spiritual dissonance, in leading worship. In this state of spiritual dissonance, experienced worship leaders have become skilled in what Goffman calls the "arts of impression management."[30] Feeling disconnected from God as a worship leader can be seen as a performance disruption that impression management seeks to avoid. Leading others in worship, despite personally feeling disconnected from God, is often camouflaged by being what Goffman describes as a "disciplined performer."

---

30. Goffman, *Presentation*, 208.

The "Disciplined Performer"

For Emily, singing as an expression of worship is an important factor in choosing a church. She loves to sing and has been involved in worship teams throughout her church life. Singing is one of the first areas she looks to get involved in within a church. Emily discusses one of her more difficult experiences of involvement in the worship team at a church she attended while working overseas:

Did you have any sense of connection to God through the worship there?

EMILY: *No, the worship was hard work. There were just a couple of instruments and it wasn't particularly well put together. And while I loved singing and I wanted to be involved in it, it wasn't easy every week. Sometimes it flowed and sometimes it was just hard work. And so I was sort of a bit distracted. And actually, when I started singing up the front, I couldn't really focus on God anyway. Sort of conscious of the job that I had to do leading worship. I think that whole time for me, it stands out as trying to get connected, that whole sort of two years.*

Emily is a "disciplined performer" insofar as she suppresses her spontaneous feelings in order to give the appearance of sticking to the affective line, the expressive status quo, established by her team's performance. For Emily, singing as part of this particular music team was not worship, but rather a job to fulfil. It was during this time that Emily entered into what she sees as her "desert experience of faith." However, this situation regarding her spiritual life did not manifest in her role as a worship singer and leader. As Goffman states, "It is crucial for the maintenance of the team's performance that each member of the team possess dramaturgical discipline and exercise it in presenting [their] own part."[31]

This sense of performance contrasted strongly with Emily's experience of worship at Soho Evangelical in the UK. The leader of the music team was one of Emily's flatmates, and so the team would meet in their home to practice. Emily was still going through a desert period of faith when she began attending Soho. She would often sit in with the team and sing with them. As she felt herself entering into a better place with God, her

31. Goffman, *Performance*, 216.

confidence returned, and she became a part of the music team and loved it. However, it was not an automatic entry into the team. As Emily explained,

EMILY: *In London, you sort of had to audition in a sense to get in. But it was more than that, it was also, they watched your life as well. And see for me, I'd been . . . a number had known me for quite a few months and I just wasn't in the right place to actually to go up on stage and sing and they knew that, and they knew where I was at. And then there just came a point where the leader said to me—she said, "I think you're ready." And I was like, "Yeah, I think I am." And it was just the right time. And that was really neat. It felt hard in the beginning, 'cause I thought, they know I can sing, and they are always telling me I can sing, yet they are holding me back. But I soon realized that it was right, because I wasn't in a good place with God and it would have been just me up there singing as opposed to me worshipping. And so I really valued that leadership that was just placing restrictions on me and then leading me into one of my [spiritual] giftings. So that was quite cool.*

Watching people's lives to gauge whether someone is ready to be involved in worship ministry, or perhaps needs to be relieved from worship duties, creates in-group solidarity. Such accountability to a group of people or specific church leaders can be viewed as the spiritual aspect of dramaturgical discipline that Goffman speaks of, which is crucial for the maintenance of the team's performance.[32] One technique of impression management, according to Goffman, is "for the team to choose members who are loyal and disciplined, and a second one is for the team to acquire a clear idea as to how much loyalty and discipline it can rely on from the membership as a whole."[33] However, Emily felt that some of the churches she has been involved with could have had higher standards for choosing team members:

EMILY: *As a musician or a singer, I struggled with churches in the past because their attitude was, if people want to serve the Lord, then anyone should be able to serve the Lord, and so people would be in the music team who had no talents or abilities whatsoever. And they were willing, but technically I felt they shouldn't have been there, because it was hard for the*

32. Ibid. 216–18.
33. Ibid., 218.

congregation. It sounded awful, it was distracting, they weren't leading people into worship.

The way worship is led by the worship leader and musicians contributes enormously to the congregation's mode of engagement. Music played poorly or people leading out of tune can become a distraction and obstacle for people wanting to enter into a place of worship.

The Show Must Go On

Esther began to develop a "heart for worship" from her early involvement in the worship team at church when she was thirteen to fourteen years old. Esther's involvement deepened her sense of belonging as she got to know people across a range of ages. She used to love playing church music at home for fun and thinking about and relating to God through music. Esther would screen out many songs in selecting titles to sing at Spurgeon Baptist by assessing whether they were theologically sound. The "Jesus is my girlfriend" type songs did not make the cut. But during her time of leading worship at Spurgeon Baptist, Esther was surprised at how easily she could fake it:

ESTHER: *And I found that my own worship was not always the best. Which partly disillusioned me as well, just because I could fake it, and people would still comment to me about how they loved to watch me worship, you know. I just found that interesting. It was not supposed to be between me and others. It was supposed to be between them and God. They're just enjoying that you're worshipping, but you are not, you know.*

So what kind of insight did that give you in relation to worship, being able to manipulate people through music? Did that change what you thought about worship?

ESTHER: *Yeah, you can [manipulate people through worship]. Yeah, I think it has. Like, I think there are different ways of worshipping through music anyway. And I think people are responsible for how they respond to that themselves as well. But there needs to be real humility and worship in people, like people who are leading that kind of thing need to be honest about their sincerity I think. Otherwise, I think that is partly why other people don't worship. Like partly you are . . . you do seem to have an influence on that.*

It is important to consider how the listening situation is framed by context, and how that situation impacts whether people engage or do not engage with worship. Music theory argues that the listening situation itself creates meaning. The musical culture and rules of a genre influence modes of listening and engagement. Thus, while the resulting feeling might be the same, the meaning behind that feeling can be fundamentally different.

Authentic Engagement

However the worship "show" is managed, it is expected to be authentic. Timothy's story pulls together some of what we have discussed so far in relation to worship by illustrating this desire for authentic spiritual engagement. Timothy, unlike his wife Ruth, did not come from a Christian background. He was fifteen when he went to church for the first time, and that was an unconscious decision. Timothy retold the story of how he ended up at a church with some amusement. Timothy was being bullied at school and at home, and did not have anyone to talk to about it, which was causing him to feel lonely and isolated. When he was fifteen, Timothy made a friend who accepted him rather than leaving him on the social fringe of school, often picked on and rarely befriended. They were both musicians; Timothy played the clarinet. Timothy's friend, Samuel, invited Timothy to play in his band, which played on Sundays. Timothy was excited about being invited to play, although he thought the performance date was a little odd. When Sunday night arrived, Samuel picked Timothy up, and to his surprise, pulled up at Flaxbush Baptist Church. Not only had Timothy never been to a church before, but he also had no concept of God. God, and religion in general, was not a topic of conversation within his home, nor in his larger social environment at school and with his peers. As Timothy explained,

TIMOTHY: *Anyway, so here I am, and I had been playing in Dixieland bands and jazz and stuff in pubs. So I went to this church service and just played like I normally do, which was Dixie. I played Dixie clarinet, it's all over the top and really out there and the pastor really loved it because they had this, like, singing hymns and stuff, and you had this clarinet going bam blee blan do wa all over the top of it. And they really loved it, and I loved the fact that they loved it. And so for me, it was a place of acceptance, you know, and being appreciated for the gifts I had, where I didn't have that at home. So they gave me a Bible and I smuggled it into the house and it was a crazy time. And I became a Christian at a friend's house about six months later.*

Timothy had come a long way since that first experience of playing in a church worship band. At thirty-nine, Timothy had become a talented and experienced worship leader. Timothy knew the rules of the worship genre; he had been immersed in the musical culture of church for over twenty years. When I interviewed Timothy and Ruth, they had just started attending New Hope Pentecostal. Both were reluctant leavers from a church that they were previously deeply involved in. Timothy was one of the regular worship leaders. They were both feeling burnt out by the time they left Docklands Community Church and wanted a period of no official involvement in the next church they went to. This sobering experience made it difficult to enter into worship in a church environment. It had only been more recently that Timothy had begun to feel that connection in worship again:

TIMOTHY: *As I soak, I'm rediscovering again. Just rediscovering the connection I think. It's funny 'cause when you're serving in a church environment, I think it's very easy to just get in the habit of just doing it, it's a process, man. Even with worship, I can stand up there and I know what buttons to push and I think that's just shit at the end of the day, seriously that's just the worst when you start doing that.*

Timothy knows how to be a disciplined performer; but playing by these rules is not what brings authenticity. Authenticity and realness are two concepts that the participants in this study consistently sought after, dual themes they constantly referred to and returned to. Authenticity, as Timothy explained, is not only meaning what he is singing about but also feeling it. Authenticity is often contrasted with "faking it," leading worship but not worshipping personally, either due to distraction or sometimes from a sense of feeling disconnected from God.

Often it is possible to maintain a front or perception that does not reflect the worship leader's spiritual reality through the art of impression management.[34] Impression management is made easier by the fact that the audience only sees the performance, with no knowledge of the rest of the performer's life or insight into how they might be feeling as they lead

---

34. Goffman, *Presentation*, 221.

worship. Authenticity, to continue to reference Goffman, is about the front room and the back room lining up. The authentic performance is not a mask. Impression management, then, is not about giving off a false impression, but rather a performance that genuinely reflects and represents the individual character. In dramaturgical terms, one plays oneself.[35] In this sense, authenticity is not only a feeling, but also has to do with meaning.

Lyrics: Voice, the Subjective "I" and "We"

Popular music theorist Simon Frith draws our attention to the social role of lyrics when he writes, "If music gives lyrics their linguistic vitality, lyrics give songs their social *use*."[36] People's engagement with worship demonstrates a struggle over meaning: both to make sense of religious metaphors, and most importantly, to make worship connect meaningfully with their own lived experience. The same song can mean different things to different people, depending on their scheme of interpretation and their cultural and spiritual capital, which includes their own biography. Frith argues that a song is always a performance and that the words of a song are heard in someone's accent.[37] Songs are a form of speech, and speech acts, according to Frith, bear meaning both semantically and through structures of sound to signify emotions and character. We do not read lyrics randomly or subjectively, independent of the song's context. As Frith points out, "The lyricist sets up the situation—through her use of language, her construction of character—in a way that, in part, determines the response we make, the nature of our engagement."[38]

When it comes to church worship, congregations become more than an audience who simply listens; they become worshippers who sing. Worship songs position the congregation as the singers. The *voice* of a worship song is no longer that of the lyricist, the author of the song, but that of the congregation. The "I" and "we" of worship songs is claiming the "I" and "we" of the worshipper(s). The investment of representation being asked of the worshipper as the singer is distinctive to other songs where our engagement can take place as a listener to a conversation or story and separation of ourselves from the protagonist. The "I" in worship songs is

35. Although even this can be role that we play, as Goffman notes.

36. Frith, *Music*, 123.

37. Ibid., 120.

38. Frith, *Performing*, 184.

asking the singer, the worshipper, to become the "I" doing the addressing, often expressing feelings or exclamations of praise or action towards God. By making worship matter, worshippers, like the fan, "authorize" songs and liturgy to speak for them. The voice in worship songs thus moves beyond that of spokesperson or a surrogate voice evident in popular music. The worshipper not only gives authority to the voice, but also claims the voice as his or her own.

Worship songs provide a conventional language for use in worship, much like Horton's suggestion that popular love songs have provided "a conventional language for use in dating,"[39] or as Frith puts it, "they give people the romantic terms in which to articulate and so experience their emotions."[40] Frith further contends that audiences often feel words and music that are then developed by the imagination. Paul, an experienced worship leader, described music as being "like a gift, it is a language; it is a way of talking. For me, playing is just like a different way of talking to God."

While Daniel made it clear that worship for him involved his whole way of life, singing in church is an important way in which he expressed worship to God. In fact, for Daniel, the practice of gathering on a Sunday is an expression of worship. For Daniel, Sunday worship is a way of saying "I am setting this time aside for you God." As Daniel explained, "I love singing. It helps me communicate, through other people's words, the way I do actually feel about God. I love it when worship songs are written by people in my church to communicate heartfelt things."

Simply singing the words of a song, or "saying stuff," and singing a song as an expression of what you want to say involves an entirely different mode of engagement:

> EUGENE: *A lot of it does come down to the actual lyrics itself. Say you might have a song that is quite wordy and doesn't say much. Then you might have a song that focuses on the holiness of God and that is quite a different experience, or a focused experience, if you like. Like listening to songs, say in the car and stuff, the songs that mean the most are the ones where you connect with the lyrics and actually understand the lyrics. It's like, that's what I actually mean here, I'm not just saying stuff.*

This kind of critical engagement often took place for participants in choosing whether to authorize the "I" in a worship song to speak for

39. Horton, "Dialogue," 569.
40. Frith, *Music*, 123.

them. The song has to authentically express what they mean or feel for it to be sung with authority. Authenticity is required because worship is an expression of thanks or praise to God. It is like singing a love song when one is not in love, or to a beloved when one's heart is not in it. The words fall empty. What is missing is "subjective meaning," or the meaning that is added by "voice" of the song itself: a voice that has been given authority to speak on behalf of the singer or listener. Because of this subjective voice in worship, people want to mean what they are singing or saying. People are being asked to take a song that somebody else has written and offer it up to God as their own. This is where the breakdown of meaning and connection began for a number of interview participants. They can no longer become the "I" with any sense of authenticity because as singers and as worshippers, they feel a dislocation between the reality of their lived experience and the spiritual reality the song expresses. This spiritual dissonance sometimes leads to a mode of disengagement.

Mode of Disengagement: Struggle Over Meaning

Caleb described himself as being "sold out for Jesus" from about sixteen years old through his first few years at university. He was passionate about his faith and it was obvious to people that he loved Jesus without having to mention it. Worship was something that he enjoyed and would really get into. He had some strong spiritual experiences of God during times of worship. Looking back on those experiences, Caleb explained that "I could probably write off a few of those, but some of them I can't." These days, however, Caleb finds himself switching off during worship. I asked him if he felt he had lost something from his younger days of connecting to God through worship. Caleb replied,

CALEB: *I think so. I think I'm not so energetic and passionate about it. And in some ways I kind of feel like I'm OK with that. I'm not quite sure if I'm actually, if . . . I haven't quite decided if not having that energy or passion is because I'm less into Jesus and God or whether or not I just . . . I don't really buy that expression of faith. I'm not quite sure which it is. Maybe it is a bit of both. Because I don't think my heart is as warm as it was back then. And I don't know if that's youth or adulthood or what.*

Caleb talked about his mind wandering during worship. Although he still sang the songs, his mind was not engaged but instead could be focused on something completely different, much like having the radio on in the background. Caleb does try at times to enter into the worship and the songs. However, part of the problem for Caleb is the metaphoric dimension of worship songs: "I always kind of find myself thinking, well, what am I supposed to think about? If I sing 'greater God,' am I supposed to kind of think about awesome landscapes or something? I don't know. I mean see, a lot of people probably wouldn't even think about it, they would sing the words, and yeah, I'm worshipping God, and I guess I do. But I don't know."

Caleb has been immersed in the Christian worship culture since his youth. He has played in church worship bands and understands the musical culture. Yet now Caleb seems to have lost the scheme of interpretation that makes sense of the metaphors in many contemporary Christian worship songs. His critical engagement seeks to construct tangible, realistic image of God from the metaphors that he is being asked to sing.

Likewise, Jody was critical of certain lyrics that no longer made sense to her:

JODY: *And there are the whole other fluffy things that make no sense at all in songs. Like, let me think. I could sum this up for you by a very popular song, "Over the mountains and the seas your river flows with love for me." And what is that? "Your river flows with love for me; and I will open up my heart and let the Healer set me free." That line is OK. But the mountains and the river running thing . . . What is that? I used to sing that with absolute integrity. And as a teenager I could sing any of those "I give you my heart forever" sort of songs with absolute integrity. But not now.*

"What is that?" Remains a valid question and one that is asked by a number of those I interviewed. For some participants like Jody, the metaphors have become empty, hollowed out images that no longer signify beyond themselves. So a river running with love, for example, might signify or evoke an image of a river, but the linguistic signification of love is absent. The metaphoric river, it would seem, does not flow with love, but only water. Worship songs are often laden with such metaphors and religious terms that aim to articulate the experience of worship. When worshippers fail to connect the religious terms or metaphors to their own understanding of reality and lived experience, or interpret them to be misleading theology, or as a religious sentiment or claim that they themselves cannot share, then worshippers deny the song authority to speak for them.

Critical Mode of Engagement

Marva Dawn argues that churches are dumbing down church through the music they sing. She asks, "Does our choice of worship music increase or reduce our capacity to listen or to think theologically? Does superficial music dumb down the faith? Does our music nurture sensitivity to God?"[41] Raymond Gawronski's summarizes the "shallowness" of worship songs Dawn addresses, writing,

> Written, no doubt, within the past twenty years, it is a piece of that resigned sentimentality that is characteristic of "easy listening music." Although pleasant enough, it is spiritual Wonder Bread: It utterly lacks roots, depth, sustenance. It is all right as a starter, to open the heart to prayer. But unless fed by some solid food . . . serious seekers will turn elsewhere.[42]

The concerns Dawn and Gawronski express speak to the educational role of worship, or the belief that worship and liturgy expresses theology. The pedagogical function of worship songs is what Brian Smith has referred to as "theology off the wall."[43] Percy makes a helpful distinction between the *didactic* and *emotive* function of worship.[44] For example, the function of worship within charismatic Christianity, which has had a widespread influence on the worship culture and song selection in the majority of New Zealand churches, is emotive. As Percy says, "it is a vehicle to move people closer to God, to 'release' them, to stir the heart. Consequently, most songs in modern revivalism are devoid of serious doctrinal content: they express feelings about or to God."[45] Percy contrasts this emotive function of worship against the didactic function of classic revival worship under Wesley, Moody, or Edwards in which theology was both taught in hymns and sung by converts.

While I would not go as far as Dawn does in saying "Shallow music forms shallow people,"[46] the lyrics of many contemporary worship songs do convey a lightness that offers very little in the way of theology, but can be highly emotive. As Percy has suggested in relation to charismatic wor-

41. Dawn, *Reaching*, 176.

42. Gawronski, "Orthodox," 14.

43. Smith, "Theology."

44. Percy, "Place," 104.

45. Ibid.

46. Dawn, *Reaching*, 175.

ship, it "is essentially a matter of the heart, and works best when it travels lightly."[47] Dawn fails to consider how worshippers themselves engage with worship and "shallow" worship songs. This critical mode of engagement, which includes the strategy of "opting out" of singing particular songs or lines of a song, suggests that meaning-making and interpretation of worship songs is more complex than Dawn allows for.

In the critical mode of engagement, the emotive function of worship needs to be complimented with its didactic function. What a songs says becomes equally as important, sometimes more so, than the emotional experience it might elicit. This critical mode of engagement sometimes starts with worship leaders themselves as they "screen" songs to sing during worship:

JONATHAN: *Being involved in worship has made me quite sensitized to the quality and what impact it has in terms of its content and in terms of its relevance to people. And I've always been a stickler for rejecting worship songs where I disagree with the words. And that included some very popular songs at various times.*

Were there quite a few of those?

JONATHAN: *Oh yeah.*

So what would be some of the things that would cause you to reject a song?

JONATHAN: *There's a lot of songs, and there's a whole discourse on this, the very famous quote about "Jesus is my girlfriend" songs of the 1990s, where you just basically . . .*

REBECCA: *I love Jesus, he loves me, we're all a happy family* [laughs].

JONATHAN: *Yeah, we're sort of running through the meadow with Jesus and its happy tulips and they've got, you know, the sound track on, and wow, it's just great. And the other thing is songs that don't say anything, songs that have very little content.*

47. Percy, "Place," 102.

The content of the songs is important for those engaging critically with the lyrics. Roger finds a number of the songs he sings in church "mind-numbing boring," and "removed from reality." I asked him to explain in what ways they are removed from reality. He replied,

ROGER: *They don't talk about things that are. They just, it's just sort of fluffy words banded together with a good rhythm. Rather than something that engages us and helps us praise God, or reflect on God, or move us towards God's mission, or help us engage with other people. Which I think are the key things, but they just don't do that.*

An increasingly common experience for young adults, particularly those, like Roger, for whom the lyrics hold significant weight in evaluating a song, is to switch off, or "opt out" of singing if the lyrics are not true to life. The gathering together to intentionally worship God is an important aspect of church for Roger. Roger currently experiences connection and disconnection through the same service or set of songs. Certain songs will annoy him, which leads to frustration by distracting him from focusing on worshipping God.

Critical engagement involves reflecting on what one is being asked to sing and whether it is a valid and authentic expression of one's personal faith journey:

SANTOS: *I used to get a strong sense when I was singing worship songs of some words that might sound good, or on paper might look very good and fit with the song, but I found very, very difficult to sing because of connotations, or because I couldn't particularly agree with them.*

ANTONIA: *Yeah, you can't relate to them.*

SANTOS: *Exactly. They are quite abstract.*

So singing for you both no longer connects you with God? Do you feel the words are disconnected from your reality and experience?

SANTOS: *I think so.*

ANTONIA: *There are some good songs, but yeah, for the most part . . .*

SANTOS: *Logos Baptist still sings songs and maybe I'll sign along with them. I just find that singing along, there's some very serious sentiments, there's some very intense sentiments that are put so tritely to melodic Christian music that I find incredibly difficult to lah lah lah along to. I mean, what you are committing to is actually—it seems so trite and it seems so manufactured without having a genuine, this is what I really want to say or how I really feel.*

What comes through clearly in Santos and Antonia's conversation is a strong sense of disconnection from worship songs due to the lyrics. This disconnection is, at one level, encouraging. It is based on young adults' thoughtfulness and reflectiveness in their engagement with worship, as well as their desire for integrity and authenticity in what they are signing. One of the strategies used in the critical mode of engagement with worship is selective engagement.

Selective Engagement

As the name suggests, "selective engagement" involves selection of which parts of worship to engage in. Because selective engagement is based on the religious sensibility of owned faith, it is not an act of religious consumption, of simply choosing what one likes and leaving the rest. Rather, selective engagement is a characteristic of the critical mode of engagement as well as the desire for authenticity. This distinction is illustrated by Cameron's choice to "opt out" of singing certain songs:

How important are the lyrics of what you sing?

CAMERON: *Interesting question. I think lyrics need to be relevant. They need to be theologically correct, because some songs, particularly modern songs, aren't all that correct. And the focus of them can often be on me and things like that rather than on God, and on what he does and how great he is.*

Do you struggle to sing those songs?

CAMERON: *Sometimes I do. Yeah.*

What do you do in those times?

CAMERON: *Sometimes I just won't sing them. I mean I will stand, but you know . . . opt out.*

Paul, who has been a worship leader for over fifteen years, provided an insightful understanding of the function and limits of worship lyrics:

PAUL: *It is important that we are careful about our songs. But at the same time, a song does not try to describe everything about "X." It will just kind of go splatter. And it kind of depends on how you are feeling at that time. They should be a helpful lyric that is actually helpful to the church. It has to build up the body; if not, don't do it in church. Maybe sing it to them or put it on a CD. A lyric is never going to be completely balanced or fair. I think people trying to put that onto songs is a bit of a waste of time. But at the same time, if it is a lyric that I don't like, then I just don't sing it. That's cool. You are always trying to capture as many people as you can. You can't expect church to be everything I want it to be, or all things to all people. And I think that about the lyrics as well.*

Delimiting worship lyrics in this way reveals the way Paul, as a worship leader, prioritizes the corporate dimension to worship over individualized self-expression. Sourcing worship songs with this collective focus can present challenges for worship leaders if David Wells' argument that contemporary worship is "deeply privatized"[48] is correct. Wells argues that "Worship is less about ascribing praise to God for who he is than it is celebrating what we know of him from within our own experience."[49] My findings suggest that participants share a preference for worship that is focused on who God is. Furthermore, Wells fails to take into account that even when worship songs focus on the individual, they are still sung collectively.

Selective engagement, while motivated in part by how one might be feeling during a time of worship, or personal preference, is also motivated by a desire for authenticity. My interviews suggest that selective engagement is based on how participants feel towards God and whether the

48. Wells, *Losing*, 44. "One indication of this," Wells argues, based on a content analysis of worship songs, "is that the Church, the collective people of God, features in only 1.2 percent of songs; what dominates overwhelmingly is the private, individualized, and interior sense of God. By contrast, 21.6 percent of the classical hymns were explicitly about the Church" (*Losing*, 44).

49. Ibid., 46.

feelings or commitments being expressed and declared in a song genuinely reflect those of the individual worshipper. For others, a form of selective engagement is based not so much on not feeling a certain way, or not liking a song, as it is on a struggle over meaning.

Mind-Heart Engagement

In some of the interviews, participants expressed caution about the emotional state of worship. It is not that people do not want this emotional experience, but rather that they need worship to be more than that. Worship needs to engage their mind as well. When the mind is engaged, then they feel that they are given space to think about God and their life with more reflection:

Do you find you are becoming more critical of the lyrics and the words you are singing?

DYLAN: *Yeah. I guess one of my things about worship is I'm cautious about worship that tries to just induce an emotional state in you rather than engaging your mind as well. I guess it is one of my prejudices that I'm a sort of a person who likes to think things through mentally. So I think worship isn't just an emotional experience, it's a directing of our lives to God, turning God-ward, and for me that isn't something that just takes place in singing. But I like a good sing as much as the next guy.*

What goes on for you when you worship?

NAOMI: *I think for me, I do really like worship, but sometimes I feel it is a bit emotional. It is about eliciting emotions. It gets quite intense and there is a lot of hype. I don't like that. I realize that people are not being insincere with that. But I think that worship doesn't have to be an emotional experience. It is affirming the goodness of God. But then other times it will be the thing that really makes me feel emotional, but often when I feel emotion, it is when I feel really sensitive to the Spirit. And I really love it. I love music. It's not that I don't love music; I love music.*

Deliberate, thoughtfully chosen words facilitated people's mind-heart engagement with worship:

ANTONIA: *I like the worship aspects of it. There's a lot of alternative types of worship. Some of them are kind of experiential, so you can go and wash your hands and then cover yourself in mud and then wash it off again and, you know, all that kind of stuff.*

As opposed to just singing?

ANTONIA: *Yeah. And a lot of the words that are used in the worship time or the words that are used for the confession time are relevant . . .*

SANTOS: *They are very deliberate, aren't they?*

ANTONIA: *They help you to relate your life experience to God, or sort of bring your own life experience and kind of see it in a context where you can have God's input or, you know, ask for forgiveness or whatever.*

SANTOS: *Often there are many things that you come across in the last week, or month, or two months, or however long it was since you were last in a contemplative worship space [laughs] that is great to be able to reflect on or pray about or think about or meditate on. I find that much more helpful, and certainly the words that are used are deliberately chosen for their meaning and connotation. And having something that you can read through and deliberately think about and choose, you think, yeah, I like that take on it.*

It is this mind-heart engagement that enables Antonia and Santos to relate their life experience to God. Like Naomi and Dylan, mind-heart engagement facilitates a level of authenticity that is sometimes missing for them when worship is limited to an emotional experience. The authenticity comes through having time to digest and reflect on what they are saying, or when space is given over to silence and reflection so that they can offer up their own prayers and thoughts to God. Daniel, like many participants I interviewed, would like to see a wider range of worship forms that engage the mind as well as the heart: "But I would like to see more use of Bible reading and prayer in worship. Even some of the candle things have helped me to slow down and focus on God. Sometimes when I can't pray, lighting a candle has helped me as a symbol that I can leave my struggles with God. Just that little flame there is saying that it is with God."

Atmospheric Engagement: Meaning Beyond the Lyrics

Another strategy participants used to engage with worship aside from lyrics was that of "soaking" in the atmosphere of worship. The music provides a spiritual (sacred) acoustic envelope, much like Barthes analysis of music as *jouissance*, or pleasure,[50] and Karbusicky's notion of "aesthetic enjoyment"[51] whereby listeners are overwhelmed by sound. To some extent, atmospheric engagement brings us full circle to collective effervescence, albeit a subtler kind. Being part of the collective gathering is not mentioned explicitly in the interviews as it was for those describing an experience of collective effervescence. Nonetheless, a revitalizing of the spiritual life still occurred for participants who found themselves drawn into the environment created by the collective gathering. Antonia, who had began to disengage with the worship at her church through familiarity with the songs ("I had sung those songs so many times I was just quite ready to have a break from that"), was still able to worship God through atmospheric engagement. "I still enjoyed being there. I remember the last service I attended at Flaxbush before I left. I was just in the congregation and I don't think I sang much. I still enjoyed the environment, I still felt like there was a connection there. So between myself and God and that sort of stuff, I was sort of over the singing."

Although Antonia was disengaged with the content of the worship songs, she still felt connected to God and to the faith community through the worship environment. The atmosphere, and especially the acoustic environment provided by a church service, enables a "mode of listening" to use Stockfelt's[52] phrase, that is contemplative and allows for "soaking" in the communal dimension of worship independently of the worship songs themselves. This is also part of a selective mode of engagement. In this way, the music culture of worship facilitated an appropriate mode of listening for Antonia that enabled a spiritual experience of worship.[53]

Meaning is not dependent upon the lyrics of worship songs. Meaning does not have to be organized around the words, but can instead be organized around the music itself and the environment created by it. Music

50. Barthes, *Image*, 179.

51. Karbusicky, "Interaction," 646.

52. Stockfelt, "Adequate," 132.

53. Stockfelt has shown how the meaning of music changes in different listening situations as people apply "modes of listening" appropriate for different contexts such as a church, concert hall, iPod, car, cinema, or café ("Adequate" 132).

has a *mood, a feel* about it that people connect with and create meaning from. The way music moves us enables us not only to "feel" worshipful, for example, but also to express and offer up worship to God without words. It is a position of worship encouraged by God in the Psalms: "Be still and know that I am God" (Psalms 46:10). The lyrics of a song, then, can fade into the background as the music itself rises to the forefront and speaks its own spiritual language.

Because the practice of worship is more about the overall experience created by the social situation of gathering, atmospheric engagement enables people to worship independently of the song lyrics. For Christina, worship is "more than just singing. It feels alive. I think if you are feeling a bit down, that gets you in the mood . . . just your response to the worship more than the lyrics." While the lyrics of a song are also important to Joshua, he can still engage God in worship through atmospheric engagement even when the words are not meaningful to him: "so often if it's a song that I think is just trash lyrics, I'm quite happy to stand there in silence and just kind of close my eyes and lift my soul to a position of worship—as opposed to thinking whoever wrote this song is a trash songwriter, you know, what's he trying to do? [laughs]." Joshua, like Antonia, is able to participate in worship through atmospheric engagement. Joshua combines atmospheric engagement with selective engagement that allows him to remain engaged in worship even when there are songs that he elects not to sing because of the lyrics.

In this chapter we have explored the way that embedded faith, characterized by a religious sensibility, is expressed through various modes of engagement when it comes to worship within a church service. The religious sensibility towards the religious practice of worship is one of investment. The nature of investment is seen in the attention and consideration participants give in deciding whether to sing particular songs or not. The collective effervescence that can occur through corporate worship as a re-creative effervescent assembly still holds much promise and potential. Unfortunately, however, the extent of dis-engagement from worship experienced by a majority of participants suggests that contemporary styles of worship no longer facilitates this group's worship of God in a congregational setting.

Modes of engagement operate as strategies for people who seek to enter into worship through singing but who cannot always sing certain songs they feel lack authenticity or truth. Selective and atmospheric engagement demonstrate how owned faith can remain embedded in the corporate practice of worship even when one is experiencing disengagement at another level. The next chapter continues with an exploration of modes of (dis)engagement in relation to preaching.

7

Preaching and
Interpretive Communities

I was interested in exploring the role that preaching plays in people's faith journeys and how much preaching influenced church selection. Everyone I interviewed affirmed the importance of "good" preaching. Of course, what makes preaching either good or bad is sometimes a matter of perspective. The preparation of a sermon text and a congregation's interpretation of a sermon is shaped and influenced by Fish's notion of "interpretive communities." Interpretive communities provide strategies for both preaching and listening to a sermon. Preaching is not only one of the main ways that churches retell their story as a community of memory, it also provides them with a particular understanding of faith and life.

Congregations are an active audience when it comes to listening to a sermon. That is to say, congregations are actively involved in the production of meaning from preaching. They are socially situated individuals whose listening is framed by shared cultural meanings and practices. According to Stuart Hall, the consumption or reception of messages is itself a "moment" of the production process. Hall argues that consumption of messages predominates over their production "because it is the 'point of departure for the realization' of the message."[1] Meaning is socially determined. This chapter explores not so much what makes preaching good or bad, although this issue is articulated in places, but rather participants' reception and interpretation of sermons through the theoretical framework of interpretive faith communities. After all, preaching takes place within a

1. Hall, "Encoding," 168.

particular social context. That is, in a local church as an interpretive faith community of memory.

The "Preacher is the Message"

In the '60s, Marshall McLuhan coined the phrase, "The medium is the message,"[2] to explain the way technology becomes an extension of our natural senses in the communication process. According to McLuhan, the medium has an impact on content and the way we understand and interpret media messages. McLuhan's theory can be adapted to the preacher, such that "the preacher is the message." In other words, the preacher, as well as his or her life, style of preaching, theological perspective, and worldview all become part of the message in both the encoding and decoding stages. The personality and character of the preacher, along with their style, which Goffman refers to as the "textual self,"[3] influences the way a sermon is "heard" and how it is interpreted. Goffman describes the textual self as being "the sense of the person that seems to stand behind the textual statements made and which incidentally give these statements authority. Typically this is a self of relatively long standing, one the speaker was involved in long before the current occasion of talk."[4] Sean's comments below demonstrate the way that the textual self of the preacher becomes an extension of his or her message:

What do you like about the sermons at your church? Are you learning from them?

SEAN: *Yeah, definitely. I really appreciate Jermaine, he's real. He's had some real hard times in his life previously. He understands that there [are] a lot of people in not so good a space sometimes. He relates to most people. I like the fact that he comes from a non-Christian background. His faith has pretty much been derived from his later years of his life. He's got a great ability to connect with a crowd through comedy. Comedy is quite important, because if you can make them laugh then you've got them listening, obviously, and then straight after he nails it—he does it so often—he has this whole series of comedy, and the whole thing is attached*

2. McLuhan, *Understanding Media*.
3. Goffman, *Forms*, 173.
4. Ibid.

to what he is saying, and then he will hit you with quite a sobering thought about life with God, and it is such an effective means to do it. I think he is a great speaker and I really enjoy what he has to say.

From Sean's comments, it is evident that Jermaine's textual self created a positive receptivity to his sermons. Sean knows that Jermaine has been through hard times in his life because he has shared these life experiences with the congregation and he occasionally draws on them to illustrate a point in a sermon.

The significance of the preacher's textual self on the reception of a sermon message is illustrated by Carlos' selective approach to church attendance based on who was preaching:

CARLOS: *I found Samuel to be really inspirational, to the point where I was just noting that when Samuel was going to be speaking I would turn up.*

You wouldn't turn up if he wasn't?

CARLOS: *Yeah. I wasn't particularly keen on Frank, so I'd just miss his ones.*

Why was that? What didn't you like?

CARLOS: *I thought—not a naïveté or falseness . . . but found that if I was going to describe the thing that I didn't like about Frank, was that he seemed a little bit plastic or a little bit fake in some regards. Just based on his belief in some things which I had found to be untrue in my life.*

So it didn't meet up with your own reality?

CARLOS: *Yeah. My reality wasn't his reality.*

You didn't have that issue with Samuel?

CARLOS: *No. I found that his reality was really similar to my reality with regards to church and also to Christianity.*

How the sermon is preached and, more importantly, by whom became a deciding criterion for Carlos in choosing whether he would attend church on any given Sunday. Frank was considered "plastic" and "fake" compared to the inspiration of Samuel's sermons. These characteristics stand behind each of the preachers, influencing the authority, or lack thereof, with which their sermons are heard and interpreted. Carlos' comments also draw our attention to the way in which sermons' authority rests not only in the preacher, but also in relation to the listener's own perception of reality based on his or her own experience and knowledge.

Jonathan and Rebecca's story continues to emphasize the significance of the preacher's textual self in determining the reception of a sermon and the way it becomes an extension (both positive and negative) of the message. Shortly after getting married, Jonathan and Rebecca began looking for a new church together. Rimu Fellowship was the first church they tried. They liked it and stayed. It was Alison's preaching that initially impressed them. They did not know it at the time, but Alison was only a visiting speaker:

JONATHAN: *We really liked what she had to say.*

REBECCA: *She impressed us.*

JONATHAN: *She impressed us . . . Really impressed us with her warmth.*

REBECCA: *Especially in comparison with Nick [the pastor at their previous church]. Because I had been so frustrated hearing him and his tone of voice—his sort of middle aged man mannerisms of being quite dominant—and it really, really annoyed me. Like, I used to talk about it all the time. My parents couldn't understand what I was going on about. But I really felt offended by it. Whereas she was as a woman; she was very soft-spoken and very kind of loving, it was like she drew people to what she said through the love of what she had to say rather than through her force. And I really, really loved it. I really warmed to her style of preaching. It was the verse that she had . . . the Bible reading that she had was the same as our wedding topic.*

Rebecca's use of "warmth" and "love" verses "dominance" and "force," describe how she views the very different textual selves of the two preachers. Alison's textual self draws Rebecca in and enables her to engage with Alison's sermons. In contrast, Nick's textual self signifies for Rebecca a "dominance" and "force" which repels, frustrates, and offends her, and so distracts her from listening to what he is saying. Alison and her preaching gains the authority and respect that is withheld from Nick. Sometimes people draw on other interpretive communities that provide an alternative or opposing frame of reference and way of understanding the world. Feminist discourse can be understood as an interpretive community that provided the particular interpretive strategies Rebecca employed in critiquing the patriarchy she experienced in her church.[5]

Robert Jackall and Janice Hirota's insights into storytelling addresses Rebecca's struggle with her experience of "middle aged man mannerisms" in preachers, for as they explain,

> How stories are told and by whom they are told are more impor-
> tant than the stories themselves; one must therefore adopt, for
> instance, a feminine aesthetics of narration, "resisting" masculine
> illusions of closure, linearity, mastery, and control, and being open
> to the multiperspectival possibilities of intimate reciprocity.[6]

How a message is preached is important. This might mean removing masculine language or "middle aged man mannerisms," or it might mean "reaching for images that might yield fresh perspectives on the world"[7] and the gospel story. Alisha's comments further support Jackall and Hirota's argument that *who* tells the story is a significant factor in how the story is received. As Alisha noted, "I think the preacher at the end of the day makes the preaching. When you can see that their lives match up, then you can see that they are really genuine and being inspiring, then you want to hear what they say because it is worth listening to." Similarly, Rebecca recounted her reaction to the sermon of a possible new pastor for their church: "We hated him; we absolutely hated what he had to say. And I said to Jonathan, if he's going to be employed, then I don't want to go there because I just didn't like it at all."

The Message: Engaging the Complexities of Life

Henri Nouwen argues that one reason preachers often create more antago-
nism and frustration than sympathy with their sermons is because of their assumption of non-existent feelings.[8] Nouwen explains, "A large number of sermons start by making untested suppositions. Without any hesitance, many preachers impose feelings, ideas, questions, and problems on their

---

5. For an application of Fish's theory of interpretive communities to feminist theological thinking, see Fulkerson, "(Non-Sexist) Bible."

6. Jackall and Hirota, *Image*, 225.

7. Ibid.

8. Nouwen, *Ministry*, 40

hearers that are often completely unknown to the majority, if not to all of them."[9] Preachers, Riddell writes, "must hear and feel the questions and protests which are contained in the angst-ridden society that enfolds them; otherwise preaching takes place in a vacuum."[10] They must also hear and feel the questions coming out of their own congregations.

What is also important for preachers is an understanding of the type of faith journeys that people in their congregation are on. People's stories confirm M. Scott Peck's opening words to *The Road Less Travelled*: "Life is difficult."[11] Life does not always work out as one imagines. Furthermore, it does not always work out as people have been led to believe from the preaching they have heard in church. The life of faith is indeed a difficult one. Therefore, as Bellah et al. maintain, "A genuine community of memory will also tell painful stories of shared suffering that sometimes creates deeper identities than success."[12]

One of the characteristics of church and preaching that Caleb felt lacked realness was its over-emphasis of the good, which seemed to allow no room for the struggles and failures of life. Caleb contrasted his experience at Mount Aspiring Baptist, where he felt doubt and struggles were embraced, against his experiences of other churches:

CALEB: *I think that's what I found really good about Karl [the pastor] was that he was really real. And I think that was kind of the first preacher that I've had that was really real and he was just like you know, faith is hard. And he has been through quite a bit of disappointment himself. And it was good to have a bit more of that flavor come through in the sermons. Whereas, you kind of really don't get that as much, or it is kind of looked down upon to a certain degree in some of the charismatic and Pentecostal churches. It is seen as a little bit of a weakness to ascribe to that kind of doubt.*

How important is that realness and authenticity from up front?

CALEB: *Absolutely. Definitely. And Karl was great, you know, he was such a no-hype speaker as well. At the end of his sermons he would just open it up to the church, and he would just go, "Has anyone got any questions or*

9. Ibid., 40.

10. Riddell, *Threshold*, 120.

11. Peck, *Road Less Travelled*, 13.

12. Bellah et al., *Habits*, 153.

*comments?" which was kind of a new concept. I had never come across
that in church before, which was great and people would say things and
they would go, "What about this?" or "What about that?" And a lot of
the time Karl would just go, "Well, I don't know," you know, and I kind
of really respected him for that. He didn't try to have the answers. He
didn't try to say something that he didn't really believe. And you know,
sometimes he would let other people in the audience come up with suggestions and stuff. Or he would just give you pointers to go on. So I
guess Karl was just like, "I don't really know all the answers, I'm kind of
looking for them myself. And that's OK and we are all going together."
Whereas I guess some of the churches that I had gone to before you've
got to have the answers.*

Andrew was attracted to the transparency of the leadership at St James
Anglican:

ANDREW: *What attracted me mostly was the leadership style at this congregation. The leader always talked about his own fallibility. And he would
say what he was struggling with and all the leadership would talk about
what they were struggling with and what they can work on. This was
new to me. It wasn't new completely. Where I had always been to these
Youth Alive rallies and been to all these Pente [Pentecostal] things back
in New Zealand—it was always about these people who looked like they
were just perfect, and it just didn't seem right. When I was [in] England
and this person was always talking about their struggles and they are
meant to be leading the church, I sort of went, I like this guy. I like a
leader who actually has problems. They weren't bad problems. So that
was really great.*

Churches that do not allow space for struggle and failure, or view it as
a spiritual weakness or as a sign of unacknowledged sin in a person's life,
create an inauthentic culture. An inauthentic culture prevents people from
sharing openly and honestly about their struggles or questions of faith that
they feel will not be tolerated. It can lead to people pretending that everything is OK, that they have no problems, and situations where experience
is spiritualized in such a way as to be abstracted from reality. The preaching
culture leads to either inauthentic or authentic engagement with the life of
faith.

Familiarity Syndrome

"Redundancy of the message," according to Nouwen, is one aspect of the preacher's message that causes audiences to lack motivation and eagerness to listen. [13] Redundancy of the message is part of the familiarity syndrome by which people have already heard most sermon messages so many times that they lose even the slightest possibility of evoking a response. Young adults who have grown up in the church have heard sermons since they were Sunday school children and are likely to continue hearing many of the same sermons for as long as they remain within the church. Nouwen argues that "When a message has become so redundant that it has completely lost the ability to evoke any kind of creative response it can hardly be considered a message any longer."[14] Perhaps this is why people are searching out good preaching that can evoke a response and challenge them to grow their faith and relationship with God.

Jody was introduced to the Holy Spirit at a Presbyterian Easter camp when she was thirteen years old. It was at Easter camp that Jody witnessed another side to spiritual reality when she received the gift of tongues and saw demons cast out. Such experiences confirmed God's power and existence to Jody. She was very receptive to the preaching at Little Bay Presbyterian and eager to learn all that she could. I asked her what was good about preaching that she connected with, and Jodi answered, "I just really was soaking up Bible knowledge at that point. I was really impacted by the teaching of the Bible, you know, I just took it on board. I was just like a sponge. I took everything on board that I heard. And I tried to put it into practice."

These days, however, Jody has been finding preaching "horribly dreary" because "it is stuff that I have heard before." She went on to discuss what she felt she needed in relation to this familiarity syndrome:

JODY: *I have heard so many flipping sermons. And I know so much about Christianity and I apply so little of it. Like I apply less now than I ever did. So I think what I need is not to hear more information about what I am supposed to be doing. What I need is some encouragement to get off my butt and do it—some inspiration. And I think that inspiration is really missing. It is just information. But I need to be inspired. I am lacking that.*

13. Nouwen, *Ministry*, 38.
14. Ibid., 39.

The content of a sermon is important for Jody. But she does not feel like she is hearing anything new in sermons. Furthermore, she desires content that comes with direction. How do we put this into practice? Jody feels she is lacking in her practice of what she believes and hears. This is because, as Jody suggested, what she hears offers very little, if anything, to put into practice.

Until recently, Belinda's experience of preaching echoed Jody's. As she said to me, "You know what? I don't often get stuff out of sermons. And I actually get bored quite easily." Going on to explain why, she said, "I began switching off because I got the same message." Belinda was drawn to her current church's preaching, which she found "way more relevant" because it was practical. "I can't stand it, Belinda complained, "when people say you've just got to do this. And I'm like, well, give us examples. Like rather than spiritualize everything and over-spiritualize. How do you just keep trusting in God? Give us an example of that, you know. Make it really tangible for people."

Without offering answers to this "so what?" question or any practical applications, preaching can become vacuous, empty-sounding clichéd propositions or abstract theological discourse. As Belinda pointed out, "How do you keep trusting in God?"

Noah, like Jody and Belinda, is currently dealing with the familiarity syndrome of preaching. The main strategy Noah has responded with is a practice-orientated faith. It is about living out what he believes by putting some of the guidance that he hears in sermons into practice. It is a desire to activate his faith rather than passively believing. It is faith as a way of life.

What about the preaching? How important is that?

NOAH: Not very. Well, you have to be able to listen to it. It has got to be interesting. But I guess I kind of feel that I can't really learn too much more from what people are going to be saying. I've pretty much heard most sermons before in one way or another. The only way that I am going to be able to impact myself spiritually is if I actually get out there and put some of these things into practice in a practical way . . . So for me now to be challenged I've got to take what I've been taught and get out there and do something with it.

Engagement with a biblical text is an essential characteristic of good preaching for Nathan, who explained that "Someone could be really eloquent, but not engage with the text in any way, and I would probably feel ripped off." In contrast to Noah, who feels that he cannot learn anything new from preaching, Nathan's attitude towards preaching is one of expectancy: "I think ideally we should be coming saying God is going to speak through this person because he speaks through his word and there is something for me here. He wants to touch my life. What's it going to be? And I'm looking for it, you know." It is not enough for people to just receive theological "information" in sermons. Those I interviewed want to know what difference preaching is going to make to their lives and the lives of others.

Intellectual Engagement: Hunger for Depth

Those who have grown up in the church often hunger for greater depth. Unfortunately, many young adults I interviewed had experienced shallow or motivational-type preaching, or preaching that continuously covers the basics. Naomi grew up in a Pentecostal church that discouraged her from going to university. University was treated with suspicion, as a place that might undermine faith. Naomi disagreed and moved cities to begin her degree. Once there, Naomi's contacts encouraged her to begin going to Kauri Fellowship, where she said she appreciated "being around educated Christians." She went onto explain,

NAOMI: *I could see that I didn't have to, you know, leave your mind at the door when you come in. I really appreciated the level of . . . people were really intelligent there. It made you want to learn more and be like that, and think about things in a deeper way.*

Did that come through in the preaching?

NAOMI: *Yeah, I think it did. It did come through in the preaching. But just in the community life in general I think. I don't know how better to describe it really . . . Definitely in the preaching.*

The Pentecostal church that Naomi grew up in and Kauri Fellowship represent two very different interpretive communities. The worldview and values shared by the congregation as an interpretive community are reflected in the preaching. Naomi shared her recollections of the preaching within her Pentecostal church:

NAOMI: *I think preaching or teaching, I think they can be the same thing . . . I think for me, going back to the Bible, I guess, and still applying it to today definitely. Because it is a living document, you know? I think there is a sense growing up that sociology played a big part in the preaching, which has definitely got its place . . . Like, they became kind of like management seminars, or pursuit of excellence, which is not actually sociology, but general self-advancement, whether it is business or not. I am amazed doing Bible College now what people don't know. There is a real lack of knowledge about the Bible.*

ANDREW: *To be fair, the Pentecostal Church is very strong on Scripture.*

NAOMI: *But it is a certain interpretation of Scripture. It is Scripture as it can build you up. Selective reading of blessing and prosperity perhaps, I don't know.*

Naomi no longer ascribes to the Pentecostal interpretation of Scripture, or at least its narrow or selective use of it. It is no longer her normative framework of reference for understanding faith. The interpretive community that she now belongs to involves a deeper intellectual engagement that has a critical edge. Naomi's re-interpretation and critique of preaching in the Pentecostal context that she used to be part of illustrates how the identification of what is considered real and normative occurs within interpretive communities and how, as Fish points out, "what was normative for the members of one community would be seen as strange (if it could be seen at all) by members of another."[15]

Biblical teaching was not a strength of Living Water Apostolic, where Wendy used to attend. As Wendy described it, "The church wasn't really that big on teaching. That's what made me want to go and study theology at some point. It was very light on the teaching side of things and quite big on the preaching—the exhortation, motivational, visionary, you know— acronyms about how to do this, that, and the other." As Wendy's faith has grown, so too has her desire for hearing preaching with depth that engages the mind rather than motivational-type sermons:

15. Fish, *Text*, 15.

You mention that at that church the teaching was a little bit impoverished. What makes preaching good for you?

WENDY: *That's definitely changed over time, because initially I would have said that I quite like those motivational-type ones early on. But I soon realized I needed a lot more than that. And that is probably to do with as you grow, you need to know more. So it was initially meeting a need, because it was just very small amounts of teaching or whatever. Now days, I am far more fussy about what I like in terms of a sermon. I really get annoyed when somebody doesn't use the Bible in their preaching. And I like it if they start from Scripture and draw something out of that. It doesn't matter if it is specifically about the text of the Bible and what it means, or if they take that and use that as a starting point and sort of explain a principle, or, you know, talk about something and how it relates to that. So I don't mind either one of those. But there has to be . . . the Bible has to be in it somehow.*

I don't like ones that are purely about somebody's experiences. Although I love to hear about people's experiences, I mean, I thrive on that. It has to be—well, no, I love to hear people's experiences. I guess if the two can be combined, that's great. Or just every now and again you get to hear about somebody and their experiences. And the majority of the time I would prefer to hear actual Bible teaching.

Wendy has been disappointed with the preaching at her current church due to the sermons' lack of depth. Wendy feels that the ministers underestimate the level of the congregation's spiritual and theological understanding. From her perspective and knowledge of the congregation, she felt that "There are people at that church who want more. I think the majority of people want more. They want more depth and they are ready for it. They have the capacity for it. So I think it is being a bit watered down and it doesn't need to be."

Wendy's comment about sermons being "watered down" suggests that churches need to develop a deeper understanding of their congregational makeup. One way for churches to evaluate their congregations' faith maturity and to discover how many within the congregation are connecting with religious practices such as preaching is to engage in "reflexive monitoring of their situation" in order to develop a "reflexive ecclesiology."[16] Reflexivity is to reflect on what one is doing, in the case of preaching, to incorporate

16. Carroll, "Reflexive," 554.

collective knowledge of congregational engagement into reflection and change one's practices accordingly.

Preaching that engages listeners at an intellectual level does not shy away from critical thought. Theo is looking for an interpretive church community that does not gloss over the controversial passages of the Bible. He has yet to find one. Theo discussed some of the areas that he would like to see churches engaging and grappling with:

THEO: *Like, I don't know, how on earth does one be a Christian in our current age? And what's the Bible really on about? I don't know. I find that most churches stick to the common sense stuff that you can look at the Bible and you can read for yourself and go, "Aw, that probably means this." And where everyone goes, "Yes, amen, yes we all agree that is what that says." But I've heard all that stuff before. So I'm far more interested in delving into the . . . I want to hear people flinging mud at Paul's letters and saying well what on earth was he talking about there? And why was he being hard on women? Because all these really tough things they just gloss over . . . Which is a constant source of frustration.*

Instead of ignoring or trying to explain away problems and contradictions within a biblical text, Hudson suggests that we should ask why they are there. Questioning a biblical text in this way, Hudson argues, becomes "the radical expansion of the interpreter's horizon."[17] It also opens up the potential for intellectual engagement that in many cases has been shut down in people's experience of preaching, such as in Theo's experience.

Based on my interview findings, I would suggest that when people say they want preaching that is intellectual, they are saying they want to hear sermons that teach them something, present a fresh angle or alternative perspectives on a passage. They voice a desire for preaching that is not afraid to engage with difficult passages and is comfortable with internal biblical contradictions, ambiguities, and uncertainties. Intellectual engagement does not require all the answers, but instead leads people to explore their faith in new and deeper ways. It is a sincere wish to avoid the familiarity syndrome that comes from the repetition of sermons that offer nothing new.

Furthermore, participants' desire for intellectual engagement suggests that the pre-eminence of emotions, or "heart" in preaching at the expense of the mind may be misguided. This hunger to be engaged by the intellectual

17. Hudson, "Dance," 18.

side of Christianity points towards something that transcends historical epochs such as modernity or postmodernity. It is not a head-heart divide. I do not think this hunger is about rational or propositional versus more symbolic, emotive, or relational style of preaching. Rather, it is a desire to be led into a deeper intellectual understanding of God and faith in a way that creates a "stirring in the heart." In the words of those who encountered Jesus on the road to Emmaus shortly after his resurrection, "Were not our hearts burning within us while he talked with us on the road and opened the Scriptures to us?" (Luke 24:32).

Life Experience and Aberrant Decodings

Hall suggests that what may be seen as "distortions" or "misunderstandings" arise precisely from "the lack of equivalence" between the codes of encoding and decoding in the communicative exchange.[18] Eco calls this "aberrant decodings."[19] Aberrant decodings occur whenever the social situation between the encoders and decoders is significantly different. Nouwen argues that a difficult problem to overcome in preaching is preoccupation with a theological point of view. Nouwen points out "that not only those who preach but also those who listen have their own 'theologies.'"[20] Such theologies, or ways of understanding faith, can create a lack of equivalence between the encoded sermon and decoded reception, or interpretation, by individuals in the congregation. This lack of equivalence and aberrant decodings generates polysemic meanings. Polysemy, however, as Hall makes clear, is not is not to be confused with pluralism: "Connotative codes are not equal among themselves. Any society/culture tends, with varying degrees of closure, to impose its classifications of the social and cultural and political world. These constitute a dominant cultural order, though it is neither univocal nor uncontested."[21]

In the context of preaching, interpretive strategies employed in listening to a sermon are not those of an individual free agent, even individuals who have their own "theologies," as Nouwen puts it. These strategies, Fish explains, are community property, as is the individual, insofar as they

18. Hall, "Encoding," 169.
19. Eco, "Semiotic."
20. Nouwen, *Ministry*, 42.
21. Hall, "Encoding," 172.

simultaneously enable and limit the operations of consciousness.[22] Such limits provided by interpretive church communities, however, do not always go uncontested.

Some of the young adults I interviewed struggled at times with where a preacher chose to draw such closure to meaning in their sermons. Sean, for the most part, would be challenged by the preaching at Flaxbush Baptist. At other times, however, Sean said that "There was a point where I got over him laying down 'my way or the highway' sort of style." Likewise, Joel, who also attends Flaxbush Baptist, found that the preaching "is too black-and-white for my liking." Joel explained what he meant by this, saying,

JOEL: *There is one answer which can be rationally put together. There's none of that, "Some of you may believe this some of you may believe that." I mean it's, you know, it's that tendency towards a concept of a creed, not necessarily dictated by a denomination, but maybe dictated by a pastor. The "Nick King [the pastor] creed," for example. But having said that, you need something. There has to be some . . . I'm totally stuck in the middle on this one. There has to be constraints, otherwise your faith just falls to pieces. So what do you choose to put the constraints on? And I'm not sure I feel comfortable where Nick sometimes chooses to place the constraints. What is that solid framework that we hang everything off? I think that he's creating the framework plus the hanging with his sermons, and I think I'd like to see a sermon that was more of a solid framework and less things hung on it, and leaving it up to us to hang the things on it.*

Young adults like Sean and Joel tend to react negatively to being told what to do in a sermon, especially if the sermon closes off alternative ways of understanding a topic or passage of Scripture under discussion. Brueggemann's idea of "funding the postmodern imagination" speaks to Joel's desire to hear sermons that leave more room for him to hang things on. Instead of presenting a full alternative world to people, which Brueggemann dismisses as imperialistic, we need to offer truth in little pieces, "out of which people can put life together in fresh configurations."[23] Brueggemann is asking us to reconsider, from a postmodern context, what the meeting of liturgy and proclamation is all about:

22. Fish, *Text*, 14.
23. Brueggemann, *Bible*, 20.

> That meeting is not, in my urging, a place to come to affirm the great absolutes that are allied with a modernist hegemony. It is not a place for claims that are so large and comprehensive that they ring hollow in a context of our general failure, demise, and disease. It is rather a place where people come to receive new materials, or old materials freshly voiced, that will fund, feed, nurture, nourish, legitimate, and authorize a *counterimagination of the world*.[24]

Funding a postmodern imagination in preaching will, as Sweet suggests, draw "fewer conclusions than it does entertain possibilities. It is the preaching of departures, beckonings, thresholds . . . to a people On the Way."[25] Or to paraphrase Joel, it is a preaching that provides a solid framework, but not necessarily the things to hang on it. However the interpretive position of a faith community will determine their openness to such suggestions.

Mount Aspiring Baptist was a church that funded the postmodern imagination. Caleb described the pastor at Mount Aspiring Baptist as the best speaker he had ever heard. It was his preaching that drew him to his current church, which is one of the few places that Caleb says he would listen to the whole sermon all the way through. He also connected to the people there, who Caleb said "shared the same journey with me." Caleb described this shared faith journey as one in which people had "been a bit exposed to the charismatic thing. And they had been kind of taken along with that for awhile, but then they'd kind of grown out of it, or, you know, got a bit tired of it." Growing "tired" of charismatic Christianity is evidence of the way that "charismatic renewal is subject to the normative Weberian constraints that apparently govern charisma, namely eventual routinization."[26] Percy describes this process of routinization by noting that "What begins as fresh, authentic, groundbreaking and novel—all legitimate descriptions of Charismatic phenomena—can soon become ritualized, replicated, domesticated and fossilized."[27] It is this routinization that can lead to people becoming tired, skeptical, and weary of charismatic Christianity, as it has done for Caleb and others at Mount Aspiring Baptist.

Mount Aspiring Baptist was an interpretive community that Caleb connected with. Caleb's journey, which has grown out of the

24. Ibid., 20.

25. Sweet, *Soul*, 215.

26. Percy, "Place," 97.

27. Ibid.

charismatic-evangelical style of faith, fits Tomlinson's description of a "post-evangelical." Tomlinson defines a post-evangelical as someone who takes "as a given, many of the assumptions of evangelical faith, while at the same time moving beyond its perceived limitations."[28] Caleb has moved beyond the black-and-white absolute limits of truth and scriptural interpretation held by evangelicals. Caleb now feels an openness to alternative interpretations that is more situational and confirmed by life experience. Caleb did concede that "there is maybe a place for charismatic and Pentecostal churches and churches like that," for people who do not think as he does. Caleb suggested that it was his sceptical nature that drew him to churches like Mount Aspiring Baptist instead.

Seasons of faith can create a lack of equivalence between the message and its reception. The social situation of the listener influences what is heard. For example, Emily's self-described "desert experience of faith" impacted how she heard sermons:

You talked about becoming disillusioned with the preaching predominantly in terms of a lack of depth. What created that sense of disillusionment?

EMILY: *I think I was probably caught up in everything else. And there were a few other speakers around, where if you went along on Sunday and they were speaking, it was like you had hit the jackpot, and it would be a really good service. And there was enough of that happening to keep me going. But I also think that that last year of university for me, or the last year that I was at that church, I had started to head into what I now term my desert experience. So I probably wasn't in a very good place anyway. And so it probably just made everything worse, really, that there was nothing from the pulpit that was inspiring me. And because in my own life, like it was dry, everything was dry Weet-Bix and I couldn't inspire myself, so to speak. Yeah, it all went a little downhill.*

The fact that for Emily, everything was "dry Weet-Bix," is an indicator of the way the experiential has come to dominate interpretation of reality for many young adults. A more extreme situation than lack of equivalence in response to preaching is that of "interpretive rupture."

28. Tomlinson, *Post-Evangelical*, 7.

Interpretive Rupture

Experiencing a different interpretive faith community as a result of church switching caused some of the young adults to call previous ways of understanding God, faith, and church into question. When the influence of young adults' previous faith community remained strong, however, resistance to a new interpretive framework was likely. But when participants' experiences confirmed new interpretations and teachings on faith and God, generating cognitive dissonance, then what I have called "interpretive rupture" was likely. Interpretive rupture involves a critical distancing from one's previous interpretive framework, particularly regarding specific issues faith that have been called into question or found from experience to be untrue. Interpretive rupture can be a disorientating experience. It involves reorienting oneself according to new interpretive bearings. Interpretive rupture results in a "lack of equivalence" between interpretive faith communities, particularly when experience brings a change in a person's social situation or understanding of faith.

Ruth experienced interpretive rupture when she moved to another church that provided a very different interpretive faith community compared to her previous church. Ruth went to Saint Simon Bible Chapel, a Brethren church, in her adolescence and describes it as having been "traditional and patriarchal." However, during this stage of her life, Ruth did not question the patriarchal nature of the church and its leadership structure. Not knowing any differently, Ruth accepted patriarchy's ideological dimension, viewing it as normal and universal. This acceptance lasted until Ruth was seventeen and moved away from home. She attended Victory Pentecostal Church, whose culture was completely unlike what she had been used to at Saint Simon Bible Chapel. Ruth not only saw women in leadership, but also began to hear stories of healing as she learned about the gifts of the Holy Spirit. This was a striking contrast to Saint Simon Bible Chapel, which did not acknowledge (let alone teach about) healing or the gifts of the Holy Spirit. In encountering this new interpretive faith community, Ruth said she was suddenly faced with questions about "What is true?" and "What is the reality?"

At one of Victory Pentecostal Church's healing services, Ruth not only experienced the Holy Spirit for the first time, but also received healing for a back disease. Ruth recalls:

RUTH: *I remember sitting at the back with my legs crossed and my arms fold-ed, determined that I was only there to observe and it was just a load of hogwash, basically. Until, of course, they do the altar call, and then all of a sudden I find that I'm up there. And even before the guy started pray-ing for me, I realized that it was actually my heart that needed healing, not my back, which was what I had the issues with. I had a disease in my back. And I don't think I ever doubted the fact that God could heal if he wanted to, and I think that's a bit of a cop out because it kind of gives you an out, but the question was always, "Would he heal?" So anyway, I went up and this gentleman prayed for me, and I had a vision of my back and this white light going down my back. And up until this day, I had to have my back manipulated two or three times a day—just cracked back into place—and my mum used to do it at home. And from that day on, I haven't had to have it done again, so you know, there are those sort of things. So you can't go back to something like Saint Simon Chapel where they won't even acknowledge that a healing has taken place.*

At first, Ruth did not want to believe what she was hearing at Victory Pentecostal Church as she began to experience cognitive dissonance. The interpretive rupture brought about by her healing resolved some of this dissonance, which allowed Ruth to discard the teachings of her previous church surrounding healing and gifts of the Holy Spirit and instead em-brace the teaching of Victory Pentecostal Church. Ruth's story illustrates the way that church congregations can be "at once a major source of cogni-tive dissonance for the individual and a major vehicle for eliminating and reducing the dissonance that may exist."[29]

Ruth's healing broadened her understanding and experience of God and faith. The experience became a critical filter through which she now evaluates sermons and theology. Her story now no longer fitted within the interpretive strategies of Saint Simon Chapel, which did not acknowledge healing and continued to operate within a patriarchal structure. Preaching reflects the culture and theology of a church. If a church does not believe in healing or the gifts of the Spirit, then these theological topics are not going to be preached on, except perhaps to deny their reality. In contrast, churches that believe in healing and the gifts of the Holy Spirit will offer prayer ministry for healing and preach sermons that proclaim the ongoing work of the Holy Spirit.

29. Festinger, *Theory*, 177.

Surprisingly, Ruth and her husband Timothy did return to Saint Simon Chapel when they moved back to the area. Upon her returned to Saint Simon Chapel, Ruth did not experience interpretive dissonance. Instead, Ruth can now critically engage with the teachings of Saint Simon Chapel and their interpretation of Scripture without further dissonance. Ruth now ascribes to very few of the church's teaching and no longer agrees with the prohibition of women in leadership. The couple went back because of familiarity and to pick up established relationships. It is possible to be connected socially to a church community through relationships while being disconnected as an "outsider" both theologically and interpretively. Ruth and Timothy could thus be considered "theologically disengaged adherents." What is also apparent in several of the interviews is the way in which belonging is often defined as belonging to a group of people in the church rather than to the church as a whole. In Ruth and Timothy's situation, there is a sense of belonging socially and relationally, but not theologically or interpretively.

Interpretive Rupture and Spiritual Dissonance

Carlos experienced interpretive rupture not through encountering an alternative or opposing interpretive faith community, but instead through trying to live out what he was hearing in sermons in his own church. During his time at Koru Pentecostal, Carlos heard numerous sermons on successful Christian living and aspects of the prosperity gospel that taught him if one gives to God (through the church) then he will give back:

CARLOS: *And so I got inspired [from the preaching] and that was definitely driving the motivation to go into business for myself. So I went into business full-time and I formed my own company a few years before that. So I sunk a lot of time, investment, and money. Basically I soaked up all of my personal savings to survive and invest in this idea that I had for a company. And then, when I couldn't push it any further, couldn't borrow any more money, couldn't take it anywhere, I gave up. And that was a really devastating experience for me because all the teaching and all the beliefs that I had heard at Koru Pentecostal saying that "God wants you to succeed, God wants you to have a huge business, you've just got to give more away to get this and all that." I had bought into that kind of thinking.*

Were you giving quite a bit away for your business to succeed?

CARLOS: *Yes, definitely, and not in a blackmail way. I just expected—you know, they're saying that you're going to receive this, and ask and you shall receive. I just blindly believed that because I had done so much, that it was just all going to fall into place. That was the time that I had started up this other relationship with this girl in the leadership. So it was just a mixed-up period of time where a lot of what I assumed to be right wasn't found to be so. And a lot of stuff that I had been told would happen didn't happen.*

According to Festinger, the "Processes of social communication and social influence are . . . inextricably interwoven with processes of creation and reduction of dissonance."[30] Carlos was deeply hurt by his sense of failure and the spiritual dissonance it caused:

CARLOS: *I just felt really broken and really just wanted to tell God, "Fuck you! This is too painful."*

Did you?

CARLOS: *No, I was too scared to, eh. That was back in the stage where I was expecting to turn into a pillar of salt if I told God to fuck off, eh [laughs]. So that just was fantastic [sarcastic tone]. That fuelled a huge belt of depression. Just what the hell had happened? I had done everything that they said.*

Did you blame God?

CARLOS: *Possibly. I think it was a mixture. I blamed myself and I blamed God.*

What about the leaders that were preaching the success message?

CARLOS: *No. I didn't think about it at all . . . Until I went back that one time. And I saw the culture that I was in. And the things they had been speaking. And just realized that I had been a sucker for what they were saying. They weren't very strong on critical thinking, critical analysis, perspectives outside of church. Basically, their scenario would be "If you*

30. Ibid.

put God first in your life then he's going to sort you out. You can't fail."
So I put God first. I had done everything I possibly could have imagined
to make it work and failed.

Did you feel quite misled?

CARLOS: *Yeah! But not at the time. It took me a while to actually get a per-*
spective on what happened and why it happened.

The interpretive rupture Carlos experienced from Koru Pentecostal's
theology of success began his detachment from his previous reliance on the
pastors as external sources of authority whom he had "blindly believed."
What Sharon Parks has called the "tyranny of the they," began to be under-
mined when this relocation of authority took place within Carlos and he
started to submit the preaching to an executive ego.[31] Reflecting back, Carlos views the experience as a good one in a holistic kind of way. However,
it has made Carlos deeply sceptical about what you get "sold" at church.
Carlos now makes certain that "You believe it for yourself. And to make
sure, in essence, that you don't believe everything hook, line, and sinker.
That you don't get so engrossed in what someone else tells you that you
forget to believe what you believe."

With this new sense of self-authority and reflexivity, Carlos has
shifted from listening to sermons where he simply believes what is said
unquestioningly, to listening critically by filtering the message through his
own experiential reality. Carlos' comments surrounding Koru Pentecostal
demonstrate this new critical perspective: "They definitely extract certain
Scriptures to encourage their point of view at the neglect of other Scriptures. Actually, I found that Koru Pente was very, very shallow in Scriptural
teaching. It was a lot more motivational teaching."

Changing interpretive communities through church switching is one
of the strategies young adults employed to reduce dissonance. Preaching
was often responsible for the cognitive dissonance that Carlos and some
of the other young adults I interviewed experienced. Switching to another
church from Koru Pentecostal was a refreshing move for Carlos. Carlos
described it as "phenomenal to have some depth in the teaching and critical
analysis of what they were saying."

Personal experience is an important frame of reference for people in
responding to a sermon. As such, churches that offer an experience of God

31. Parks, cited in Fowler, *Stages*, 154.

or the Spirit as part of their ministry need to be more sensitive to how they frame the invitation. It is not uncommon for pastors to present the call to come forward for prayer or "ministry" in a way that guarantees a particular encounter with God. The pastor might say something like, "I feel like there are people here who are tired and spiritually dry. Come forward for prayer, God wants to refresh you." Carlos explains that this is an area of church that he struggles with because

CARLOS: *I've been up to so many alter calls, or so many experience-based alter calls, where you go up and supposedly get an experience with God and then your life is back to normal and you're OK with everything. And I actually hold, not a resentment, just . . . I probably hold a level of disappointment that I've been up to so many of those alter calls at the front and never had anything happen. And so that, as an experience, is always a part of my Christianity, is not essential to whatever I believe because it's been knocked out of me so many times. My expectation of that actually working is low.*

So did you go up to the front?

CARLOS: *No. I actually walked out.*

So it was something that grated?

CARLOS: *Yeah, it does really grate me, eh. It gets my wick.*

So what grates for you?

CARLOS: *I actually think they are promising something that they can't deliver. They are promising an experience of God and saying that will really help you. Not saying it's essential, but they're telling you that God wants to give you this experience, and then you go up believing that God wants to give you this experience, and it doesn't happen. And so someone is not living up to their promise.*

An important theme that emerges out of Carlos' story is the way that life experience becomes a stronger lens for evaluating and assessing sermons. The reality preached is measured against a person's lived reality. If there is a lack of equivalence between the two, then aberrant decodings occur or the sermon maybe discredited altogether.

Life experience has resulted in Caleb rethinking what he had previously been taught in the churches he has been affiliated with over the years. Caleb stopped going to church during his final few years at university. He got to a point where he got over church and Christianity. This was a result of spiritual burnout from quite extraordinary expectations of his faith. Caleb's enthusiasm and the devotion he put into practicing and developing his faith came through strongly as he shared his story. "I think I was still trying to be some legend Christian person," said Caleb. "So I was, you know, I suppose I was pretty hard out. Like I'd go away for weekends to pray and, you know, like rent huts and just clear off and go and try and seek God for the future and all this sort of stuff . . . And I guess that probably just had to give after a while."

Considering Caleb's high expectations of what his faith should look like and what he should be experiencing, it is unsurprising that Caleb experienced spiritual dissonance in the form of a "gulf" between expectations and reality. Festinger argues that individuals strive towards consistency within themselves. This consistency exists, for the most part, between what a person knows or believes and how they act and chose to live.[32] Caleb found consistency by letting go of many of his expectations of faith and leaving the church for a time.

Caleb was challenged by a sermon he heard recently about having expectations of God. However, Caleb now interpreted that message much differently than he would have during his charismatic days.

CALEB: *But I don't, I definitely don't expect any pay back for anything I do for God or anything like that. I'm past that kind of thinking or mentality. But you know, I'd been raised up on that sort of teaching that says, "Take one step towards and he'll take a thousand steps towards you," you know, all of those really cliché sayings. And that kind of flavor would come through in a lot of the early teaching that I listened to. And now I just don't ascribe to it . . . that sales pitch that if you do this and that, God will bless you and God will honor you and God will stand by you. I mean yeah, maybe he does, but I don't really know what that looks like.*

---

32. Festinger notes, however, that people "are not always successful in explaining away or in rationalizing inconsistencies to themselves. For one reason or another, attempts to achieve consistency may fail. The inconsistency then simply continues to exist. Under such circumstances—that is, in the presence of inconsistency—there is psychological discomfort" ("Theory," 2).

Caleb has done more than just rethink the "sales pitch" that if you live in a particular way then God will bless you; he now no longer ascribes to it at all. At the time of our interview, Caleb had started going to a church that holds a similar view and understanding of faith as he did.

The young adults interviewed for this research give preaching serious consideration when choosing a church. Preaching remains an important source of spiritual growth, challenge, and inspiration. Viewing churches as interpretive communities of memory adds insight into the role preaching plays in the switching process and can help us understand why young adults are attracted to one church over another, or can no longer stay in their current church community. The challenge for preachers is to accurately assess where the congregation as a whole stands in relation to their understanding and knowledge of faith. Are people predominantly new to the faith? Or have they been followers of Jesus and involved in church for most of their lives, as the majority of my participants had been? Reflexive ecclesiology has much to offer to the practice of preaching in churches.

Familiarity syndrome of sermons can be addressed through relevant applications to people's everyday life. This includes the importance of engaging with struggles, doubts, and failure in ways that do not simply spiritualize such difficulties with Christian jargon that young adults decode as vacuous language, inauthentic and lacking realness. Young adults are testing what they hear against life experience, and cognitive dissonance can occur when they attempt to put what they hear in preaching into practice. One of the strategies for dealing with spiritual and cognitive dissonance is to switch churches. It is hard for a person to remain in a church where interpretive rupture has occurred, especially when the teaching has been tried and found wanting, often to the pain, confusion, and grief of the person. People look for an interpretive community that reflects who they are, their values and understanding of faith, and one that is also consistent with their experiential reality.

8

Church Two-Timing

There was a period of about a year and a half when, every Sunday morning, I attended an average-sized Baptist church of around one hundred to 150 people, consisting of families and a growing number of young adults along with several older people. Come Sunday evening, I would head off to an informal Anglican service whose demographics predominantly consisted of young adults (twenty- and thirty-somethings). The Anglican church seemed to grow every week and would regularly have two hundred to 250-plus people attending on a Sunday night. Although the services at the respective churches had some stylistic differences, and even sensory differences stimulated by very different church buildings, my reason for going was not to experience such differences. Instead, my practice of what I call "church two-timing" was relationally motivated. I became involved in Milford Baptist Church through a good friend who is the pastor there. My attraction to Saint Paul's Anglican was the young adult demographic. While my motives for attending Saint Paul's were largely social, I was also regularly encouraged spiritually there. Church two-timing enabled me to maintain and develop friendships with people at the two churches. My church two-timing was made easier by the fact that Milford Baptist did not have an evening service. However, I did not expect that my research would lead me to encounter so many other church two-timers. Out of the fifty young adults I interviewed, twelve were, or have been, involved in church two-timing.

The Concept of Church Two-Timing

Church two-timing is the practice of attending two churches simultaneously. People involved in church two-timing attend two churches regularly, often involving different denominations but not always involving different expressions of faith. Church two-timing consists of a primary church and a secondary church. A person's commitment, involvement, and sense of belonging are associated with the primary church. In contrast, there is no or very little sense of obligation or desire to become involved in the secondary church. As I discuss below, there are some exceptions to this pattern, for some of the young adults I interviewed did feel a sense of belonging and community at both their primary and secondary churches.

The concept of church two-timing is not without its connotative problems, and so needs some further clarification. Church two-timing is not meant pejoratively. Rather, it is meant to express the relational dimension and tensions the practice can entail. Two-timing, then, is a relational metaphor applied to church affiliation, but without the associated negative connotations of "unfaithfulness" or "cheating" on another person (or in this case, church). Such connotations aside, the concept does capture something of the tensions and questions of loyalty that arise for some people when attending two churches. Distinguishing between primary and secondary churches extends this relational metaphor, because people have a different relationship to each of their churches. Primary and secondary churches serve different functions, and the experiences of the young adults I interviewed suggests that people often have different modes of engagement with each of their two churches. Engagement with the primary church appears to be more holistic in terms of people's integration into the life of the faith community beyond the church service. In contrast, engagement with the secondary church tends to be more selective and predominantly limited to the church service.

The Tension of Church Two-Timing

Alisha is a twenty-three-year-old single woman who has been involved in various churches throughout her life. When I asked whether her reasons for going to church had changed over the years, she said that she now approaches church with "less of a consumer-orientated mentality" and "a little less selfishly." When Alisha first came to Auckland, New Zealand's biggest city, she considered herself a "religious consumer" in her approach to finding a church. Church was about what could best meet her spiritual needs, including certain criteria such as preaching and worship. Now, however, as Alisha explains, "It's more about what you can contribute as well. How I can be the most effective as well as being challenged and encouraged."

With a "spiritual marketplace" of over 230 churches to choose from in Auckland, Alisha was not short on choices. This increased range of choice in churches raises the likelihood that people will be able to find a variety of churches that match their needs in terms of both individual commitment and church community. The practice of two-timing takes place within this spiritual marketplace as people are drawn to attend different churches to find a more complete fit to what they are looking for.

Over a six-month period, Alisha attended two distinctly different churches: Totara Baptist and New Hope Pentecostal. The two churches were demographically different, and as one might expect, differed stylistically. New Hope Pentecostal had hundreds of youth and young adults attending worship with contemporary, lively, high-energy music. The morning services attracted around six hundred to seven hundred people and the evening service drew about eight hundred to one thousand. Totara Baptist, by comparison, hardly had any youth, let alone young adults. When Alisha started going, there were typically three to four young adults in a total congregation of less than one hundred. She ended up attending Totara Baptist at the invitation of a friend. Alisha's story is an example of how relational connections are often more of a determining factor in people's decision-making process about church affiliation than denominational considerations.

However, church two-timing created a sense of tension for Alisha:

ALISHA: *So the more I did it [attended both churches], the more confused I got as to what church I wanted to go to, and so I knew I had to decide because I knew it was bugging me a lot. I was very close to going to the New Hope Pentecostal. But I didn't, because I felt that whole connection to that family again at Totara Baptist. And I knew that it wouldn't benefit me if I left Totara Baptist at that stage of my life. I need to stick around. So I totally stopped going to New Hope because it was confusing me too much.*

Divided loyalties?

ALISHA: Yeah, and I was confused about the whole thing. So I thought I'd just stick to one and commit myself to that one, because I was constantly comparing Totara to New Hope and vice versa, and they are completely different churches and serve completely different purposes. It wasn't helpful.

Choosing Totara Baptist over New Hope Pentecostal was a surprising choice. Alisha felt that New Hope Pentecostal targeted her age group and in a way that she felt comfortable inviting her friends who had no church background to join her there. As she described it, "It's a cool church. It's meeting that cultural need of my age group with the music, and everyone's young and has got cool clothes and it's the whole image thing, and its quite appealing in that sense." The importance Alisha gives to the symbolic dimension of church is captured in her phrase "it's the whole image thing." New Hope reflected Alisha's identity more closely than Totara Baptist, especially in the sense of taste: style of music, clothes, and overall image. But the attraction and distinction of New Hope was in more than just taste, it was also in the church's demographic makeup consisting of people her own age and in a similar stage of life. The "symbolic search," as discussed in earlier chapters, is undertaken to find a church that reflects the identity of the individual: What does this church suggest about who I am?[1]

Despite New Hope Pentecostal being a good symbolic fit for Alisha, she became increasingly aware of a growing tension between having a consumer mentality and being more committed to a church:

ALISHA: I had that mentality a little bit, like it met my needs in these areas. And a lot of friends were saying, "Well, is Totara Baptist meeting your needs?" And in some ways it wasn't, so that's what got me thinking, you know. I think that at the end of the day, I learned that that should not really be the reason, what you can get out of it all the time—that's just consumerism. How uncool is that?

Religious consumerism, for Alisha and others I interviewed, misses the heart of what church is all about. Church is seen as a place to give as well as to receive. Church is not understood as a "religious service provider," but rather as a faith community and a place to gather to worship God together.

---

1. See Hopewell, *Congregations*, 29.

After all, it was the intimacy of the community at Totara Baptist that drew Alisha in, together with the opportunity to be involved, that became the decisive factor in her decision to attend this church exclusively. What is interesting is participants' conscious awareness and acknowledgment of when they feel that they are simply consuming and then the action taken to change this "mentality" of consumption as Alisha described it. To some extent, the tension Alisha felt from church two-timing stemmed from her sense that it was motivated by a consumer mentality towards church. Alisha's reaction against a consumer mentality in choosing a church based on whether it met her personal needs lends weight to Paul Johnson's argument for the need to consider the market model of religion, where people are seen as "religious consumers," in partnership with the concept of religious communities.[2]

Questions of Belonging

Alan is a twenty-three-year-old who came to faith when he was nineteen. He is from an unchurched background and family. His first experience of church was at a large Pentecostal church at a service of over one thousand people that a friend invited him to attend at university. Another friend invited Alan to Totara Baptist Church. He started attending the same two churches as Alisha had: New Hope Pentecostal and Totara Baptist, each very different in both style and demographics. Stylistically, Alan found Totara Baptist to be a struggle:

ALAN: *I was struggling, 'cause I was going to New Hope Pentecostal, which is really charismatic and bouncy, bouncy church. We always have lots of noise and music and "Let's just be really expressive of our faith." Whereas Totara Baptist was almost the complete opposite where it's "Let's play the organ, one person on the organ, let's not lift our hands up in church, and let's just . . ." It was a really traditional service. It reinforced my previous expectations of what church was like. I went from seeing, like, "Praise Be" on TV and going there is no way I am going to that . . . I couldn't understand why young people would want to go to a church like Totara Baptist. I couldn't understand it at all.*

2. Johnson, "Religious Markets."

From a market model perspective and as a religious consumer, Totara Baptist Church had little to offer, particularly stylistically, to young people and young adults. Somewhat surprisingly, Alan also eventually ended up choosing to attend this smaller Baptist church over the vibrant Pentecostal church that he had originally considered far more relevant to his life. Like Alisha, Alan was drawn into the community at Totara Baptist, which began with a deep impression left by the pastor of the church:

ALAN: *I had a conversation with him once, the first time he met me, and about two months later he remembered everything we talked about. It was really cool having somebody as a pastor that I could just talk to, and he'd remember everything about me and come over and say, "Hello, come out and have coffee." Nothing against the pastor at New Hope. He's just got five thousand people he has to get around, which is never going to happen.*

Size preferences do matter for many people when it comes to deciding on a church, and there are attractions and advantages that come with being part of either a small or large congregation. Alan was originally attracted to New Hope Pentecostal Church by the sense of vibrancy and energy its large size created. But he was also attracted to the intimacy he experienced in Totara Baptist Church. Alan explained, "I wasn't wanting to grow into Totara Baptist, it was growing into me. Like the family at Totara was just awesome. Like, I would walk in and people would remember my name, and they just all remembered what I had been doing and what I was hoping to do with my life."

In addition to this experience of community at Totara Baptist, Alan appreciated the space and creative freedom the smaller church afforded its handful of young adults to try new things. This contrasted sharply with New Hope, where size of the congregation meant that people who wanted to get involved in something like playing in the worship band had to undergo a lengthy process. Research on religion of young adults has found that having "entrepreneurial" or "innovative" institutional space in which to create religious expressions based on lifestyle interests or issues pertaining to a particular stage of life is important to an increasing number of people in this age group.[3] Over time, however, Alan began to feel a conflict of interests from his practice of church two-timing. Two-timing raised the question of belonging for Alan. He got to a point where he asked himself, "What is my

3. See Flory and Miller, *GenX*, and Flory and Miller, *Finding Faith*.

own church?" He did not know how to answer. He felt like he could not give his full commitment to either church because of this ambiguity. In the end, Alan decided that he had to give one up, and so he stopped attending New Hope Pentecostal Church.

Christina did not experience the confusion that Alisha did, or questions of belonging that Alan faced in her own practice of church two-timing. Christina was clear on what her primary and secondary churches were. Christina was committed to Totara Baptist, which she described as her "home church." The tension for Christina arose out of her motive for going to her secondary church, All Saints:

You also went to All Saints for a period. What was behind that?

CHRISTINA: *Wrong motivation. I was still learning who I was in God, and still felt that I needed to be in a relationship to be complete. And part of going to All Saints was meeting new people and not primarily on the hunt, but I guess just expanding a little bit. So I've stopped going. I knew my intentions were wrong. I think if my intentions, even the smallest intention, is wrong then I don't feel right going.*

How we frame and understand our motives can result in the same action being a source of tension. Christina judged going to a church to find a partner as wrong, and so she stopped going to All Saints. For other participants, going to church to find a partner was a perfectly justifiable motive. For Mills, motives and social actions are integrally linked: "The motives actually used in justifying or criticizing an act definitely link it to situations, integrate one man's action with another's, and line up conduct with norms. The societally sustained motive-surrogates of situations are both constraints and inducements."[4]

How does going to church to find a partner, or to meet new people, come to be categorized as a "wrong motive"? There is usually a range of reasons that motivate people to go to church, some of which have been discussed throughout this book. Motives for going to church cannot be simply reduced to spiritual and religious reasons. Motives often include practical reasons, such as friendship and finding a partner. "Mixed motives," are not the same as "wrong motives." Perhaps Christina had heard sermons about the "right" reasons for coming to church and used such a frame of reference to conclude that her dominant reasons for going to All Saints fell outside of

---

4. Mill, "Situated," 908.

this. However Christina came to conclude that her motives were "wrong," it was reason enough to stop attending All Saints and hence stop the practice of church two-timing.

To return to Alan's story, he had started dating a woman from New Hope Pentecostal and started church two-timing again. This followed a brief interlude of only attending Totara Baptist, where he had resolved the question of belonging. Now Alan articulates a spiritual motive for attendance at New Hope: one of spiritual nourishment. Alan was inspired by the worship and energy at New Hope and realized how much he had missed it. It provided a strong contrast with the Baptist church. However, his commitment remained at Totara Baptist. He used the Pentecostal church to fuel his own energy, passion, and enthusiasm for serving at the Baptist church. The roles of the primary and secondary church were more clearly defined this time around, which helped Alan avoid the a conflict of interests and questions of belonging that Alan had previously experienced from church two-timing. Alan explains:

ALAN: *At the start of this year I was just like, "Man, where are we going with this? Are we looking to excel it or not?" And then New Hope Pentecostal came along, the girl came along, and I was like, "Wow, I've missed this so much," and I was going along Friday night, Sunday after the morning service at Totara Baptist, then Sunday night as well. So I was going to four or five services a week 'cause I was totally into it. I went to their church camp and I went to Totara's church camp, and it was just . . . going to New Hope ignited my passion for God like I don't even know how many times over . . . one hundred times over. It gave me this huge buzz to go back into Totara Baptist and to feed what I was getting from New Hope back into Totara.*

We see in Alisha and Alan's stories commitment and involvement in a church community. This communal orientation of embedded faith is also an expression of the constituted and covenanted self, and only makes sense in the context of community. Both the constituted self and the covenanted self find expression within a church community and stand in contrast to the individualistic nature of the religious consumer.[5] If we were to view affili-

5. See also Flory and Miller, "Embodied Spirituality," and Belzer et al., who argue that the faith of those participating in congregational life only makes sense within the context of a faith community rather than as an individualized spiritual quest, or privatized faith, in "Congregations That Get It."

ation with a secondary church on its own, then, by all accounts it appears to have the hallmarks of the unencumbered self, based upon the pure, undetermined choice, free of tradition, obligation, or commitment. However, when viewed within the practice of church two-timing, the unencumbered self is in fact a covenanted self anchored to a primary church community.

Inspired by One Church to Serve at Another

Amy and Bob, a couple who are now in their thirties, started church two-timing in their teenage years. They both attended their respective family churches, which for Bob was more out of a sense of "pressure from Mum and Dad." The advantage of church two-timing for Bob and Amy was that it enabled them to go to a church with their family, fulfilling family expectations and obligations, while at the same time belong to another church independent of their parents' gaze. Bob made friends with a group of teenagers from a church on the other side of Auckland from where he lived. Bob began attending this church with his friends, having to catch three to four different buses in order to attend. This secondary church, Rimu Baptist, ended up becoming his primary church as he became more and more involved in the youth group there. His family church, Harvest Pentecostal, had a noticeable absence of young people. Church two-timing for Bob was not about experiencing denominational differences between the Pentecostal and Baptist churches; rather, each church signified a different mode of attendance based on his different relationship with each church: family versus friends. Attending Harvest Pentecostal was a religious practice signifying family time that Bob attended out of a sense of obligation. In contrast, attending Rimu Baptist signified Bob's voluntary decision to attend church with his friends as he began to pursue his own faith journey independently from his parents.

Bob left Rimu Baptist after having attended for six years, shortly after breaking up with his girlfriend, who also attended the church. Bob remembered going back to the church two weeks later and feeling that, "It just didn't seem like my church anymore. It was just sort of an instant . . . I didn't feel right going there." Bob said that he immediately changed churches and began going to Koru Pentecostal Church with one of his friends. They had already been going there periodically through some of their other friends and knew that they liked the church and its strong focus on youth.

Bob started dating another girl who was involved in the youth ministry at Saint Joseph's Presbyterian Church, where he had also begun helping out. Both of them attended Koru Pentecostal in the evenings. One of the things that attracted Bob to this youth-focused church was anonymity:

BOB: *I think what attracted me was just being an anonymous part of the church. Because I was heavily involved in Rimu Baptist and with the way Mum and Dad and Uncle Tom had made a stamp on Harvest Pentecostal, I couldn't really walk into a Pentecostal church at that time and be anonymous. I was always Clive Hewson's son, or Uncle Tom's nephew. And that brought good reactions and bad reactions. And at Koru Pentecostal I was just some guy in the congregation.*

Koru Pentecostal became Amy and Bob's secondary church as their commitments and responsibilities grew at their primary church, Saint Joseph's Presbyterian. The senior pastor at Saint Joseph's knew that Bob and Amy were also attending Koru Pentecostal, and as Bob explained, "She released us to do that and was quite happy for us to do that." I asked Bob whether having that support from the senior pastor was encouraging, to which he replied:

BOB: *Yeah, it was really encouraging because we had the best of both worlds. We got to go and minister and give out to a congregation and then in the evening come and get fed by a completely different congregation without any strings attached. And in my mind that's the best of both worlds. Because having worked in different churches, when you are at church you are on the job, you know, and it's sometimes very difficult to worship when you are worried about the microphone falling over or something because you work there, you know what I mean? And that was another group that came here, people that were in ministry in other churches.*

Amy went on to explain that often it was ministers and elders who were church two-timing, going "to just soak in the worship and not have to worry about whether it's their day on board or not." Bob described this approach to the secondary church as being like a smorgasbord: "Where you turn up and help yourself and go home." Bob's description of church being "like a smorgasbord" where one may simply help oneself to what one wants and leave the rest is the ideal setting for a religious consumer. However, Bob and Amy's story is more complex than simple religious consumerism. They were connected to the leadership at Koru Pentecostal, where they found support for their work with young people at Saint Joseph's Church. Amy's comments show that two-timing can provide spiritual benefits for church leaders. Church leaders and people involved in ministry in their primary church are equipped, refreshed, and often inspired in their faith by their secondary church, which can benefit their involvement in their primary church.

It is possible to see Bob's "helping himself" at the religious smorgasbord and other church leaders going to "just soak in worship" at one church in order to serve at another as what cultural theorist Michel de Certeau has called "secondary production."[6] Secondary production, according to de Certeau, is the domain of consumers, which I extend here to worshippers in a church service. The focus and attention of secondary production is on what the consumer "makes" or "does" with what they consume. So Bob takes what he wants from his secondary church and "uses" it to energize and refresh him spiritually. Having been refreshed and refuelled this way, Bob feels he is able to keep giving and serving in his primary church, Saint Joseph's Presbyterian. A genuine desire to go to a church service to worship God is in itself an act of offering something to the "Divine Other" rather than taking, and is hence why I am reluctant to use "religious consumption" to describe Bob and Amy's church two-timing.

For Bob and Amy, the practice of church two-timing enables the couple to worship God at Koru Pentecostal free of the distraction and responsibility they experience in their involvement at Saint Joseph's Presbyterian. Unlike Alisha and Alan, Bob and Amy did not experience any of the tensions that so often come along with church two-timing. For Bob and Amy, having the best of both worlds included sharing a sense of belonging and community at both churches.

What is interesting in Amy and Bob's practice of two-timing is that the leadership of the two churches was very supportive and encouraged them in what they were doing. The leadership at their primary church realized the important role that the secondary church played in spiritually refreshing Amy and Bob. As Amy explains regarding the primary church, "They [the leadership of the Presbyterian church] were like, 'There is no one your age here, so obviously that sense of community and friendship is important for you there. You know, we love that it is filling you up and that you've got good teaching and care because what you are learning there, that skill is coming out here and blessing us.'"

6. de Certeau, *Practice of Everyday Life*, xiii.

The leadership at Koru Pentecostal took on a supporting role as the couple's secondary church, providing encouragement and even pastoral care for Amy and Bob and the ministry they had among young people at Saint Joseph's Presbyterian:

AMY: *The old leadership at Koru Pentecostal were extremely pastoral to us and they released us to do the work we were doing at the Presbyterian church. And so I was basically, like, this missionary to the Presbyterians and they cared for us and counseled us and included us in all the leadership developments that were happening, and prayed for what we were doing and were stoked for what we were doing with the Presies and supported it. But the new wave of leadership just could not get their head around it.*

Both churches Amy and Bob attended had recently undergone leadership changes. The new leadership was not supportive of the couple's two-timing. Some of the resources that were shared between the two churches as a result of Bob and Amy's dual affiliation have now come to an end. This has resulted in Amy and Bob feeling disconnected to both churches and feeling it is perhaps time to change to another church (singular) altogether. Currently, they are in a place of limbo as they decide what their next move will be in relation to church attendance.

Jack ended up church two-timing because his girlfriend went to a different church than he attended. There was a brief period when Jack was involved in both churches, but he soon realized that his primary church would not understand: "I didn't really tell people at Flaxbush Baptist that I was helping with that [group at Koru Pentecostal] because you are helping outside of Flaxbush and that's not what you did. But I obviously did enough within Flaxbush that people didn't notice that I was doing something else." Apart from this brief period, Jack's formal church involvement was solely at Flaxbush Baptist. Jack's secondary church inspired, or as he said, "re-inspired" him to serve in youth ministry at his primary church, Flaxbush Baptist: "I never felt a belonging in Koru Pentecostal, but I felt like I could charge myself there in a way that I had lost at Flaxbush, to take a renewed passion back to keep doing what we were doing, but try and put something new into it each time."

Jack went on to explain where that passion came from:

JACK: *I think at Koru, you saw people more alive in their faith from a visual perspective. It was more of a charismatic approach to worship and just their lives. I mean, you look at the depth of their theology and it was probably, now that I look back, incredibly shallow in comparison to what I had been experiencing at Flaxbush. But there was a reality in that that I needed to be refreshed by. And it was that refreshing which I felt like I could come back and then apply the theology, which I had learned and then re-input back into an environment of service. So I was able to do what I was doing but out of a bit of passion rather than, aw man, no one else is going to fill this void.*

It is only in hindsight that Jack describes the theology and teaching at Koru as being "shallow." At the time, Jack said that "I was taking what I could, the goodness out of it, rather than picking it for what it wasn't. So I wasn't necessarily critiquing a lack of [depth]." Jack's engagement at Koru was with the experiential side of the service. It also mitigated a shift in Jack's "vocabulary of motive" from serving out of love or "passion" to a motive of "duty and obligation." Considering Jack's comments, we might suggest that, for Jack, the former motive signifies enthusiasm and life, while the later signifies unwillingness and burden. Or to put it another way, serving out of passion provides an energy and enthusiasm that had been noticeably absent in Jack when he had served out of a sense of obligation alone.

Exploring the Wider Church Landscape

Dylan, a twenty-seven-year-old who has been involved in Immanuel Bible Chapel all his life, has, as he says, "always been a bit sceptical about the whole shop around until you find a church that kind of does it for you." Immanuel Bible Chapel is a small brethren church of about fifty to sixty people of all age groups, but only a handful of youth and young adults. There is no evening service. Dylan acknowledges that it would be nice to go to a church where there were more people of his age and stage of life. One of the main reasons that he stays at Immanuel Bible Chapel is that he feels there is work to be done in his current church. For Dylan, church isn't just about having his own needs and wants met spiritually:

Have you looked around at all?

DYLAN: *Yeah. I go to other churches as well, just sometimes in the evenings to hear some preaching, partly because I'm involved in the kids program on Sunday mornings. I'm never in church in the morning to hear the speaker. Half the time it's my Dad, so I probably get the message there.*

Over lunch at home?

DYLAN: *Yeah. So I never get to hear the speaker. So sometimes I visit other churches and move around to hear and see what is going on in other places, and sometimes that is very encouraging.*

Church two-timing enables Dylan to visit other churches in the evenings to hear preaching, which he misses out on in his primary church. He also occasionally borrows a van to take a group of young people on these church expeditions. This is an easier alternative than trying to start an evening service for these young people, who remain committed to this family church. Not only does church two-timing in this situation save a drain on limited human resources, it also has the potential to encourage the young people of Immanuel Bible Chapel to remain involved in this smaller church rather than migrating to any number of youth-focused churches around Auckland.

Dylan's strategy of taking young people to a secondary church is not without risks, as Belinda's story illustrates. Belinda started church two-timing as a thirteen-year-old through her youth group leader at Rata Baptist Church, who took a group of teenagers from their home church to Koru Pentecostal Church in the evenings. Belinda found Rata Baptist to be more personally relevant than Saint Luke's Methodist, which she had attended with her mother before switching to Rata Baptist, and she soon found the Koru Pentecostal to be more relevant than Rata. Being more relevant for Belinda meant that the church was "more fun than Rata Baptist, and had way more young people."

It was not long before Belinda switched to Koru Pentecostal completely. Belinda's sense of connection to Rata Baptist had been to a group of young people there, most of whom were now going to Koru Pentecostal. The community she had belonged to at Rata Baptist was no longer there. Belinda started to connect with people at Koru Pentecostal and make new friends. From a teenager's perspective, Koru Pentecostal provided a very different interpretive faith community:

BELINDA: *And then I began going to Koru all the time. I started connecting with people and making friends. Again I guess they had a different message. They have a real sort of ethos—is that the right word? And they had a whole bunch of different values. They were really focused on young people and investing in them.*

Belinda's story allows us to begin to understand the important role that demographics play in making a church relevant. This is another example of demographic relevance. Relevance has a strong social component, because the demographic makeup of a church can determine the issues covered and certainly shapes the church culture. Koru Pentecostal's demographic shaped its youth culture and focus. It is also an example of the growing visibility of aged-based religious patterns, which Roozen and Hadaway have described as the "creation of an enduring stratification of religious expression by age."[7] When the relevance of a church is strongly associated with its demographics—namely, consisting of people the same age and stage of life—then people can end up switching churches as a consequence of the stage of life disconnect.

For Dylan, the practice of church two-timing involves a different church on the side each week, though there are periods where he does not attend another church in the evenings at all. Dylan's secondary churches can be seen as a form of "spiritual clubbing," where people check out trendy spiritual places just as they might check out new and exciting clubs in the urban nightlife landscape. In today's deregulated spiritual marketplace, it is argued that individuals are approaching church in very different ways than they have in the past. A number of religious observers and sociologist have used "religious consumerism" to describe this changing orientation.[8] While church two-timing is certainly a different approach to church, people like Dylan do not make sense of visiting other churches in terms of religious consumption. Although his comment, "getting those things from other places," such as preaching—a stylistic expression of worship attractive and relevant to his stage of life—could easily be interpreted from a consumer perspective. But for Dylan, two-timing is interpreted through both his commitment to his smaller church and his engagement with preaching and

7. Roozen and Hadaway, "Individuals," 31.

8. See Roof, *Spiritual Marketplace*, and Lineham, "Three Types."

worship at other churches as an important practice of faith. In this way, Dylan's secondary churches provide a source of spiritual nourishment.

The Spiritual Bricoleur

Caleb, who attended a Methodist church with his family growing up, began church two-timing during his later adolescent years and continued throughout university. For Caleb, two-timing was about getting a spiritual "top up" as well as enjoying the diversity of perspective and expression of faith:

CALEB: *It was just a thing; it was kind of like a top up, or a bit of a different slice of things. And I carried that on when I went to university. In fact I kind of made a point of going, of diversifying. The different churches that I went to . . . I decided that I didn't want to subscribe to any one church culture. So I went to a Methodist church, which was quite traditional, but again the youth group was quite charismatic . . . Then I went to a Baptist church, which was, well it was Baptist, so that was more middle of the road. And then sometimes I would go to a Catholic church with my friend as well, but not that often, but periodically. I decided that I didn't want to just have Pentecostal teaching, or just have the Baptist teaching. I kind of wanted to have a few different viewpoints and stuff. Sometimes we'd go to another Baptist church as well.*

Caleb's decision and attitude to not "subscribe to any one church culture" is representative of those for whom denominational loyalty and identity is becoming increasingly unimportant. Despite the increased social and cultural similarities among many different churches and Caleb's reluctance to ascribe to a denominational identity, his experience suggests that noticeable denominational differences are still apparent. In fact, Caleb sought out these differences to enrich his understanding of faith. At times, different church perspectives on various issues such as the Holy Spirit would cause him confusion. But for the most part, Caleb appreciated the breadth of teaching and various perspectives on life and faith.

Like Dylan, Caleb did not consider himself a religious consumer in his practice of two-timing. Caleb's engagement with the faith traditions of different denominations is a form of the "bricolage" that Levi-Strauss analyzed in *The Savage Mind*, that is, an arrangement made with "whatever is at hand," a production that bears no relation to any particular project, but continues to build upon "the remains of previous constructions or destructions."[9] Caleb then, can be considered something of a "spiritual bricoleur," as he cobbles together spiritual insights and perspectives gathered from Methodist, Baptist, Pentecostal, and Catholic churches to explore his faith and how he lives it out.

A Process of Transition

For others I interviewed, such as Grace, church two-timing is a stage of transition from one church to another as commitments in a primary church come to an end. Grace grew up in a Christian family and has been actively involved in church since her early adolescence. Two-timing for Grace occurred over a brief six-week period and was triggered by a growing disconnection with her group of friends at Brooklyn Baptist Church, where she said, "I wasn't getting the connections anymore because people were at different stages of life." Grace elaborated on this stage of life disconnect by discussing how most of her friends at Brooklyn Baptist had either recently married or were beginning to have children. Grace engaged in two-timing, as she says, almost "unconsciously." Some other friends had started going to Trinity Church and invited Grace along. She would only go when she wasn't facilitating the evening service at Brooklyn Baptist. Grace exemplifies the covenanted self through her commitment to others at Brooklyn Baptist: "I didn't want to just pull out and leave everyone in the lurch for that. So it was a commitment to keep going really, an obligation I guess."

Grace's strong sense of commitment to a church faith community is typical of others I interviewed. However, her sense of belonging was diminishing as she began to make new connections at Trinity. "It was refreshing to have a new social circle of people that were in the same stage as life as me . . . and that they were single and didn't have mental health issues and [were] easy to chat to." Disconnection from a group of people one previously felt close and connected to is a painful process. Grace continued to go to her primary church more out of a sense of obligation than from the deeper sense of belonging or connectedness that she had previously experienced there. For Grace, two-timing as a process of transition was a refreshing experience. As Grace's story shows, attending church with people in a similar stage of life can become more important than simply people the same age.

9. Levi-Strauss, *Savage Mind*, 17.

Church Two-Timing for a Season

Paul has been very involved in Jubilee Pentecostal Church since he was about fifteen years old. He had been hearing rumors about Saint Barnabas' Anglican Church for a couple of years, but had never managed to attend a church service. He eventually was ale to visit a few evening services and he "felt like God [was] saying, 'This is where I want you to be for now.'" Paul said that one of his motives was to meet people his own age, something his primary church was missing. Paul's original thought was to switch churches from Jubilee Pentecostal to Saint Barnabas' Anglican. However, what ended up happening, Paul says, was that "within about three or four months it had helped me connect back even more into my church [Jubilee Pentecostal] in the morning."

For Paul, two-timing was "like trying to having two sets of parents." He went on to say, "It [two-timing] can be helpful. In the normal course of events, you wouldn't do that. But you would if there was something wrong with the first parents or something wrong with the child. To me, it is similar. And to me, it is also inherently temporary." Paul went on to explain that "What has made it work for me is I have just used Saint Barnabas' as my bit on the side." Paul was upfront with the leadership regarding his commitment and availability to help out with the worship:

PAUL: *I felt like it was good to set the expectation and said, "Look, I am here for a time. I want to be useful to you when I am here." I feel like being here is more about me. It is about having a wider group of people to connect with. I felt that God was really into that. Because it contrasts with my earlier experience, where church is not a social club, I am not here for that. And yet, in this circumstance, I felt that God was really, really for me going there. So I did feel, like, a level of direction to go there. But I feel like there will come a time where it will be quite natural just to choose.*

Paul only decided to get involved in worship at Saint Barnabas' when he had made a decision not to leave Jubilee. He still views Jubilee Pentecostal as his primary church, and calls it his "home church."

Jubilee Pentecostal only has a morning service, which made it possible for Paul to attended Saint Barnabas'. He attends Jubilee Pentecostal every Sunday morning, but only attends Saint Barnabas' two or three times a month. Paul said that most people he spoke to at Jubilee Pentecostal were supportive of him going to Saint Barnabas' as well. Others, however, "just don't get it." The leadership at Saint Barnabas' are also supportive of Paul's two-timing, possibly because he was upfront and clear about what he was doing and why. Unlike most of the people I interviewed who had engaged in church two-timing, Paul is involved in both his primary and his secondary church. However, there is still a clear distinction between the roles the two churches play in Paul's life:

PAUL: *Like, for me, one thing that is crucial to two-timing success is you need to be grounded in one place. Part of the reason for church is the accountability. Not weirdly so. But if you start to go off the rails, people can actually say, "Hey," and have actually got a bit of force to pull you back. I think it is important to be under authority. So for me, that is Jubilee Pentecostal. So I am more involved there. I give a paltry amount to Saint Barnabas'. But most of my giving has stayed with Jubilee Pentecostal. It is still my church. I am not as involved as I could be. And that is why, for me, two-timing has to be inherently temporary. It means that you are just split between your parents and that just stops you being as involved as you could be. And I am not saying that you should be super involved. I think that is my bent.*

Although Paul does not consider two-timing to be sustainable long-term for himself, he highlighted some of the benefits that two-timing had enabled:

PAUL: *I just think it is useful for Jubilee Pentecostal for me to be at Saint Barnabas'. I have brought some of the songs back. I have brought some of the philosophies back. I just think me being in two places has some benefits. It has meant that I am not leading the group and I haven't wanted to for a variety of reasons . . . There were just a number of advantages. Getting somewhere where I didn't have a whole lot of history, because everyone knew me at the Jubilee Pentecostal.*

The attraction of going somewhere without "a whole lot of history" for Paul shares similarities to Bob and Amy's enjoyment of the anonymity they originally found at their secondary church. Having no history at Saint Barnabas' Anglican meant not only no role expectations, but more importantly for Paul, the ability to participate in church free from associations with his ex-role of having separated from his wife.

One of the issues raised by two-timing for Paul has to do with involvement. "I think," Paul said, "that there is a reality about it that if you are in two places, you can't spend time, you can't focus, you don't know where you will end up. I am ninety percent sure that I will stop attending Saint Barnabas' and just go to Jubilee Pentecostal. I would never be an elder. It does create some barriers. It just places some natural limitations on how much you can get involved." Paul's own life circumstances make two-timing attractive in the short term. As Paul said, "I always thought that I would go to Saint Barnabas' Anglican and then reassess. I have done that and stayed. I will probably do another reassessment at about two years."

Creating Space for the Two-Timer

Church two-timing requires churches to be open and welcome to worshippers who may be in search of a secondary church to meet their spiritual or social needs. People considering church two-timing may not be looking to get involved in the secondary church. Tension arises for the church two-timer when there is a sense of divided loyalties, a conflict of interest, or when a person feels that they have to decide which church to commit to. If two-timers desire a sense of belonging within a secondary church, then belonging needs to be more loosely defined—free of expectations and formal involvement.

Church two-timing offers potential encouragement to smaller churches with very few young adults that do not wish to lose these valued members of the congregation. The practice of church two-timing offers an alternative to young adults considering church switching from a small church that may offer few peers to a church that has a larger young adult demographic (and is perhaps more attractive stylistically—at least in terms of church music). This alternative calls for churches to allow creative space for young adults to get involved in church life and services with a genuine sense of ownership, but also allowing young adults to seek out a secondary church that will provide them with demographic support. Especially for smaller churches, allowing this kind of church two-timing may reduce their chances of losing young adults from their congregations.

Bob and Amy's experience demonstrates there is the potential for secondary churches to support ministries in church two-timers' primary churches. In order for this potential to be realized, churches cannot afford to have an attitude of competition with other churches—an attitude which the language of the spiritual marketplace's competition for market share in religious consumers implies. Instead, primary churches must respond to the trend of church two-timing by understanding the ways in which a secondary church can spiritually refresh and sustain people who are involved in ministering and serving in their primary church. It is out of this understanding that a primary church can support the practice of church two-timing among some of its members without being threatened by or incorrectly condemning the practice as an act of religious consumption.

The practice of two-timing brings with it implications for re-thinking what it means to belong, to be involved, as well as issues of commitment to church. Church two-timing emphasizes the depth of commitment people have to their primary church and can be considered as a strategy that can make such commitment possible. I would like to suggest that one place to begin involves a change in perspective. Rather than judging peoples' association to a secondary church as that of a "religious consumer," let us instead view them as short-term or even long-term guests.

Appendix

Methodology

Life Story Interviews

> We tell ourselves stories in order to live ... We interpret what we see, select the
> most workable of the multiple choices. We live entirely, especially if we
> are writers, by the imposition of a narrative line upon disparate images,
> by the "ideas" with which we have learned to freeze the shifting
> phantasmagoria which is our actual experience.[1]
>
> —JOAN DIDION

Our biography, our sense of identity is formed through telling our stories which are embedded in the story of the communities in which we participate. This book has explored the way Christian faith journeys of members of generations X and Y are embedded within church communities. In order to investigate and understand why generations X and Y choose to embed their faith in a church community in-depth religious life story interviews were considered the best methodological approach.

Conducting life story interviews provides insight and understanding into how faith is impacted and changed through life experience inside and outside the church and the consequences of this for embedded faith. Religious life stories also enabled me to explore the relationship between

---

1. Didion, *White Album*, 185.

embedded faith and the phenomenon of multiple switching. The life story approach enabled me to "track" the multiple church switcher while at the same time providing insight into the nature and challenges for embedded faith over the course of a lifetime.

My methodology was qualitative and inductive in nature and is informed by phenomenology, reflexivity, and the life story approach. Life stories utilise a qualitative approach which emphasises the use of open-ended questions to allow the participant to tell their story. Life stories highlight the most important experiences, influences, issues and themes as well as lessons of a lifetime.[2] As James Gee maintains, "One of the ways—probably *the* primary way—human beings make sense of their experience is by casting it in narrative form."[3] In relation to my topic, life stories portray religion and faith as lived experience and not just something believed abstracted from practice.

Phenomenology has had an important influence on the sociology of religion. A phenomenological approach seeks to understand the human experience of faith and the transcendent, giving priority to the believer's frame of reference and definition of reality. Ninian Smart defines phenomenology as an attitude of informed empathy as it seeks to "bring out what religious acts mean to the actors."[4] This approach influenced how I engaged with the participants' stories in writing up the book. Their experiences are understood as valid experiences. As such I have not critically challenged participants own accounts, judgments and reflections on their experience of faith and church. This does not mean, however, that I do not highlight contradictions sometimes evident in participants' stories, or compare and contrast stories to each other.

In order to allow the participants to tell their story, interviews were semi-structured and informal. There were certain areas that I wanted to cover but I did so by allowing the conversations to remain as open as possible. The first question that I always began with was, "*Tell me about your life and faith journey and your experiences of church.*" From this point on each interview had a degree of uniqueness in relation to the order of questions that followed.

Reflexivity is also an important methodological aspect to my research. Reflexivity acknowledges the researcher as an active participant in the

2. Atkinson, *Life Story*.

3. Gee, "Narrativization," 11.

4. Smart, *Dimensions*, 2.

research process. According to Denzin and Lincoln (1998) the reflexive turn in qualitative sociology has created the space whereby it is now possible to write the researcher into the world they investigate as an active participant in the research process. Reflexivity enables me to draw on my own experience and spiritual development in both the interview itself and in making sense out of the interview life stories of the participants.[5]

Finding the Participants

I found all of the interviewees through my social networks built up over the years of church involvement. The majority of participants I know personally and had already spoken to them about my PhD research. All those I asked were willing and happy to be interviewed. Some of the participants became involved through informal snowballing as people I knew spoke to others about my research and they said they would be willing to be interviewed. Participants had to be currently involved with a church congregation and, obviously, a member of either the GenX or the older end of the GenY birth cohort (20 years old and over). The research topic on faith and church is an important area for the participants and they were happy to be able to contribute from their own experience.

Using personal networks in my research meant that I was a 'social insider' to many of the people I interviewed. This has had distinct advantages; I am part of their social world and they are part of mine. This influences the questions that I can and did ask of some participants that were based on my knowledge of them and things that they were thinking about, experiences that they have had and told me about, or knowing that they have switched churches and from what to where. It also enabled me to ask questions about areas of life that a participant had over looked or not thought about in telling their story. Here are a couple of responses in answer to the question,

How have you found being interviewed by someone you know?

NATHAN: *Yeah good. I feel safe. I can tell, and I think you are able to ask questions well because of your knowledge of me.*

EUGENE: *It is probably more helpful to be honest. Like I don't know that I would be afraid to tell a stranger my story. But it is helpful to know*

5. See Hertz, *Reflexivity and Voice.*

that, to know you and your background too. And the fact that you are a Christian and able to understand some of the . . . ask the right questions I suppose, in many respects and delve a bit deeper.

It is generally acknowledged in the research literature that insider status can provide access to information, and sometimes people, that are inaccessible to an outsider. Most participants said that being interviewed by someone they knew made it easier for them, increased trust, and helped them to feel relaxed. Nesha Haniff argues that insiderness provides an advantage over the limits of outsiderness through being able to understand the hidden meanings and developing a deep level of trust with participants.[6] Understanding hidden meanings, or simply just understanding as an insider was recognised by participants. As Noah commented on being interviewed by myself, "It is good. Because you understand me a little bit anyway . . . maybe a bit more comfortable; the fact that you are a Christian anyway and understand what I am saying. If the person was not a Christian they probably wouldn't understand half the answers I am saying, because they don't understand church culture and Christian faith."

The Interviews

I gained ethics approval from the University of Auckland Ethics Committee for my research. Consent forms were signed by participants before interviews began. The interviews lasted from one to three hours. Most interviews lasted around two hours. Fifty religious biographies produced a vast amount of material to read through, code, theme and analyse. Using Nvivo 7, a qualitative software program, for coding and theming the interviews greatly enhanced this process. Making sense of the stories is what Norman Denzin calls the *art of interpretation*.[7] 'The practice of this art allows the field-worker-as-*bricoleur* to translate what has been learned into a body of textual work that communicates these understandings to the reader.'[8]

People's narratives and religious life stories told during an interview are always a snapshot of people's lives. The interviews engage people at a particular moment in time from which they reflect back on their life. People tell their story reflecting back in a particular space, a social location of

6. Haniff, "Native Anthropology."

7. Denzin, "Art and Politics," 447.

8. Ibid.

the present. The present creates a certain distance from the past and more recent experiences can come to dominate the past, and hence the interview. As Theo's comment below demonstrates significant aspects of a person's story can be forgotten or overlooked in an interview that is attempting to cover a life story. At the end of the interview I asked him, "Any thoughts or reflections on the interview process?" Theo said, "There are some crucial incidences that I haven't talked about that take a while to recall. Now they will come to mind afterwards. And I have been on such a journey that it is hard to boil it all down in one instance."

How we remember and tell our story raises the epistemological concern of what Miroslav Volf describes as "remembering rightly." Volf explains,

> We are not just shaped *by* memories; we ourselves *shape* the memories that shape us . . . and since we do so, the consequences are significant; for because we shape our memories, our identities cannot exist simply in *what* we remember. The question of *how* we remember also comes into play. Because we can react to our memories and shape them, we are larger than our memories.[9]

People re-interpret their past through the lens of the present. New knowledge and experiences are drawn on to make sense of the past, just as the past can be drawn on to make sense of present reality. People expressed in the interview that how they interpret particular events now is not how they would have understood them at the time. Earlier spiritual experiences, for example, are an area that some participants look back on and re-interpret quite differently now, as was evident in a number of people's comments and reflections. This re-interpretation might include questioning the experience itself, or having new vocabulary and understanding in which to make sense of past experiences.

Furthermore, in contrast to the story that has an ending in the interview, the story of the participant continues. The place in their faith journey and thoughts, attitudes, and affiliation with church at the time of the interview is probably not always an indication of where they are going to stay. I know for a fact that this is certainly the case for a number of participants. Their story, and hopefully their faith journey, continues to unfold as it is lived out in the everyday realties of their lives.

9. Volf, *Memory*, 25.

Bibliography

Ammerman, Nancy. *Congregation and Community*. New Brunswick: Rutgers University Press, 1997.

———. "Culture and Identity in the Congregation." In *Studying Congregations: A New Handbook*, edited by Nancy Ammerman et al., 78–104. Nashville: Abingdon, 1998.

———. "Organized Religion in a Voluntaristic Society." *Sociology of Religion* 58 (1997) 203–15.

———. *Pillars of Faith: American Congregations and Their Partners*. Berkeley: University of California Press, 2005.

Arnett, Ronald C. *Communication and Community: Implications of Martin Buber's Dialogue*. Carbondale: Southern Illinois University Press, 1986.

Assmann, Jan. *Religion and Cultural Memory: Ten Studies*. Translated by Rodney Livingstone. Cultural Memory in the Present. Stanford: Stanford University Press, 2006.

Atkinson, Robert. *The Life Story Interview*. Qualitative Research Methods 44. Thousand Oaks, CA: Sage, 1998.

Auer, Bernhard M. "A Letter from the Publisher." *Time*, January 6, 1967, 11.

Babchuk, Nicholas, and Hugh Whitt. "R-Order and Religious Switching." *Journal for the Scientific Study of Religion* 29 (1990) 246–54.

Barna, George, and Mark Hatch. *Boiling Point: It Only Takes One Degree: Monitoring Cultural Shifts in the Twenty-First Century*. Ventura, CA: Regal, 2001.

Barthes, Roland. *Image, Music, Text*. Translated by Stephen Heath. New York: Hill & Wang, 1977.

Bauman, Zygmunt. *Community: Seeking Safety in an Insecure World*. Themes for the 21st Century. Cambridge: Polity, 2001.

———. "Europe and North America." In *Faith in a Society of Instant Gratification*, edited by M. Junker-Kenny and M. Tomka, 3–9. London: SCM, 1999.

———. *Liquid Modernity*. Cambridge: Polity, 2000.

Beaudoin, Tom. *Virtual Faith: The Irreverent Spiritual Quest of Generation X*. San Francisco: Jossey-Bass, 1998.

Bell, Martin. "Comparing Population Mobility in Australia and New Zealand." *Journal of Population Research and New Zealand Population Review* (2002) 169–93.

Bellah, Robert N., et al. *Habits of the Heart: Individualism and Commitment in American Life*. Berkeley: University of California Press, 1985.

Belzer, Tobin, et al. "Congregations That Get It: Understanding Religious Identities in the Next Generation." In *Passing on the Faith: Transforming Traditions for the Next Generation of Jews, Christians, and Muslims*, edited by J. Heft, 103–22. New York: Fordham University Press, 2006.

Bennett, Stephen Earl, et al. "Generations and Change: Some Initial Observations." In *After the Boom: The Politics of Generation X*, edited by S. C. Craig and S. E. Bennett, 1–19. Lanham, MD: Rowman & Littlefield, 1997.

Berger, Peter L. *The Heretical Imperative: Contemporary Possibilities of Religious Affirmation*. Garden City, NY: Anchor/Doubleday, 1980.

———. *A Rumor of Angels: Modern Society and the Rediscovery of the Supernatural*. Garden City, NY: Anchor, 1969.

Besecke, Kelly. "Seeing Invisible Religion: Religion as a Societal Conversation about Transcendental Meaning." *Sociological Theory* 23 (2005) 179–96.

Bibby, Reginald W. "Going, Going, Gone: The Impact of Geographical Mobility on Religious Involvement." *Review of Religious Research* 38 (1997) 289–307.

Bibby, Reginald W., and Merlin Beinkerhoff. "The Circulation of the Saints: A Study of People Who Join Conservative Churches." *Journal for the Scientific Study of Religion* 12 (1973) 273–83.

Brueggemann, Walter. *The Bible and Postmodern Imagination: Texts under Negotiation*. Minneapolis: Fortress, 1993.

———. *The Covenanted Self: Explorations in Law and Covenant*. Minneapolis: Fortress, 1999.

Carroll, Jackson. "Reflexive Ecclesiology: A Challenge to Applied Research in Religious Organizations." *Journal for the Study of Religion* 39 (2000) 545–57.

Carroll, Jackson, and Wade Clark Roof. *Bridging Divided Worlds: Generational Cultures in Congregations*. San Francisco: Jossey-Bass, 2002.

Cnaan, Ram, et al. "Bowling Alone but Serving Together: The Congregational Norm of Community Involvement." In *Religion as Social Capital: Producing the Common Good*, edited by C. E. Smidt, 19–31. Waco, TX: Baylor University Press, 2003.

Coupland, Douglas. *Generation X: Tales for an Accelerated Culture*. London: Abacus, 1996.

———. "Generation X'd." *Details*, June 1995. Available from http://coupland.tripod.com/details1.html

Craig, Stephen C., and Stephen Earl Bennett. *After the Boom: The Politics of Generation X, People, Passions, and Power*. Lanham, MD: Rowman & Littlefield, 1997.

Crouch, Andy. "Generation Misinformation." *Christianity Today*, May 21, 2001, 83.

Davie, Grace. *Religion in Britain Since 1945: Believing without Belonging, Making Contemporary Britain*. Oxford: Blackwell, 1994.

Dawn, Marva. *Reaching Out without Dumbing Down: A Theology of Worship for the Turn-of-the-Century Culture*. Grand Rapids: Eerdmans, 1995.

de Certeau, Michel. *The Practice of Everyday Life*. Berkeley: University of California Press, 1984.

de Vaus, David. "The Impact of Geographical Mobility on Adolescent Religious Orientation: An Australian Study." *Review of Religious Research* 23 (1982) 391–403.

Denzin, Norman K. "The Art and Politics of Interpretation." In *Approaches to Qualitative Research: A Reader on Theory and Practice*, edited by S. N. Hesse-Biber and P. Leavy, 447–72. New York: Oxford University Press, 2004.

Denzin, Norman K., and Yvonna S. Lincoln. *The Handbook of Qualitative Research*. 2nd ed. Thousand Oaks: Sage Publications, 2000.

Didion, Joan. *We Tell Ourselves Stories in Order to Live: Collected Nonfiction*. New York: Knopf, 2006.

Durkheim, Emile. *The Elementary Forms of Religious Life*. Translated by C. Cosman. Oxford: Oxford University Press, 2001.

Durkheim, Emile, and W. S. F. Pickering. *Durkheim on Religion: A Selection of Readings with Bibliographies.* London: Routledge & Kegan Paul, 1975.

Ebaugh, Helen Rose Fuchs. *Becoming an Ex: The Process of Role Exit.* Chicago: University of Chicago Press, 1988.

Eco, Umberto. "Towards a Semiotic Inquiry into the Television Message." In *Communication Studies: An Introductory Reader*, edited by J. Corner and J. Hawthorn, 131–49. London: Arnold, 1980.

Esler, Anthony. *The Youth Revolution: The Conflict of Generations in Modern History.* Lexington: Heath, 1974.

Fabbri, Franco. "A Theory of Musical Genres: Two Applications." In *Popular Music Perspectives*, edited by D. Horn, P. Tagg, and Marian Green, 52–81. Göteborg: International Association for the Study of Popular Music, 1981.

Festinger, Leon. *A Theory of Cognitive Dissonance.* Evanston, IL: Row, Peterson, 1957.

Fish, Stanley Eugene. *Is There a Text in This Class? The Authority of Interpretive Communities.* Cambridge: Harvard University Press, 1980.

Flory, Richard W., and Donald E. Miller. *Finding Faith: The Spiritual Quest of the Post-Boomer Generation.* New Brunswick: Rutgers University Press, 2008.

———. "The Embodied Spirituality of the Post-Boomer Generations." In *A Sociology of Spirituality*, edited by Kieran Flanagan and Peter C. Jupp, 201–19. Aldershot, UK: Ashgate, 2007.

———. *GenX Religion.* New York: Routledge, 2000.

Foote, Nelson. "Identification as the Basis for a Theory of Motivation." *American Sociological Review* 16 (1951) 14–21.

Foster, Richard. *Celebration of Discipline: The Path to Spiritual Growth.* San Francisco: Harper & Row, 1978.

Fowler, James W. *Stages of Faith: The Psychology of Human Development and the Quest for Meaning.* San Francisco: HarperSanFrancisco, 1995.

Friedman, Maurice. *The Confirmation of Otherness.* New York: Pilgrim, 1983.

Frith, Simon. *Music for Pleasure: Essays in the Sociology of Pop.* Cambridge: Polity in association with Blackwell, 1988.

———. *Performing Rites: On the Value of Popular Music.* Cambridge: Harvard University Press, 1996.

Fulkerson, Mary McClintock. "Is There a (Non-Sexist) Bible in This Church? A Feminist Case for the Priority of Interpretive." In *Modern Theology* 14 (1998) 225–42.

Fussell, Paul. *Class: A Guide through the American Status System.* New York: Simon & Schuster, 1983.

Gallagher, Sally. "Building Traditions: Comparing Space, Ritual, and Community in Three Congregations." *Review of Religious Research* 47 (2005) 70–85.

Gawronski, Raymond. "Why Orthodox Catholics Look to Zen." *New Oxford Review* 60 (1993) 13–16.

Gee, James. "The Narrativization of Experience in the Oral Style." *Journal of Education* 167 (1985) 9–35.

Giles, Jeff, and Susan Miller. "Generalizations X." *Newsweek* 123 (1994) 64–72.

Goffman, Erving. *Behavior in Public Places; Notes on the Social Organization of Gatherings.* New York: Free Press of Glencoe, 1963.

———. *Forms of Talk.* Philadelphia: University of Pennsylvania Press, 1981.

———. *The Presentation of Self in Everyday Life.* New York: Anchor, 1959.

Green, Lucy. *Music on Deaf Ears: Musical Meaning, Ideology, Education, Music and Society.* Manchester: Manchester University Press, 1988.

Grenz, Stanley. "The Community of God: A Vision of the Church in the Postmodern Age." *Crux* 28 (1992) 19–26.

———. *Created for Community: Connecting Christian Belief with Christian Living.* Grand Rapids: Baker, 1996.

Grossberg, Lawrence. "Is There a Fan in the House? The Affective Sensibility of Fandom." In *Adoring Audience: Fan Culture and Popular Media*, edited by Lisa A. Lewis, 50–69. London: Routledge, 1992.

Hadaway, C. Kirk. "Denominational Switching and Religiosity." *Review of Religious Research* 21 (1980) 451–61.

———. "Church Growth in North America: The Character of a Religious Marketplace." In *Church & Denominational Growth*, edited by David A. Roozen and C. Kirk Hadaway, 346–58. Nashville: Abingdon, 1993.

Hahn, Todd, and David Verhaagen. *Reckless Hope: Understanding and Reaching Baby Busters.* Grand Rapids: Baker, 1996.

Hall, Stuart. "Encoding/Decoding." In *Media and Cultural Studies: Keyworks*, edited by G. Durham and D. Kellner, 166–76. Malden, MA: Blackwell, 2001.

Haniff, Nesha Z. "Toward a Native Anthropology: Methodological Notes on a Study of Successful Caribbean Women by an Insider." *Anthropology & Humanism Quarterly* 10 (1985) 107–13.

Hauerwas, Stanley. *A Better Hope: Resources for a Church Confronting Capitalism, Democracy, and Postmodernity.* Grand Rapids: Brazos, 2000.

———. *Unleashing the Scripture: Freeing the Bible from Captivity to America.* Nashville: Abingdon, 1993.

Hauerwas, Stanley, and William H. Willimon. *Resident Aliens: Life in the Christian Colony.* Nashville: Abingdon, 1989.

———. *Where Resident Aliens Live.* Nashville: Abingdon, 1996.

Heelas, Paul, and Linda Woodhead. *The Spiritual Revolution: Why Religion Is Giving Way to Spirituality, Religion and Spirituality in the Modern World.* Malden, MA: Blackwell, 2005.

Heft, James, editor. *Passing on the Faith: Transforming Traditions for the Next Generation of Jews, Christians, and Muslims.* New York: Fordham University Press, 2006.

Heilman, Samuel. *Synagogue Life: A Study in Symbolic Interaction.* Chicago: University of Chicago Press, 1973.

Hertz, Rosanna. *Reflexivity & Voice.* Thousand Oaks, CA: Sage, 1997.

Hervieu-Léger, Danièle. *Religion as a Chain of Memory.* New Brunswick, NJ: Rutgers University Press, 2000.

Hobsbawm, Eric. "The Cult of Identity Politics." *New Left Review* 217 (1996) 38–47.

Hoge, Dean, et al. "Types of Denominational Switching among Protestant Young Adults." *Journal for the Scientific Study of Religion* 34 (1995) 253–58.

Hoge, Dean, and Thomas O'Conner. "Denominational Identity from Age Sixteen to Age Thirty-Eight." *Sociology of Religion* 65 (2004) 77–85.

Hopewell, James F. *Congregations: Stories and Structures.* Philadelphia: Fortress, 1987.

Horton, Donald. "The Dialogue of Courtship in Popular Songs." *The American Journal of Sociology* 62 (1957) 569–78.

Hudson, Don. "The Dance of Truth: Postmodernism and the Evangelical." *Mars Hill Review* 12 (1998) 13–22.

Hunt, Stephen *Alternative Religions: A Sociological Introduction*. Aldershot, UK: Ashgate, 2003.

Jackall, Robert, and Janice M. Hirota. *Image Makers: Advertising, Public Relations, and the Ethos of Advocacy*. Chicago: University of Chicago Press, 2000.

Jamieson, Alan. *Churchless Faith: Faith Journeys Beyond Evangelical, Pentecostal & Charismatic Churches*. Wellington, NZ: Philip Garside, 2000.

Johnson, D. Paul. "From Religious Markets to Religious Communities: Contrasting Implications for Applied Research." *Review of Religious Research* 44 (2003) 325–40.

Johnstone, Carlton. "Emerging Generations and the Challenge of Being Witnesses in Our Time" Available from http://www.methodist.org.nz/files/docs/mission%20and%20ecum/carlton%20johnstone.pdf

———. "Faith Crossroads and Social Networks: The Transition from Inherited Faith to Owned Faith." *Journal of Youth and Theology* 8 (2009) 43–59.

———. "Modes of Engagement with Worship." *Stimulus*, 18 November (2010) 10–18.

———. "Understanding the Practice of Church Two-Timing." *International Journal for the Study of the Christian Church*, 9 (2009) 17–31.

Karbusicky, Vladimir. "The Interaction between 'Reality-Work of Art-Society.'" *International Social Science Journal* 20 (1968) 644–55.

Kassabian, Anahid. "Ubiquitous Listening." In *Popular Music Studies*, edited by D. Hesmondhalgh. London: Arnold, 2002.

Kavanaugh, John. *Following Christ in a Consumer Society*. Maryknoll, NY: Orbis, 2006.

Kelly, J. N. D. *Early Christian Doctrines*. New York: Harper & Row, 1978.

Kelman, Herbert C. "Compliance, Identification, and Internalization: Three Processes of Attitude Change." *The Journal of Conflict Resolution* 2 (1958) 51–60.

Kilbourne, Brock, and James Richardson. "The Communalization of Religious Experience in Contemporary Religious Groups." *Journal of Community Psychology* 14 (1986) 206–212.

———. "Paradigm Conflict, Types of Conversion, and Conversion Theories." *Sociological Analysis* 50 (1989) 1–21.

Ladd, Everett Carll. "The Twentysomethings: 'Generation Myths' Revisited." *The Public Perspective* 5 (1994) 14–18.

Lévi-Strauss, Claude. *The Savage Mind*. Chicago: University of Chicago Press, 1996.

Levy, Lester, et. al. *The Generational Mirage? A Pilot Study into the Perceptions of Leadership by Generation X and Y*. Hudson Report, 2006.

Lindbeck, George A. *The Nature of Doctrine: Religion and Theology in a Postliberal Age*. Philadelphia: Westminster, 1984.

Lineham, Peter. "Three Types of Churches." In *Thinking Outside the Square: Church in Middle Earth*, edited by R. Boddé, Hugh Kempster, and John Bishop. Auckland, NZ: Jointly published by St Columba's Press and Journeyings, 2003.

Lovell, Stephen. *Generations in Twentieth-Century Europe*. New York: Palgrave Macmillan, 2007.

Maffesoli, Michel. *The Time of the Tribes: The Decline of Individualism in Mass Society*. London: Sage, 1996.

Mannheim, Karl. "The Problem of Generations." In *Essays on the Sociology of Knowledge*, edited by K. Mannheim, 276–322. London: Routledge & Kegan Paul, 1952.

Marler, Penny, and David A. Roozen. "From Church Tradition to Consumer Choice: The Gallup Surveys of the Unchurched American." In *Church and Denominational*

Growth: What Does (and Does Not) Cause Growth or Decline, edited by David A. Roozen and C. Kirk Hadaway, 253–77. Nashville: Abingdon, 1993.

Marty, Martin E. *A Nation of Behavers*. Chicago: University of Chicago Press, 1976.

Marx, Karl, and Friedrich Engels. *The Communist Manifesto*. Harmondsworth, UK: Penguin, 1967.

Mason, Michael, et al. "The Spirituality of Young Australians." *International Journal of Children's Spirituality* 12 (2007) 149–63.

McLuhan, Marshall. *Understanding Media: The Extensions of Man*. London: Sphere, 1967.

Mead, Margaret. *Culture and Commitment: A Study of the Generation Gap*. London: Panther, 1970.

———. *Culture and Commitment: The New Relationships between the Generations in the 1970s*. New York: Columbia University Press, 1978.

Mellor, Philip, and Chris Shilling. *Re-Forming the Body: Religion, Community and Modernity*. London: Sage, 1997.

Miller, Donald E., and Arpi Misha Miller. "Introduction: Understanding Generation X: Values, Politics, and Religious Commitments." In *GenX Religion*, edited by R. W. Flory and D. E. Miller, 1–12. New York: Routledge, 2000.

Mills, C. Wright. "Situated Actions and Vocabularies of Motive." *American Sociological Review* 5 (1940) 904–13.

———. *The Sociological Imagination*. Harmondsworth, UK: Penguin, 2000.

Moore, Ralph. *Friends: The Key to Reaching Generation X*. Venture, CA: Regal, 1997.

Niebuhr, H. Richard. *Radical Monotheism and Western Civilization*. Lincoln: University of Nebraska, 1960.

Nooney, Jennifer. "Keeping the Faith: Religious Transmission and Apostasy in Generation X." PhD diss., North Carolina State University, 2006.

Nouwen, Henri. *Ministry and Spirituality*. New York: Continuum, 2000.

Olaveson, Tim. "Collective Effervescence and Communitas: Processual Models of Ritual and Society in Emile Durkheim and Victor Turner." *Dialectical Anthropology* 26 (2001) 89–124.

Ortner, Sherry. "Generation X: Anthropology in a Media-Saturated World." *Cultural Anthropology* 13 (1998) 414–40.

Otto, Rudolf. *The Idea of the Holy: An Inquiry into the Non-Rational Factor in the Idea of the Divine and Its Relation to the Rational*. 2nd ed. New York: Oxford University Press, 1950.

Parks, Sharon. *The Critical Years: The Young Adult Search for a Faith to Live By*. 2nd ed. San Francisco: Harper & Row, 2000.

Peck, M. Scott. *The Road Less Travelled: A New Psychology of Love, Traditional Values and Spiritual Growth*. London: Hutchinson, 1993.

Percy, Martyn. "A Place at High Table? Assessing the Future of Charismatic Christianity." In *Predicting Religion: Christian, Secular, and Alternative Futures*, edited by Grace Davie, Paul Heelas, and Linda Woodhead, 95–109. Aldershot, UK: Ashgate, 2003.

Polanyi, Michael, and Harry Prosch. *Meaning*. Chicago: University of Chicago Press, 1975.

Prothero, Stephen. *Religious Literacy: What Every American Needs to Know and Doesn't*. New York: HarperOne, 2007.

Putnam, Robert D. *Bowling Alone: The Collapse and Revival of American Community*. London: Simon & Schuster, 2001.

Putnam, Robert D., Lewis M. Feldstein, and Don Cohen. *Better Together: Restoring the American Community*. New York: Simon & Schuster, 2003.

Richardson, James, and M. Stewart. "Conversion Process Models and the Jesus Movement." In *Conversion Careers: In and out of the New Religions*, edited by James T. Richardson, 24–42. Beverly Hills, CA: Sage, 1978.

Riddell, Michael. *Threshold of the Future: Reforming the Church in the Post-Christian West*. London: SPCK, 1998.

Rokeach, Milton. *The Open and Closed Mind*. New York: Basic Books, 1960.

Roof, Wade Clark. "Multiple Religious Switching: A Research Note." *Journal for the Scientific Study of Religion* 28 (1989) 530–35.

———. *Spiritual Marketplace: Baby Boomers and the Remaking of American Religion*. Princeton: Princeton University Press, 1999.

Roof, Wade Clark, and William McKinney. "Denominational America and the New Religious Pluralism." *Annuals of the American Academy of Political and Social Science* 480 (1985) 24–38.

Roozen, David A., and C. Kirk Hadaway. "Individuals and the Church Choice." In *Church and Denominational Growth*, edited by David A. Roozen and C. Kirk Hadaway, 241–52. Nashville: Abingdon, 1993.

Rose, Stuart. "Is the Term 'Spirituality' a Word That Everyone Uses, but Nobody Knows What Anyone Means by It?" *Journal of Contemporary Religion* 16 (2001) 193–207.

Rosing, Helmut. "Listening Behaviour and Musical Preference in the Age of Transmitted Music." *Popular Music* 4 (1984) 119–49.

Ross, Alex. "Generation Exit." *The New Yorker* April 25, 1994, 102–6.

Savage, Sara, et al. *Making Sense of Generation Y: The World View of 15- to 25-Year-Olds*. London: Church House, 2006.

Schuman, Howard, and Jacqueline Scott. "Generations and Collective Memories." *American Sociological Review* 54 (1989) 359–81.

Schutz, Alfred. "Making Music Together." In *Collected Papers II: Studies in Social Theory*, edited by A. Schutz and M. A. Natanson, 159–78. Hague: Martinus Nijhoff, 2006.

Shepherd, Nicolas. "Christian Youth Groups as Sites for Identity Work: Religious Socialisation and a Reflexive Habitus." Paper presented at the BSA Sociology of Religion Study Group Annual Conference, "Religion and Youth," Birmingham, UK, April 8–10, 2008.

Smart, Ninian. *Dimensions of the Sacred: An Anatomy of the World's Beliefs*. London: HarperCollins, 1996.

Smith, Brian. "Theology Off the Wall: From Printed Word to Projected Word." *Stimulus* 9 (2001) 2–6.

Smith, Christian, and Melinda Lundquist Denton. *Soul Searching: The Religious and Spiritual Lives of American Teenagers*. Oxford: Oxford University Press, 2005.

Smith, Wilfred Cantwell. *Faith and Belief*. Princeton: Princeton University Press, 1979.

———. *The Meaning and End of Religion; A New Approach to the Religious Traditions of Mankind*. New York: New American Library, 1964.

Stark, Rodney, and Charles Y. Glock. *American Piety: The Nature of Religious Commitment*. Berkeley: University of California Press, 1968.

Statistics New Zealand. "Quickstats About Population Mobility 2006 Census." (2007) Available from http://www.stats.govt.nz/Census/2006CensusHomePage/QuickStats/quickstats-about-a-subject/population-mobility.aspx

Stockfelt, Ola. "Adequate Modes of Listening." In *Keeping Score: Music, Disciplinarity, Culture*, edited by David Schwarz, Anahid Kassabian, and Lawrence Siegel, 129–47. Charlottesville: University Press of Virginia, 1997.

Bibliography

Strauss, William, et al. *Millennials and the Pop Culture: Strategies for a New Generation of Consumers in Music, Movies, Television, the Internet, and Video Games.* Great Falls, VA: LifeCourse Associates, 2006.

Sweet, Leonard. *Soul Tsunami: Sink or Swim in New Millennium Culture.* Grand Rapids: Zondervan, 1999.

Tambiah, Stanley J. *A Performative Approach to Ritual.* London: Oxford University Press, 1981.

Toffler, Alvin. *Future Shock.* London: Bodley Head, 1970.

Tomlinson, Dave. *The Post-Evangelical.* London: Triangle, 1995.

Torevell, David. *Losing the Sacred: Ritual, Modernity and Liturgical Reform.* Edinburgh: T. & T. Clark, 2004.

Turner, Victor. *Dramas, Fields, and Metaphors; Symbolic Action in Human Society.* Ithaca: Cornell University Press, 1974.

———. *The Ritual Process: Structure and Anti-Structure.* Chicago: Aldine, 1969.

Turner, Victor, and Edith L. B. Turner. *Image and Pilgrimage in Christian Culture: Anthropological Perspectives.* New York: Columbia University Press, 1978.

Voas, David, and Alasdair Crockett. "Religion in Britain: Neither Believing nor Belonging." *Sociology* 39 (2005) 11–28.

Volf, Miroslav. *The End of Memory: Remembering Rightly in a Violent World.* Grand Rapids: Eerdmans, 2006.

Ward, Pete. "Affective Alliance or Circuits of Power. The Production and Consumption of Contemporary Worship in Britain." *International Journal of Practical Theology,* 9 (2005) 25–39.

———. *Selling Worship: How What We Sing Has Changed the Church.* Waynesboro, GA: Paternoster, 2005.

Weber, Max. *The Sociology of Religion.* Boston: Beacon, 1963.

Welch, Michael, and John Baltzell. "Geographic Mobility, Social Integration, and Church Attendance." *Journal for the Scientific Study of Religion* 23 (1984) 75–91.

Wells, David. *Losing Our Virtue: Why the Church Must Recover Its Moral Vision.* Grand Rapids: Eerdmans, 1998.

Westerhoff, John H. *Will Our Children Have Faith?* Toronto: Morehouse, 2000.

Whelan, Winifred. "Bodily Knowing: Implications for Liturgy and Religious Education." *Religious Education* 88 (1993) 273–81.

Wolff, Richard. "A Phenomenological Study of In-Church and Televised Worship." *Journal for the Scientific Study of Religion* 38 (1999) 219–35.

Wright, G. Ernest. *The Biblical Doctrine of Man in Society.* London: SCM, 1954.

Wuthnow, Robert. *After the Baby Boomers: How Twenty- and Thirty-Somethings Are Shaping the Future of American Religion.* Princeton: Princeton University Press, 2007.

———. *Growing up Religious: Christians and Jews and Their Journeys of Faith.* Boston: Beacon, 1999.

———. "Two Traditions in the Study of Religion." *Journal for the Scientific Study of Religion* 20 (1981) 16–32.

Yoder, John Howard. *Body Politics: Five Practices of the Christian Community before the Watching World.* Scottdale: Herald Press, 1992.

"The Younger Generation." *Time,* November 5, 1951.

Zinnbauer, Brian, Kenneth Pargament, and Allie Scott. "The Emerging Meanings of Religiousness and Spirituality: Problems and Perspectives." *Journal of Personality* 67 (1999) 889–919.

Subject Index

Names Index

Names Index

Scripture Index

www.ingramcontent.com/pod-product-compliance
Lightning Source LLC
Chambersburg PA
CBHW060335100426
42812CB00003B/1003